Political Marketing

Political Marketing

Theory and Concepts

Robert P. Ormrod,
Stephan C. Henneberg and
Nicholas J. O'Shaughnessy

Los Angeles | London | New Delhi
Singapore | Washington DC

Los Angeles | London | New Delhi
Singapore | Washington DC

SAGE Publications Ltd
1 Oliver's Yard
55 City Road
London EC1Y 1SP

SAGE Publications Inc.
2455 Teller Road
Thousand Oaks, California 91320

SAGE Publications India Pvt Ltd
B 1/I 1 Mohan Cooperative Industrial Area
Mathura Road
New Delhi 110 044

SAGE Publications Asia-Pacific Pte Ltd
3 Church Street
#10-04 Samsung Hub
Singapore 049483

Editor: Matthew Waters
Editorial assistant: Nina Smith
Production editor: Sarah Cooke
Copyeditor: William Baginsky
Proofreader: Neil Dowden
Indexer: Elizabeth Ball
Marketing manager: Alison Borg
Cover design: Wendy Scott
Typeset by: C&M Digitals (P) Ltd, Chennai, India
Printed and bound by MPG Printgroup, UK

MIX
Paper from
responsible sources
FSC
www.fsc.org   FSC® C018575

Library of Congress Control Number: 2012950033

British Library Cataloguing in Publication data

A catalogue record for this book is available from the British Library

ISBN 978-0-85702-580-7
ISBN 978-0-85702-581-4 (pbk)

This book is dedicated to our parents
Paul and Linda Ormrod
Manfred and Ursula Henneberg
John and Marjorie O'Shaughnessy

Contents

About the authors

Robert P. Ormrod is Associate Professor of Business Economics at Aarhus University, Denmark. He received a PhD from Aarhus University for his work on political market orientation. Robert's primary research focus is on political marketing and he publishes regularly on this subject in both marketing and political science journals. Robert is a member of the editorial board of the *Journal of Political Marketing*.

Stephan C. Henneberg is Professor of Marketing and Strategy at the Manchester Business School, University of Manchester. He received his PhD from the Judge Business School, Cambridge. Stephan's research focuses on issues of inter-organisational strategy, business relationships and networks, and political marketing. He was the Academy of Marketing Special Interest Group Chair for Political Marketing and has organised three international conferences on the topic.

Nicholas J. O'Shaughnessy is Professor of Communication at Queen Mary, University of London. He holds degrees from London, Oxford, Columbia and Cambridge Universities. Nicholas's research focus is on political marketing and propaganda, and he is the author and co-author of numerous journal articles and a Senior Editor of the *Journal of Political Marketing*. Nicholas is the author of two classic texts in the field of political marketing, *The Phenomenon of Political Marketing* and *Politics and Propaganda: Weapons of Mass Seduction*. Nicholas is a Quondam Fellow of Hughes Hall, Cambridge University, and a Fellow of the Royal Society of Arts.

Foreword

"Wars begin when you will, but they do not end when you please"

Niccolò Machiavelli, *History of Florence*, 1521–1525

I commend this excellent book from Robert Ormrod, Stephan Henneberg and Nicholas O'Shaughnessy to you from three of the leading figures in Political Marketing Research. It is timely and sums up much of the core work in the area and suggests a more contemporary interactionalist approach and proposes some stimulating new questions and directions for the discipline. The impact on modern democracy is a critical factor which is explored well in this book and is often the most challenging one to address in our age of social marketing media, internationalisation and interactive technology development.

How do we engage voters and actively involve them in the democratic process, or is it inevitable that tactics will be used to turn off citizens from casting their vote so that the opposition can win? Removal of migrants from electoral rolls to ensure the traditional candidate is elected was a tactic in the US Presidential Election which did not work as well as some Republicans wanted. Whilst the unleashing of massive smears and innuendo against the Liberal Democrats in the press ahead of the Eastleigh bye-election in the United Kingdom in February 2013 did not change the end result, it damaged democracy and alienated many from believing the traditional media in the United Kingdom. We have seen it before, in 1996. I was called as an expert witness in the Hannifin Divorce Referendum Appeal Case in the Irish High Court in Ireland on the effectiveness of political advertising, which stimulated a growing interest in the effective measurement of campaigning as a result of the High Court Judge's ruling, that advertising/political marketing could not influence voters.

We have come a long way as result of quality work from such figures as Bruce Newman, Dennis Johnson, Phillipe Mareek, Paul Baines, Jennifer Lees-Marshment and countless others and have an established discipline of political marketing, which has a growing movement of scholars from across the management, communications and political science disciplines in addition to marketers researching. Political marketing as a concept and practice has its early origins in the United States and was first regularly used as a territorial definition within marketing by Kelley (1956). Researchers have subsequently argued that it was first seen as an applied concept in the 1950s and 1960s in the United States while others have seen its early origins as being at the beginning of the twentieth century. It is broadly seen to include both political campaigns for elections and referenda and more covert campaigning in support of lobbying, pressure groups and public affairs work, and in particular modern interest and issue group campaigning. As a result, much work in this area cuts across traditional academic boundaries and lies both within the management and marketing domains as well as politics and international business, and is often seen as a core component of corporate competitiveness and strategy. It very often challenges the boundaries of democracy.

This book helps address those key questions of how we engage voters and citizens in running their lives and democracy. I commend it to you.

Phil Harris,
Series Editor, Advanced Marketing Series
Westminster Professor of Marketing and Public Affairs, Centre for
Corporate and Public Affairs Research, University of Chester, England, UK

1 Introduction

Research is about creating knowledge. The process of knowledge creation is central to all academic fields and can be separated into two main activities: developing theories and concepts, and fact-finding (Wacker, 1998). This book discusses the first two areas of knowledge creation, namely theory and concepts. The words 'theory' and 'concepts' are often the source of concern to students, but they need not be so. The purpose of this book is to take essential elements of the academic study of political marketing and make them more accessible. In this introductory chapter, we first discuss the reasons why theory and concepts are necessary for our understanding of a research field – in our case political marketing – and then we will provide a brief overview of each of the following twelve chapters of this book.

What are theories and concepts? According to Runkel and Runkel (1984), a theory can mean many things, from a guess to a law-like system of causal relationships or explanations, whilst Bacharach (1989) states that 'A theory is a statement of relations among concepts within a set of boundary assumptions and constraints. It is no more than a linguistic device used to organize a complex empirical world' (p. 496). In this latter case, theories create meaning by organising and explaining our knowledge about the various concepts in an academic field as well as communicating what the knowledge actually means (that is, both sense-making and sense-giving). Theories and concepts are important for all research fields because they provide a framework or structure for analysis, they are efficient in that they reduce problem-solving errors and allow us to increase the amount of knowledge we have in the field, and under certain circumstances they can also provide pragmatic explanations for empirical phenomena (Wacker, 1998).

However, being pragmatic is not necessarily the same as being 'true' (Hunt, 2003). As such, the appropriateness, breadth and depth of existing theories and concepts are central to any research area, although this does not imply precision or clarity. In fact, many theories and concepts in the social sciences can be shown to be intrinsically 'messy' (Law, 2004) because of the fluid, elusive and ambiguous nature of what is being explained. However, it is important to somehow examine the quality of existing theory in order to understand the contribution of any research domain and to identify issues of current research practice.

Getting to grips with theory and concept development on a methodological level is central to any field of research, and many different general epistemological sources as well as discipline-specific discussions exist that define theories and concepts and assess their quality. Within the general marketing literature, discussions about theory-building and the relationships between marketing theory and practice are often neglected. This may explain why marketing as a research area is currently so fragmented and why so few articles in political marketing claim to tackle issues of theories of, and in, political marketing, with only limited epistemological discussions (Henneberg, 2008). This book attempts to address this fragmentation by discussing core theory and concepts in political marketing. Our assessment of theory and concept development in the field of political marketing is necessarily based on a perspective mainly derived from marketing theory and management studies (because of the background of the authors). Consequently, we will draw primarily on the general marketing and management literature, with specific sources from the wider social sciences and philosophy. A complementary political science perspective on theory and concepts in political marketing is encouraged.

Theory and concepts in political marketing

Part 1: Theoretical Issues in Political Marketing

Chapter 2, 'Defining Political Marketing', will provide a brief introduction to some of the main themes in the book, such as different interpretations of political marketing, the underlying political marketing exchange and political relationship marketing, which are covered in greater depth in Chapters 3, 4 and 8 respectively. Following this, the chapter will discuss the normative and strategic approaches to understanding stakeholders and their relationships with political actors. Finally, a definition is presented that is based on the political marketing literature rather than an adaptation of an existing definition of commercial marketing for the political context.

Chapter 3, 'Theories and Concepts in Political Marketing', will introduce you to some of the main themes in modern political marketing and set the scene for the remainder of the book. This chapter is designed to demonstrate the breadth and depth of political marketing as a research area. The first part of the chapter discusses 'wide' and 'narrow' interpretations of the nature and scope of political marketing (management). The second part of the chapter introduces seven themes that characterise theoretical and conceptual issues in political marketing and which will be covered in the book: 1) that political marketing is grounded in exchanges and interactions; 2) that there are several competing theoretical approaches to understanding political marketing; 3) that existing marketing and political science theory and concepts need to be adapted to have explanatory power for political marketing; 4) that pragmatic and abstract views of political marketing need to be integrated; 5) that political marketing theories need to cover what, how and especially why (and justify these choices); 6) that theories contextualise as well as bridge levels; and 7) that the theoretical and empirical planes need to be juxtaposed.

Chapter 4, 'The Triadic Interaction Model of Political Exchange', will outline the foundations of the political exchange. The chapter discusses how the political exchange is fundamentally different to the commercial exchange, as the political exchange consists of three interactions in separate markets rather than a dyadic exchange between two consenting actors. These three interactions take place in the electoral market (between voters and candidates or parties), the parliamentary market (between elected representatives) and the governmental market (between governments and citizens). The triadic nature of the political exchange means that all three interactions have to be successful in order for an exchange to be completed; for example, it is possible for a voter to vote for a candidate who cannot deliver on the election pledge due to having no influence in the parliament or due to environmental factors.

Chapter 5, 'Critical Perspectives on Political Marketing', will introduce you to the distinction between political marketing management (the use of tools and concepts by political actors) and political marketing (a theoretical and conceptual research 'lens'). In addition to this, Chapter 5 identifies eleven criticisms of political marketing and political marketing management that have been levelled at both by marketing and political science scholars. Some of the criticisms that concern political marketing theory and concepts are dealt with in this book, including the nature of the political exchange, the relevancy of political marketing as a research lens to understand phenomena in the political sphere, and the non-sophistication of research.

Chapter 6, 'Political Marketing and Theories of Democracy', discusses the implications of a political marketing perspective for democracy. The chapter first describes the nature of three competing approaches to political marketing, the sales-based school (focusing on selling politicians to voters at discrete events), the instrumental/managerial school (focusing on the use of strategies, tools and tactics developed from commercial marketing over the electoral cycle) and the relationship-based school (focusing on identifying and managing relationships with stakeholders in order to achieve organisational goals). After this, the chapter discusses two alternative approaches to democracy, competitive elitism and deliberative democracy. The chapter then outlines the relationship between the three schools of political marketing and the two approaches to democracy and identifies that the relationship-based school of political marketing has the largest conceptual overlap. Therefore, the chapter concludes that it is necessary for political marketing research to move away from the dominant instrumental/managerial paradigm towards a relationship-based approach.

Chapter 7, 'The Ethics of Political Marketing', examines the implications of six alternative ethical approaches to the field of political marketing, namely Kantian, consequentialism, contractualism, communitarian, objective realism and cultural relativism. Ethical questions cannot be answered definitively; their use in the context of political marketing is to define the nature of the moral issues involved and how to prioritise between these issues. The chapter argues that political marketing and political marketing management are not by definition 'bad', despite certain examples of negative advertisements pushing the boundaries of what some would consider ethically defensible. Indeed, utilitarians, objective relativists, cultural relativists and communitarians would support political marketing as it sharpens debate, is legitimated by competitive context, and the nature of the postmodern condition enforces it as it is a response to, rather than a cause of, the social and economic phenomena of these times. Freedom of speech, including economic speech, would be an argument of particular interest to communitarians. However, there are contractualist arguments: where the generation of imagery can be a substitute for political action and for the direct civic participation of citizens, the contract-violation criticisms cannot be dismissed as merely trivial. One thing is certain, however: there is no final resting place for the ethical debates surrounding the uses – and abuses – of political marketing.

Part 2: Conceptual Issues in Political Marketing

Chapter 8, 'Political Relationship Marketing', discusses how the commercial concept of relationship marketing can be developed to fit the political context. The chapter argues that despite the importance of relationships for the development and legitimacy of political actors, political marketing research is still characterised by a focus on the outdated instrumental/managerial approach which emphasises a short-term, transactional approach to understanding the role of political marketing (management) in the modern political reality. The aim of the chapter is therefore to provide arguments for the development of a rigorous conceptual framework of political relationship marketing by discussing existing, as well as potential, applications of relationship marketing within the political sphere. To achieve this, the discussion distinguishes between two perspectives on political relationship marketing: a micro-perspective which is concerned with specific entity and exchange-oriented aspects of long-term relationships in the political sphere, and a macro-perspective which is concerned with the interplay with the wider political structures and the overall political system.

Chapter 9, 'Strategic Political Postures', develops two concepts from the commercial strategy literature to the political context. These developed concepts – strategic political postures – are labelled 'leading' and 'following', and concern the extent to which a political actor bases their political offering according to their own ideology or according to the results of public opinion poll data. The developed concepts are then overlaid to produce a two-by-two grid, describing four typologies, labelled *The Convinced Ideologist*, *The Tactical Populist*, *The Political Lightweight* and *The Relationship Builder*. The convinced ideologist focuses primarily on the needs and wants of party members, basing the political offering on ideological conviction. The tactical populist adopts the opposite approach by basing the political offering on the needs and wants of external stakeholders such as voters and the media. The political lightweight has a weak focus on ideology and does not take public opinion into account; this is arguably not a viable long-term strategy. Finally, the relationship builder draws upon the arguments made in the commercial literature that understands leading and following to be activities that are complementary rather than mutually exclusive.

Chapter 10, 'Political Market Orientation', develops the commercial concept of market orientation to suit the political context. The conceptual model of political market orientation that is developed in the chapter consists of two sets of constructs, representing the behaviour of party members and the attitudes of party members to stakeholder groups in society. The four behavioural constructs focus on the way in which information is generated, passed through the political organisation, used in the development of the political offering and finally implemented. Different stakeholder groups are derived from the commercial marketing literature (voters, competing parties and party members themselves), with the addition of several groups that have not been included in previous commercial conceptualisations (the media, citizens, and lobby and interest groups) but which are argued to be central in the political context.

Chapter 11, 'Political Marketing Strategy and Party Organisational Structure', links the strategic political postures conceptual framework and the political market orientation conceptual framework to provide an integrated concept of political marketing. Each of the four strategic political postures has a specific set of important stakeholders, and a set of dynamic relationships between the stakeholders and the elements of the party structure. The tactical populist concentrates its energy on voters and the media, and the structure of its internal relationships focuses on implementing a strategy that is decided on by the party top. The opposite of this is the convinced ideologist, which concentrates on party members and stakeholder groups with a special affinity with the party; there is a focus on the inclusion of party members of all levels, but this is at the expense of listening to stakeholders outside of the party. The relationship builder attempts to reconcile these two more extreme postures by balancing the needs and wants of a wide selection of stakeholder groups. Finally, we apply the integrated concept of political marketing strategy to the network party type from the organisational theory literature on political parties in order to demonstrate how concepts derived from commercial marketing theory can complement – rather than replace – existing models from the political science literature.

Chapter 12, 'Symbolism in Political Marketing', describes the way in which symbols are used to persuade especially voters of a particular point of view in a political discussion. Symbolic acts have been at the heart of politics almost since recorded history began. What is often regarded as great political leadership is in fact the supreme sensitivity to symbols and a mastery of their manipulation. Symbolic government is a style of government where the creation of symbolic images, symbolic actions and celebratory rhetoric have become a principal concern. This is equally valid for political actors in opposition, but is more extreme in incumbents and so the chapter focuses mainly on symbolic *government*. Appearances do not just matter to the symbolic government; they are central to the way in which voters are communicated with. The symbolic government is a relatively new kind of government; this is not to say that previous governments did not frequently use symbolic images and actions, but what was once just one of several tools of government has now graduated into becoming its central organising principle, absorbing therefore much of the energy of government.

Chapter 13, 'Conclusion', draws upon the theories and concepts discussed in the preceding chapters in the book and proposes two research agendas. Taking the starting point of the 'wide' interpretation of the nature and scope of political marketing, the first research agenda discusses how topics such as relationship-building, political market orientation profiles and an understanding of the political exchange as three interlocking interactions can provide a theoretical and conceptual 'lens' through which to perceive phenomena in the political marketplace. The second research agenda concentrates on linking political marketing to issues in political marketing management, such as symbolism, values and the way in which election campaigns are increasingly 'outsourced' to lobby or single-issue groups.

References

Bacharach, S.B. (1989) 'Organizational theories: some criteria for evaluation', *Academy of Management Review*, 14: 496–515.

Henneberg, S.C. (2008) 'An epistemological perspective on research in political marketing', *Journal of Political Marketing*, 7 (2): 151–82.

Hunt, S.D. (2003) *Controversy in Marketing Theory*. New York: Sharpe.

Law, J. (2004) *After Method*. London: Routledge.

Runkel, P.J. and Runkel, M. (1984) *A Guide to Usage for Writers and Students in the Social Sciences*. Totowa, NJ: Rowman.

Wacker, J.G. (1998) 'A definition of theory: research guidelines for different theory-building research methods in operations management', *Journal of Operations Management*, 16: 361–85.

Part 1

Theoretical Issues in Political Marketing

2 Defining Political Marketing

After reading this chapter, you should be able to:

- identify existing definitions of political marketing
- explain why the concepts of exchange, relationships and stakeholders are essential to our understanding of political marketing
- define political marketing as a field of research.

Introduction

Up until now, definitions of political marketing have mirrored developments in the definition of commercial marketing (Henneberg, 2002). However, recent developments in political marketing theory have underlined the fundamental differences between political and commercial marketing (Baines et al., 2003; Henneberg and Ormrod, 2013), and therefore it is imperative to develop a definition of political marketing that takes its point of departure from political marketing theory. This raises the first issue that must be addressed by our definition: what is the explanatory realm of political marketing? Should the definition focus on a narrow interpretation of political marketing (political marketing as a set of activities) or on a wide interpretation (political marketing as a philosophy)? The second issue concerns the nature of the political exchange as fundamentally different to the commercial exchange (that is, a triadic interaction as opposed to a dyadic interaction; see Chapter 4). Does this mean that the definition of political marketing can nevertheless be based on the concept of exchange as it is understood in the commercial literature? The third issue builds on the question of a narrow or broad understanding of political marketing, as well as the nature of the political exchange: to what extent are relationships a central component of a definition of political marketing? Finally, most political marketing research focuses primarily on voters as the key stakeholder group, despite the importance of this group varying according to the position on the electoral cycle. This raises the final issue to be addressed by our definition: does one focus on normative and/or strategic approaches to identifying and categorising specific stakeholder groups or does one adopt a neutral stance, instead leaving this choice to the individual political actor?

The aim of this chapter is to develop a definition of political marketing. This aim is motivated by the need to make explicit our understanding of what political marketing is, a necessary exercise when discussing theories and concepts (and empirical methods) in political marketing. This chapter will proceed as follows. We first present five existing definitions of political marketing that have been selected to represent advances in research from the origins of academic research into political marketing in the mid-1970s to the current day. After this we discuss 'wide' and 'narrow' interpretations of political marketing, the nature of the political marketing exchange, political relationship marketing and how one can integrate the stakeholder concept into an understanding of political marketing. Finally, we propose a new definition of political marketing that takes into account the various issues that are discussed in this chapter.

Existing definitions of political marketing

In the following section we present five definitions of political marketing that we argue provide a selection of the definitions that have been proposed over the past forty years in the literature. Whilst by no means exhaustive, these definitions provide a sufficiently nuanced picture of the development of our understanding of the nature of political marketing from the original broadening of the marketing debate in the first half of the 1970s (Shama, 1976), through the change to an emphasis on relationships and exchanges in the second half of the 1990s (the 'classic' definitions proposed by Lock and Harris, 1996, and Henneberg, 2002), to current definitions that demonstrate the differences in the understanding of the fundamental nature of political marketing in the American (American Marketing Association, 2007; Hughes and Dann, 2009) and European (Winther-Nielsen, 2011) commercial marketing traditions and their political marketing counterparts.

The first definition of political marketing can be traced back to Shama (1976), who defined political marketing as 'the process by which political candidates and their ideas are directed at voters in order to satisfy their potential needs and thus gain their support for the candidate and ideas in question' (Shama, 1976: 766). This definition was developed as part of the broadening of marketing debate in the early 1970s (Levy and Kotler, 1969; Kotler, 1975). Shama's (1976) definition of political marketing mirrored its commercial counterpart in that political marketing was seen as a process rather than an organisational philosophy, with the focus on political candidates satisfying voters as the central exchange partners rather than a wider focus on relationships.

Lock and Harris's (1996) definition reflected developments in the field of commercial marketing from a transaction-based to a relationship-based approach. Lock and Harris (1996) define political marketing as both a discipline and an activity. As a discipline, political marketing is 'the study of the processes of exchanges between political entities and their environment and amongst themselves, with particular reference to the positioning of both those entities and their communications', whilst as an activity, political marketing is 'concerned with strategies for positioning and communications, and the methods through which these strategies may be realized, including the search for information into attitudes, awareness and response of target audiences' (Lock and Harris, 1996: 21–22). This definition therefore recognises that political marketing is not solely concerned with the actions of political actors through the permanent campaign and that the underlying mechanism is that of the exchange of value between political entities and environments at both the aggregate and individual level.

Henneberg (2002) proposed that 'Political marketing seeks to establish, maintain and enhance long-term political relationships at a profit for society, so that the objectives of the individual political actors and organisations involved are met. This is done by mutual exchange and fulfilment of promises' (Henneberg, 2002 103). This definition is close to that of (Grönroos, 1990) in the commercial literature, building on the relationship marketing approach (Bannon, 2005; Henneberg and O'Shaughnessy, 2009). Two key stakeholders are named: society and political actors (both individuals and organisations).

The American Marketing Association (AMA) defines political marketing as 'Marketing designed to influence target audiences to vote for a particular person, party, or proposition' (AMA, 2007).[1] This definition builds on the AMA's definition of commercial marketing as 'the activity, set of institutions, and processes for creating, communicating, delivering, and exchanging offerings that have value for customers, clients, partners, and society at large' (AMA, 2007).[2] Hughes and Dann (2009: 244) integrate and develop the AMA's (2007) definitions and propose that political marketing is 'a set of activities, processes or political institutions used by political organisations, candidates and individuals to create, communicate, deliver and exchange promises of value with voter-consumers, political party stakeholders and society at large'. The influence of the AMA's (2007) definition is apparent in the lack of an explicit reference to relationship-building in Hughes and Dann's (2009) definition; on the other hand, the role of stakeholders is

---

[1] www.marketingpower.com/Community/ARC/Pages/Additional/Definition/default. aspx, accessed 19 September 2012.

[2] www.marketingpower.com/Community/ARC/Pages/Additional/Definition/default. aspx, accessed 19 September 2012.

emphasised in the definition by identifying four groups as relevant for analysis, namely political marketers, voter/consumers, party stakeholders and society in general.

Finally, Winther-Nielsen (2011: 29) considers political marketing to be 'concerned with reciprocated exchanges of value between political entities and their environments'.[3] As such, Winther-Nielsen's (2011) definition builds on Lock and Harris' (1996) with its focus on entities and environments, and follows the modern perception of political marketing as focusing on exchanges of value. Where Winther-Nielsen's (2011) definition differs is that no specific goal is stated, in contrast to Lock and Harris' (1996) focus on political marketing as a discipline and a set of processes, and Henneberg's (2002) more general focus on relationship-building and long-term organisational aims.

Narrow and wide interpretations of political marketing

Discussions surrounding the theoretical foundations of both commercial and political marketing remain unresolved and fragmented in the academic literature, and the dominant instrumental/managerial paradigm results in the current empirical focus of research on descriptive studies of activities carried out by political actors (Henneberg, 2008). This leads us to ask the following question: is political marketing, or should political marketing be, solely concerned with getting a candidate elected, or does, or should, political marketing provide a theoretical and conceptual lens through which to understand phenomena in the political marketplace? These two interpretations of the nature and scope of political marketing can be described as 'narrow' and 'wide' approaches respectively (Henneberg, 2008).

The narrow approach focuses on political marketing management, that is, how tools from the commercial marketing literature are used to achieve political actors' tactical and strategic aims. By concentrating on marketing activities, the narrow interpretation of the nature and role of marketing in the political context reduces the explanatory realm of political marketing as a research field to the observable behaviour of political actors. This narrow interpretation, coupled with the adoption of outdated concepts and models from the field of commercial marketing (Henneberg and O'Shaughnessy, 2007), results in a body of research that is open to criticism from marketing and political scientists alike (Henneberg, 2004, 2008).

On the other hand, the wide interpretation of the nature and scope of political marketing emphasises the use of theories and concepts from the commercial marketing literature that are developed to suit the idiosyncratic nature of the political context. Marketing's role in the political organisation

---

[3] Winther-Nielsen's original definition was written in Danish; the English translation is by the authors and is authorised by Winther-Nielsen.

focuses on facilitating exchanges of value and on relationship-building with various stakeholders such as voters, competing parties or candidates and the media (Dean and Croft, 2001; Hughes and Dann, 2009). This wide interpretation of political marketing can contribute to the understanding of the political context by providing an alternative theoretical 'lens' through which to view political behaviour (Henneberg, 2004). For example, political science concentrates on structural or group characteristics when examining voter behaviour; a political marketing perspective would instead help understand how individual voters make decisions, become part of a discrete group and make sense of the political brand (Henneberg, 2008).

The five current definitions vary in their adoption of the narrow and wide interpretations of the nature and scope of political marketing. What can be seen is that, apart from the AMA (2007) definition, there has been a gradual shift in emphasis over time from a narrow interpretation towards a wide interpretation. This definitional shift has followed developments in the field of commercial marketing, from a transaction-based approach towards relationship- and network-based approaches (Henneberg, 2002). This wider interpretation has implications for our understanding of the concept of exchange: whilst a transaction-based approach to market exchanges implies a short-term perspective, the wider interpretation implies a long-term perspective that sees relationship management as a key activity. However, whilst the commercial exchange of value can be seen as a dyadic interaction, the unique characteristics of the political marketplace necessitate an understanding of the political exchange as an interaction triad.

The political marketing exchange

The definitions of political marketing discussed above are unified in that they all focus on the exchange of value as the fundamental concept in political marketing. This exchange of value is understood in the same way as it is in the commercial marketing literature, that is, as a dyadic interaction between two actors that both possess agency and enter into the exchange freely (Brennan and Henneberg, 2008). However, Henneberg and Ormrod (2013) argue that a political exchange needs to be conceptualised as three linked interactions rather than as one dyadic (buyer/seller) exchange that is characteristic of commercial market interactions. These three exchanges are the electoral interactions between voters and political actors (parties/candidates), the parliamentary interactions between political actors that have mandates in the parliament, and the governmental interactions between governments and citizens. This triadic structure to each political exchange means that it is necessary for each interaction to be successful before the political exchange is complete; not only must the political actor receive enough votes to be represented in the parliament, but the political actor has to be able to influence legislation, and environmental factors have to be amenable to the implementation of the legislation (Henneberg and Ormrod, 2013). In the following we briefly discuss the characteristics of each of the three interactions.

The electoral interaction takes place between the voter and the political actor at election time and is the most common object of political marketing research due to its salience. Unlike a commercial exchange between a business and a consumer, the electoral interaction is not characterised by balanced reciprocity as the political actor receives value immediately in the form of the vote whilst usually the voter only receives a general promise that certain behaviours will occur in return, such as the implementation of election pledges. The second key difference between the commercial exchange and the electoral interaction is how decisions are made that decide the composition of the elected assembly and thus whether the interaction is successful – whilst an individual actor or small group such as a buying centre or family make the decision in the commercial exchange, all voters take part in the decision, and the majority decision prevails (this majority depends on the voting system and vote aggregation algorithm that is used in a party system).

If the electoral interaction is successful, the candidate or party becomes represented in the parliament. Depending on the aggregated decision of the electorate, this may or may not result in the candidate or party being part of the parliamentary majority (Henneberg and Ormrod, 2013). Therefore, the characteristics of the parliamentary interaction are closely linked to the wider political system; for example, in the United States there are few parties and so majoritarian rule is the norm (or is it that because of a majoritarian system, there are only a few parties?); in European proportional representation systems such as Denmark's and Germany's, coalition governments are the norm, and so the original offering of the party or candidate in the electoral interaction is 'watered down', although this may even have been taken into account in the process surrounding the development of the political offering (Bowler and Farrell, 1992). On the micro-level, the parliamentary interaction takes place between elected representatives and is manifested in the day-to-day *realpolitik* of running a government, securing parliamentary majorities, and developing and passing legislation. As such it is possible for the electoral interaction to be successful but the nature and composition of the elected assembly may hinder the reciprocation of value by the political actor.

The final interaction occurs in the governmental market, that is, between the government and citizens as a result of the conceptualisation of the first interaction in the electoral marketplace between voters, on the one hand, and parties or candidates, on the other (Henneberg and Ormrod, 2013). In this interaction, the promised offering is reciprocated by tax revenues and other resources that are not necessarily tied to any specific spending promises. However, it is not only citizens who are affected by government legislation, as all stakeholders in society are influenced either directly or indirectly by laws that are passed, for example when income-tax increases result in lower disposable income for individual consumers. In addition to this, there are many socio-economic factors that have the potential to mediate, moderate or even prevent this interaction from being successful, such as high inflation, industrial disputes and post-election exogenous shocks to the economy.

Therefore, it is only if all three of these interactions are successfully reciprocated that a political exchange is completed. This triadic structure stands in stark contrast to the dyadic structure that characterises commercial exchanges. For example, it is possible for both the electoral and parliamentary interactions to be successful (the voter's chosen candidate or party is elected and forms part of the ruling majority), but if socio-economic forces mean that the election promise cannot be carried out, the governmental interaction cannot be completed and so the political exchange fails (the triadic exchange is the subject of Chapter 4).

Political relationship marketing

A relationship-based approach to understanding the way in which commercial organisations in business-to-business markets interact with their stakeholders was first proposed by Grönroos (1990) and has since developed into the new (service) dominant logic of marketing (Vargo and Lusch, 2004). However, despite an increased focus on the relationship and network interaction aspects of commercial exchanges, this approach has been slow to influence political marketing literature and practice. The dominant approach in political marketing remains the instrumental/managerial paradigm, despite criticisms (Bannon, 2005). Henneberg and O'Shaughnessy (2009) argue that a relationship-based approach has the potential to influence political marketing on two levels: the micro-level with its focus on interaction and exchange relationships between the political actor and individual stakeholders, and the macro-level with its focus on the wider interplay between a relationship-based approach and the structural and systemic nature of the political marketplace.

How a political party or candidate manages relationships with individual stakeholders at the micro-level is a matter of prioritisation – scarce resources mean that identifiable voter segments are more attractive than others, some coalition partners are more ideologically compatible than others, and certain stakeholders are more important from a normative perspective. Whilst Henneberg and Ormrod (2013) focus on the electorate in their discussion of micro-level issues, the concept and practical manifestation of political relationship marketing can be equally applied to stakeholders in general.

Political relationship marketing at the macro-level is associated with the extent to which the interaction between the political actor and the political system leads to a short-term focus on popular offerings at election time, or a more long-term building of relationships with key stakeholder groups. Both of these approaches are a matter of degree (a greater or lesser relationship intensity), can coexist within a single political system (e.g. Henneberg's, 2006, tactical populist and relationship builder strategic political posture types) and are dynamic (can vary across the electoral cycle or according to socio-economic developments over time). These issues are discussed in detail in Chapters 8 and 9.

Stakeholders in political marketing

Who – or what – is a stakeholder, and what is a stake? Friedman and Miles (2006) identify no less than fifty-five different definitions of the characteristics of stakeholders, ranging from definitions that focus on the implications for the performance of the organisation (Freeman, 1984) and managerial activities (Gray et al., 1996), to very broad definitions that include future generations, animals and even naturally occurring phenomena (Starik, 1994). These definitions can be placed into one of three groups, namely those definitions focusing on normative, descriptive or instrumental/strategic issues (Friedman and Miles, 2006). For political managers, a normative approach to identifying stakeholders corresponds to decisions concerning which stakeholders ought to be selected to facilitate exchange with, the descriptive approach to how managers actually select such stakeholders, and the instrumental/strategic approach to how stakeholders are identified in the strategic planning process. In practice it is most useful to concentrate on normative and strategic definitions as these allow for a measure of analysis, as opposed to simply describing the relationship between the organisation and the stakeholder, a common criticism of political marketing research (Henneberg, 2004).

Adopting a normative approach to identifying stakeholders involves asking questions about which stakeholders the political organisation *ought* to include in its deliberations about its offering. The normative approach is closely linked to questions involving values, ethics, societal norms, the number of stakeholders that are included in decision-making processes, and how these stakeholders are selected (Bishop, 2000; O'Shaughnessy, 2002). On the other hand, a strategic approach to identifying relevant stakeholders implies a goal-oriented approach where concrete, measurable success criteria can be developed. Irrespective of which approach is selected, the question remains as to how to categorise these stakeholders. Carroll (2005) discusses three general ways in which to categorise stakeholders, based upon whether the stakeholder is internal or external to the organisation, is primary or secondary to achieving the goals of the organisation, or is characterised by a mixture of the power of the stakeholder, the legitimacy of the stakeholder's claim and the urgency with which the stakeholder's claim has to be dealt with.

Despite a long history of research into stakeholder theories in relation to the commercial literature (Friedman and Miles, 2006, identify an internal

memo at the Stanford Research Institute in 1964 as providing the first definition), little research has been carried out in the political marketing literature
that specifically investigates the applicability of alternative stakeholder
approaches or categorisation schemes in the political marketing context,
despite the recognition that political candidates are dependent on more than
just exchanges of value with voters at election time (Kotler, 1975; Shama,
1976; Newman, 1994). Probably the most in-depth analysis of the role of
stakeholders in the development of a definition of political marketing was
published by Hughes and Dann (2009) who discuss the nature of stakeholders
in the political marketing context. They propose seventeen stakeholder types
developed from a review of the commercial, non-profit and social marketing
literature, using Scholem and Stewart's (2002) stakeholder mapping process.
Whilst Hughes and Dann's (2009) article suggests a specific method of identifying and classifying stakeholders, we argue that an *a priori* linking of
specific stakeholder groups to the definition of political marketing can be too
restrictive.

Whilst the actual derivation of the relevant stakeholders in the political marketing literature has remained implicit, the voter and the mass media have both
been the subject of the vast majority of research. This is unsurprising given the
relative visibility and importance of these groups to political actors, especially
at election time, but it does emphasise the goal-oriented, strategic approach to
identifying stakeholders, and implies a narrow approach to understanding the
scope of political marketing. Add to this a normative angle and the subsequent
broader understanding of the scope of political marketing, and it becomes clear
that other stakeholders such as competing parties/candidates, grassroots party
members and public sector workers can be included in conceptual models
(Newman, 1994; Dean and Croft, 2001; Henneberg, 2002; Ormrod, 2005, 2007;
Ormrod and Henneberg, 2010, 2011), and arguably that this wider perspective
is necessary given the focus of the governmental interaction of the political
marketing exchange on exogenous factors.

The question thus arises of how broad the definition of stakeholders in the
political marketplace should or can be in order to achieve the aims of the
political actor. At first glance, marketing would seem to prescribe a narrow
approach to identifying stakeholders as it focuses on achieving aims, irrespective of whether these aims are long term or not. However, taking a broad
approach to identifying and categorising stakeholders in the political marketing context may provide a more informative angle, including as it does
both normative and strategic elements. For example, using Starik's (1994)
approach would lead to the inclusion of the global economy as an independent stakeholder in political marketing; indeed, the global economy would fit
in with the majority of definitions of stakeholders in that it directly affects
and can be affected by the governmental interaction of the political marketing exchange, but the question remains as to whether this inclusion is
because the economy should be included or because it is necessary for the
success of the political candidate or party.

The discussion above points to the necessity of including both normative and strategic elements in political marketing research and practice. A goal-oriented approach is arguably more realistic in the electoral interaction as resource limitations impact on certain activities such as voter segmentation and opinion polling. However, the wider implications of legislation for all stakeholders necessitate a wider, normative view. Therefore, due to the differences between political systems, the structure and history of each system and the diverse characteristics of the stakeholders within each system, we argue that a *definition* of political marketing cannot *a priori* specify an approach to identifying and categorising stakeholders that is applicable across all political systems or even valid at all points on the electoral cycle within a political system. As such, the question of whether a political actor focuses on a particular stakeholder on normative or strategic grounds is context-specific, and therefore it is necessary to resist the temptation to argue for one approach to identifying and categorising stakeholders over another; what is essential, however, is that the stakeholder concept is included within the definition of political marketing.

Defining political marketing

From the above discussion we can identify several characteristics of a definition of political marketing that bears more or less resemblance to existing definitions of political marketing. First, the concept of exchange has been argued to be fundamentally different in the political context; instead of the exchange as a dyad underpinning a commercial marketing understanding, we posit three linked interactions that result in one political system exchange. Relationships are essential to facilitating these exchanges, and so it is necessary to distinguish between political marketing at the micro- and macro-levels. Furthermore, the nature of the political exchange and the implications of adopting a perspective based on relationships and interactions necessitate both a wide interpretation of political marketing as a research 'lens' or perspective through which to observe phenomena in the political sphere *and* a strategic approach. Finally, this wide interpretation of the scope of political marketing research leads to the inclusion of stakeholders in the normative and strategic considerations of political actors.

From the above discussion, we propose the following definition of political marketing:

> Political marketing is a perspective from which to understand phenomena in the political sphere, and an approach that seeks to facilitate political exchanges of value through interactions in the electoral, parliamentary and governmental markets to manage relationships with stakeholders.

As with the majority of previous definitions of political marketing, exchanges of value, relationships and stakeholders are core elements of our definition. However, our definition differs in several key ways. First, the exchange component is understood as a triadic interaction rather than a dyadic exchange. Second, political relationships are dynamically managed, a characteristic that does not dictate a specific duration or intensity. Finally, there is a non-specific understanding of stakeholders that allows for differences at the systemic and organisational level, and from normative and strategic approaches.

Conclusions, limitations and implications

In this chapter, we have proposed a definition of political marketing that builds upon a broad approach to understanding the scope of political marketing and focuses on the importance of exchanges of value, relationship management and a non-specific approach to stakeholder identification. Our definition is novel in that it builds directly on political marketing theory rather than on an adaptation of existing definitions of commercial marketing. A limitation of our work is that we do not provide an in-depth discussion of whether political actors *should* use political marketing, although in our defence it has long been accepted in the political marketing literature (and more recently in the political science literature) that political actors do not really have a choice as to whether to use tools and concepts developed from the realm of commercial marketing (Sheth in Newman, 1994). Finally, the implications of our work for political marketing research is that our definition provides a perspective that is based upon the idiosyncratic characteristics of the political marketplace.

Discussion questions

- Why do we need a definition of political marketing?
- Read the five definitions of political marketing that are discussed in this chapter. In which ways does the new definition developed in this chapter differ from each of the five previous definitions?
- Choose a political party or candidate in your country. Which stakeholders *should* the party or candidate take into consideration, and which stakeholders are *necessary* to the success of the party or candidate?]

Key terms

Wide approach to political marketing	Political marketing exchange
	Political marketing definition
Narrow approach to political marketing	Political relationship marketing
	Stakeholders

Further reading

Chapters 3, 4 and 8 provide an in-depth treatment of 'wide' and 'narrow' interpretations of political marketing, the political marketing exchange and political relationship marketing respectively.

Friedman and Miles (2006) provide a good introduction to alternative approaches to understanding, identifying and categorising stakeholders, and the issues that this raises for (primarily commercial) organisations.

Henneberg (2002) provides an in-depth treatment of the various ways in which a relationship-based definition of political marketing can be linked to concepts and practical applications in political marketing.

References

American Marketing Association (2007) 'Definition of marketing', www.marketingpower. com/Community/ARC/Pages/Additional/Definition/default.aspx, accessed 19 September 2012.

Baines, P.R., Brennan, R. and Egan, J. (2003) '"Market" classification and political campaigning: some strategic implications', *Journal of Political Marketing*, 2 (2): 47–66.

Bannon, D.P. (2005) 'Relationship marketing and the political process', *Journal of Political Marketing*, 4 (2): 85–102.

Bishop, J.D. (2000) 'A framework for discussing normative theories of business ethics', *Business Ethics Quarterly*, 10 (3): 563–91.

Bowler, S. and Farrell, D.M. (1992) *Electoral Strategies and Political Marketing*. London: Macmillan.

Brennan, R. and Henneberg, S.C. (2008) 'Does political marketing need the concept of customer value?' *Marketing Intelligence & Planning*, 26 (6): 559–72.

Carroll, A.B. (2005) 'Stakeholder management: background and advances', in P. Harris and C.S. Fleischer (eds), *The Handbook of Public Affairs*. London: Sage, 501–16.

Dean, D. and Croft, R. (2001) 'Friends and relations: long-term approaches to political campaigning', *European Journal of Marketing*, 35 (11): 1197–216.

Freeman, R.E. (1984) *Strategic Management: a Stakeholder Approach*. Boston: Pitman.

Friedman, A.L and Miles, S. (2006) *Stakeholders: Theory and Practice*. Oxford: Oxford University Press.

Gray, R.H., Owen, D.L. and Adams, C. (1996) *Accounting and Accountability: Changes and Challenges in Corporate Social and Environmental Reporting*. Hemel Hempstead: Prentice-Hall.

Grönroos, C. (1990) 'Relationship marketing: the strategy continuum', *Journal of Business Research*, 20: 3–11.

Henneberg, S.C. (2002) 'The idea of political marketing', in S.C. Henneberg and N.J. O'Shaughnessy (eds), *The Idea of Political Marketing*. Westport, CT: Praeger, 93–170.

Henneberg, S.C. (2004) 'The views of an *advocatus dei*: political marketing and its crit-ics', *Journal of Public Affairs*, 4 (3): 225–43.

Henneberg, S.C. (2006) 'Leading or following? A theoretical analysis of political mar-keting postures', *Journal of Political Marketing*, 5 (3): 29–46.

Henneberg, S.C. (2008) 'An epistemological perspective on political marketing', *Journal of Political Marketing*, 7 (2): 151–82.

Henneberg, S.C. and Ormrod, R.P. (2013) 'The triadic interaction model of political marketing exchange', *Marketing Theory*.

Henneberg, S.C. and O'Shaughnessy, N.J. (2007) 'Theory and concept develop-ment in political marketing: issues and agenda', *Journal of Political Marketing*, 6 (2/3): 5–32.

Henneberg, S.C. and O'Shaughnessy, N.J. (2009) 'Political relationship marketing: some macro/micro thoughts', *Journal of Marketing Management*, 25 (1/2): 5–29.

Hughes, A. and Dann, S. (2009) 'Political marketing and stakeholder engagement', *Marketing Theory*, 9 (2): 243–56.

Kotler, P. (1975) 'Overview of political candidate marketing', *Advances in Consumer Research*, 2: 761–70.

Kotler, P. and Levy, S. (1969) 'Broadening the concept of marketing', *Journal of Marketing*, 33: 10–15.

Lock, A. and Harris, P. (1996) 'Political marketing – *vive la différence!*', *European Journal of Marketing*, 30 (10/11): 14–24.

Newman, B.I. (1994) *The Marketing of the President*. Thousand Oaks, CA: Sage.

Ormrod, R.P. (2005) 'A conceptual model of political market orientation', *Journal of Nonprofit and Public Sector Marketing*, 14 (1/2): 47–64.

Ormrod, R.P. (2007) 'Political market orientation and its commercial cousin: close family or distant relatives?', *Journal of Political Marketing*, 6 (2/3): 69–90.

Ormrod, R.P. and Henneberg, S.C. (2010) 'Strategic political postures and political market orientation: towards an integrated concept of political marketing strategy', *Journal of Political Marketing*, 9 (4): 294–313.

Ormrod, R.P. and Henneberg, S.C. (2011) 'An investigation into the relationship between political activity levels and political market orientation', *European Journal of Marketing*, 44 (3/4): 382–400.

O'Shaughnessy, N.J. (2002) 'The marketing of political marketing', in N.J. O'Shaughnessy and S.C. Henneberg (eds), *The Idea of Political Marketing*. Westport, CT: Praeger, 209–20.

Scholem, P. and Stewart, D. (2002) 'Towards a measurement framework for stake-holder-issue identification and salience', Australia and New Zealand Marketing Academy Conference, Melbourne.

Shama, A. (1976) 'The marketing of political candidates', *Journal of the Academy of Marketing Science*, 4 (4): 764–77.

Sheth, J.N. (1994) 'Preface', in B.I. Newman, *The Marketing of the President*. Thousand Oaks, CA: Sage.

Starik, M. (1994) 'Essay by Mark Starik: the Toronto Conference: Reflections on stake-holder theory', *Business and Society*, 33 (1): 89–95.

Vargo, S.L. and Lusch, R.F. (2004) 'Evolving to a new dominant logic for marketing', *Journal of Marketing*, 68 (1): 1–17.

Winther-Nielsen, S. (2011) *Politisk Marketing: Personer, Partier og Praksis*. Copenhagen: Karnov Group.

3 Theories and Concepts in Political Marketing

After reading this chapter, you should be able to:

- state the characteristics of modern political marketing management
- distinguish between wide and narrow interpretations of political marketing
- identify seven key themes in political marketing.

Introduction

Marketing theory has been influenced by many different disciplines, but it has also contributed to the development of other academic areas within management studies and beyond. While there is a considerable stock of knowledge concerning political marketing management, especially in the areas of campaign management, political strategies and comparative political marketing management, the essence of political marketing theory remains somewhat opaque. This is sometimes explained by the notion that 'traditional marketing frameworks do not fit neatly into a political marketing configuration' (Dean and Croft, 2001: 1197). Furthermore, there is no clear understanding of the ontological and epistemological implications of a marketing perspective on politics due to the primary research focus on descriptive studies that attempt to explain what political actors actually do (Marland, 2003). This refers to the fact that marketing theory makes specific assumptions about the 'fabric of reality' (ontology) and how knowledge claims can be made about this reality (epistemology). These assumptions can be applied to politics and constitute a political marketing perspective. In this chapter, we argue that the managerial focus is only one element of political marketing theory. What has been neglected is an epistemological view of political marketing as a 'research lens', a meta-theoretical vehicle for making sense of the political sphere. In order to develop this argument, we first provide a concise overview of the state of affairs in political marketing, followed by a discussion of 'narrow' and 'wide' interpretations of the nature and scope of political marketing research. We will then discuss seven key themes that we consider to be essential research foci.

The state of affairs in political marketing

It has often been argued that the application of marketing tools and instruments in politics is nothing new (Baines and Egan, 2001). This may or may not be the case, but what certainly has changed in the last twenty-five years is not just the magnitude of political marketing management but the belief that political actors not only act in marketing terms but also think in marketing terms; they themselves as well as outside experts believe that they *do* marketing management (even if they may not admit it publicly), and they try to integrate their use of marketing instruments in a coherent marketing strategy (Dermody and Scullion, 2001). This is notwithstanding the idea that much of their marketing knowledge might be 'political folk wisdom' (Scammell, 1999: 738). In this context, political actors include not only political parties, politicians and political consultants, but also governments, single-issue groups, lobbying organisations and so on, and political marketing applications have moved from solely a communication tool to an integrated way of managing politics, be it policy development, permanent campaigning or even governing. Six main developments of applications of political marketing management can be generalised for most democratic political systems in the last two decades:

- an increased sophistication of communication and 'spin'
- an emphasis on product and image management, including candidate positioning and policy development
- an increased sophistication of news management, that is, the use of 'free' media
- a more coherent and planned political marketing strategy development
- an intensified and integrated use of political market research
- an emphasis on political marketing organisation and professionalisation of political management.

However, most political actors are far from possessing an integrated and sophisticated understanding of marketing applications for their specific political exchange situations. Political marketing management has caused some parties and candidates to adopt a simplistic and populistic 'follower' mentality, contributing to the disenchantment of the electorate and a resulting cynicism regarding politics in general (Henneberg, 2006).

Serious, intensive and coordinated research activities on how marketing can be applied to politics is a fairly recent addition to the area of social and non-profit marketing. The academic field of political marketing started to form in the late 1980s and concentrated on topical events and in-depth analyses of marketing instruments, but none offered a general theory of political marketing. However, research on political marketing management quickly gained momentum, driven mainly by the increasing use of marketing applications by political parties and candidates. Although technological drivers, especially in the media arena, are often quoted as being the main reason for this acceleration, various changes in the political sphere fostered this development, such as lower levels of party identification and higher electoral volatility. Furthermore, increased competitive pressure in the political market with single-issue groups for resources such as volunteer labour and member subscriptions, less differentiation between political offerings and a general professionalisation of political marketing management activities characterise modern political markets (Panebianco, 1988). To provide an understanding of these phenomena and the reactions of political actors to them, research on political marketing management became an established sub-discipline of marketing, especially in France, the UK, Germany, Australia, New Zealand and the USA (Perloff, 1999). The need to describe and understand these phenomena instigated numerous academic articles, books and conferences. So whilst the institutional requirements for the development of political marketing theory are in place, an assessment of current research on political marketing shows shortcomings.

A distinct bias in the research foci of marketing instrument usage in campaign situations obscures more general and theoretical discussions. Whilst communication activities, market research tools and other political marketing instruments and activities have been well analysed and compared, this has been undertaken on a descriptive level. Higher-level concept development or prescriptive studies are rare. Furthermore, more fundamental issues such as ethical dimensions of political marketing, the underlying exchange mechanisms and the interaction of marketing activities with the political system have remained under-researched. As such, political marketing 'theories' have not been developed in any depth and so empirical work is not well anchored. Many crucial discussions about definitions have remained unresolved, not due to competing positions and interpretations but because of negligence and inactivity in these areas. Furthermore, a tendency towards ossification exists as many political marketing studies use an oversimplistic instrumental/managerial interpretation of marketing, oriented towards the '4P' marketing mix of product, price, promotion and place (see Baines et al., 2011: 15). This causes a decoupling of research in political marketing from fresh developments in commercial marketing theory, be it on conceptual or epistemological levels. For example, relational marketing concepts which have gained importance in commercial marketing theory in the last decades do not find their equivalent in political marketing (Bannon, 2005). Several arguments have been put forward that theoretical and applied research on political marketing need to be more innovative. In the next section of this chapter, we will examine 'narrow' and 'wide' interpretations of the scope and nature of political marketing theory.

Narrow and wide interpretations of political marketing

Essentially, the different aspects of political marketing theory can be exemplified by the two different possible research objects that political marketing theory could focus on: political marketing management, on the one hand, and political exchanges, on the other. Whilst the first research object concerns managerial aspects of marketing in politics, the second is concerned with an epistemological stance and is therefore not limited to marketing applications but encompasses all political interactions and exchanges. Together they provide the core for a holistic theory of political marketing (Henneberg, 2002).

The initial aspect of a political marketing theory takes its impetus from existing practice in the political sphere: political marketing management. It manifests itself in such diverse activities as focusing campaign strategies on the salient political issues of swing voters or through the application of sophisticated segmentation techniques, through a consequent voter orientation, the application of celebrity endorsement strategies as part of an integrated marketing communication or the institution of powerful directors of communication and campaign consultants. Furthermore, political actors, political communicators and to some extent the electorate believe that marketing activities have become an essential part of political management in many situations. This belief has now entered the mainstream through endless discussions and analyses of the ill-defined concept of 'spin' in the media (Harris, 2001).

As a result of these (perceived or real) occurrences of marketing practice and language in politics, the use of marketing theory as a means of explaining these phenomena seems obvious. Whilst political science (or other related disciplines) have little to say about topics such as segmentation, brand management or strategic capability management, they fit easily into an explanatory scheme that is based explicitly on management and marketing theory. As such, political marketing theory is a necessary (if not sufficient) way of getting to grips with some of the modern developments in democratic life. It allows us to describe certain political phenomena in a way that political science is not able to. Furthermore, as part of the established tradition of commercial marketing theory, political marketing theory can integrate a descriptive understanding of political marketing management with a prescriptive theory, that is, a theory that can help political actors to apply political marketing management techniques effectively and efficiently. Such a research view has been entitled a 'Theory of Political Marketing Management' by Henneberg (2002). However, this theory cannot break out of its self-induced narrow focus on marketing activities, relegating everything else in politics to the level of unknowns or exogenous variables. Hence, in such a narrow interpretation the wider political environment that frames the application of commercial marketing management to the political sphere remains somewhat 'alien' and ill defined in its relationship with marketing theory.

On the other hand, a wide interpretation of the nature and scope of political marketing attempts to understand the whole of politics, that is, its constituting exchange and interaction structures, not just political marketing management practice. This is done via the application of the underlying concepts of marketing theory through a marketing oriented epistemology. Such a claim needs justification that can best be provided by looking at some of the embedded elements.

First, a wide interpretation of political marketing theory is not solely concerned with marketing activities, but tries to integrate these activities with the political environment in which they are used. Therefore, only an holistic understanding of all political activities, interactions and exchanges, players, structures and so on will be sufficient to understand the specific ramifications of and for political marketing management. Such a development seems necessary in light of the frequent claims that political marketing theory has not as yet developed any meaningful ethical frameworks or analyses regarding the implications of political marketing activities on macro-level structural variables of politics such as the party system, voting behaviour, the media landscape and power distributions in society (Henneberg, 2004).

Second, a wide interpretation of political marketing theory is concerned with epistemology, that is, the 'enquiry into our knowledge of being' (Ackroyd and Fleetwood, 2000: 6). This is not to say that political marketing *is* an epistemology but rather that certain ontological and epistemological positions can be connected with a political marketing perspective, for example the specific and fundamental issues that establish the identity of the field of political marketing. The constituting elements or premises of commercial marketing theory provide such a position as outlined below, although not all of these principles are uncontested in the commercial marketing literature. These positions, in so far as they differ from those of political science, provide a new and innovative way of understanding the political sphere. As with all ontological/epistemological stances, limitations exist in as much as they obscure certain issues and highlight others, and therefore need to be supplemented by alternative perspectives.

Third, political marketing theory as a way of understanding political interactions and exchanges in general has to be seen as part of a methodological pluralism. The implication is not that a marketing-related epistemology would explain the political sphere better than a political science, sociological or psychological epistemology. However, evaluative judgements need to be employed with regard to the appropriateness of certain epistemological positions in the face of a specific phenomenon, for example seeking an understanding of the impact of negative political advertising on voter decision-making processes in order to provide guidelines for self-regulating bodies of political advertisers. Hence, this is concerned with the respective explanatory power of different epistemological stances in a concrete situation and for a given purpose. As an abstract concept, no preferences can be deduced beyond that.

Therefore, a political marketing theory of politics would not supersede but complement other (such as political science) theories. It would be more appropriate in explaining certain elements of political life whilst others would not be covered in the same depth, rigour or quality. Additionally, certain explanations might contradict those of political science directly, without it being clear which claim is of higher appropriateness, thus stimulating further discussions. As such, a wide political marketing theory would consist of theories of middle-range and would have no ambition to provide any general theories. Understood in this epistemologically oriented way, a theory of political marketing cannot be anything but a sense-making framework, that is, a way of knowing. Whilst these theoretical considerations can only present political marketing theory as a possibility for enriching our understanding of politics, the ontological and epistemological essence of a political marketing theory needs to be described in order to gauge an understanding of how far these provide a specific and valuable lens for the gaining of knowledge in the political sphere.

The character of marketing as focusing on exchange (theory) provides an ontological foundation for political marketing. The assumption is that 'reality' is made up of actors (or forces) in relation to each other. Everything achieves its characteristics and qualities within a web of (multiple) 'pairings' (Bagozzi, 1975). Marketing, in its simplest form, cannot be carried out by one actor alone; it is always an exchange between actors. Thus, the corresponding epistemology would prescribe an enquiry that looks at dyads (or networks of relationships) as the main focus of analysis. While these dyads/networks consist of actors, the exchange focus of political marketing means that, for example, research on political campaigns should not focus on the political marketing activities of parties/candidates, but take into consideration that the political marketing exchange consists of three interactions in the electoral, parliamentary and governmental marketplaces. Perceptions, interpretations and representations of activities and other meaning-laden properties such as intentions, positions and resources within the political exchange become the defining epistemological characteristics of political marketing enquiry.

Related to this point is the ontological assumption of a 'qualified' market exchange. A managerial perspective of political marketing is linked to a traditional (micro-economic) market understanding as a clearing mechanism, prescribing the exchange characteristics of independent actors with self-interested goal functions which they maximise in episodic and unrelated transactions. However, political marketing theory characterises interactions and exchanges between interdependent actors and structures. This would also encompass cooperation and collaboration, and in some cases also collusion, which in traditional markets are deemed to be anomalies. Furthermore, an increased emphasis on time dynamics is implied: not only single transactions are analysed but also the totality of interactions and exchanges constructed within relationships over time. Historical determinants, as well as future-oriented considerations, become real forces within these market exchanges.

A third element is concerned with the embeddedness of politics, especially its relationship with social and other narrative models of representation. It can be posited that the political sphere does not exist independently of other cultural and social aspects of life (Butler and Collins, 1999). The interactions and interdependencies of politics on the economy, the legal system and social and cultural experiences give a clear indication for the arbitrariness of any attempt to disentangle politics from its contextual frame (Mancini and Swanson, 1996). As this condition is existent on both an epistemological level (in the way we attempt to gain insights about politics) and on an ontological level (the fabric of politics as is), any political as well as social marketing enquiry needs to look at interconnected systems; and cannot focus simply on an arbitrarily delineated political sphere (Brenkert, 2002). This complexity makes simple and uni-dimensional explanations very unlikely. Furthermore, it becomes difficult for political marketing theory to find clear-cut 'horizons' for its explanatory purpose.

Lastly, the structural connectedness of the management of politics and politics itself is ontologically anchored in political marketing theory. The difference between content and packaging in politics is treated as spurious. Any political management or marketing activity relates inevitably to policy/politics content either through considerations regarding development, execution or assessment of policies, and is recognised as such by other actors. On the other hand, policy-making and governing encompass management issues. So any enquiry in political marketing can be said to look at aspects of politics that in a narrow sense do not have anything to do with marketing instruments. As such, political marketing theory cannot limit itself to political marketing management as the application of tools and concepts from commercial marketing to the political context. Directly linked to this is a recognition that marketing is not a neutral aspect or tool of politics and that ethical considerations have to be an integral part of any political marketing theory.

The delineation of wide and narrow understandings of political marketing theory has implications for political marketing research, especially with respect to the current state of affairs of the discipline. It is the main contention of this chapter that the current realities of research on political marketing can be explained through connecting them with the two different perspectives on political marketing theory. The underpinning idea is that the shortcomings of current research are linked to a research community that subscribes to the narrow interpretation of political marketing theory that is concerned with understanding marketing activities in politics. While this happens predominantly implicitly, this managerial stance is widespread, not only with researchers but also commentators on, or opponents of, political marketing, and so political marketing actually mirrors the most limiting aspects of mainstream marketing. Political marketing theory has not yet been employed or conceptually discussed widely and this lack of research causes the field of political marketing to be short-sighted and without a solid, theoretical foundation. The main implication of this chapter is that research on political marketing needs to be broadened in order to enhance knowledge development in political marketing. In the following section we discuss seven key themes that we perceive to be central to the advancement of the discipline of political marketing.

Key themes in political marketing

Theme 1: grounding in exchanges and interactions

Whilst commercial marketing theory can now look back on decades of theory and concept development which manifest themselves in different schools of marketing thought (Wilkie and Moore, 2003), this is not the case for political marketing thought. The research domain of political marketing was made possible on the theoretical level by the 'broadening debate' of marketing in the 1970s, but it was not until the 1990s that political marketing became the focus of serious research. As the historical development of political marketing stems from commercial marketing, marketing theory provides the ontological rationale for political marketing and it is therefore important to link the knowledge gained from political marketing research with underlying and fundamental marketing concepts (Henneberg, 2008). As a core concept in commercial marketing theory concerns the exchange and interactions, this needs to be represented in research on political marketing. Commercial marketing theories use distinct tenets about the underlying monadic, dyadic or network exchange processes that shape and restrict marketing interactions. Such an understanding of the structural characteristics, based on social exchange theory, provides clear ontological delineations and partitioning for theory development in political marketing.

A critical analysis of the assumptions that guide theory and concept development in political marketing is necessary in order to avoid the development of conceptual models with little epistemological discussion of the fundamental assumptions of each model. However, such a discussion of assumptions regarding the epistemological grounding is rare in political marketing research (Baines and Egan, 2001). Furthermore, it seems as if our understanding of the nature of exchanges and interactions in political marketing is underdeveloped. The grounding of research in clear discussions of exchange and interaction characteristics and their differences from traditional marketing exchanges has rarely been attempted. The fundamental question of the political marketing exchange characteristics which lies at the heart of filling the metaphor of the 'political market' with life has not been clarified theoretically in enough depth. This is true for campaign exchanges as well as for other relevant interactions, especially the service implementation of policies (governmental political marketing). This limitation means research in political marketing is not rigorous enough with regard to the underlying exchange morphology which determines theory and concept-building efforts.

Theme 2: pluralism of theoretical marketing approaches

When it comes to underlying marketing theories, it must be noted that marketing is somewhat eclectic: many different theories and schools exist that are based on differing perspectives that are often incompatible. Marketing as a 'magpie discipline' borrows theories from other disciplines such as economics, psychology and sociology, and what is needed is a further step, using these borrowed theories to provide insights from which to build specific theories of political marketing which can be the foundation of a theory-driven discipline (Burton, 2005). At present there are many competing theories of commercial marketing and with this comes the ability to sustain multiple research approaches, something that can be seen to have a positive and liberating effect on the discipline. For example, despite the existence of several schools of thought in the late 1980s, this did not stop the development of relationship marketing approaches (Grönroos, 1994) or interaction and network theories of marketing (Ford and Håkansson, 2006). Pluralism within a discipline is not necessarily a problem, as having multiple perspectives can increase the understanding of different facets of the research field. However, the eclectic nature of marketing also makes it a 'low-paradigm' field (Weick, 1995) in which dominant approaches are weakly defined and detailed with regard to other approaches.

Political marketing theories and concepts are obviously highly influenced by research in marketing. However, it has been observed before that an instrumental view of marketing management is dominating political marketing research. An adaptation to the political market of the 4Ps framework and the marketing mix paradigm is crowding out other research streams of marketing. As such, political marketing theory is developing into a 'strong' paradigm, focused on a singular approach that is, however, often seen as obsolete or naïve in mainstream marketing theory. Pluralism of marketing schools is not used enough in political marketing, that is, functional, relational, or network-oriented concepts are rare in political marketing theory development (Henneberg, 2007).

Theme 3: adaptation of existing marketing and political science theory and concepts

The issue of multiple theoretical approaches is doubled in the area of political marketing: theories that are developed from both marketing and political science can be used, and these theories and concepts can also be overlaid, integrated and compared. As such, political marketing theories and concepts depend on borrowing and adaptation of existing theories from both marketing and political science. Although this is dependent on the exchange characteristics of the political market, such an integrating nature of theory and concept development from different disciplines remains an important aspect of contemporary political marketing research. This problem is further compounded owing to the very different ways in which both commercial and political marketing are understood and that some of their theories are incompatible. However, the existence of multiple ways of understanding the research field can increase theory-building creativity by searching out similarities and friction points in alternative theories.

Unfortunately, research on these alternative theoretical positions in political marketing is not high on the research agenda, as research carried out by marketers and by political scientists remains isolated from each other. Not many truly 'interdisciplinary' research groups or projects exist in the field of political marketing. Consequently, integrated or adapted theories that bridge the disciplinary divide are rare. In fact, there are currently two different ways of thinking about political marketing that exist, which are not integrated except on the most superficial level (Dean and Croft, 2001). State-of-the-art theories and concepts are not used across disciplinary borders to challenge existing theories and concepts in political marketing and to develop new theories and concepts. For example, important marketing concepts like market orientation, the service-dominant logic of marketing and value-network concepts are only starting to creep into political marketing research. However, with the development and acceptance of political marketing as an established sub-field of marketing theory and political science, this can go some way to encouraging cross-disciplinary research.

Theme 4: integration of pragmatic and abstract discipline views

Another issue of political marketing research concerns the aim of this research: should it be the development of theories and concepts that are ultimately capable of being applied by political marketing practitioners, for example candidates, governments, single-issue groups and their marketing advisers, or should it be about understanding politics through a marketing approach (Henneberg, 2008)? Although the former, more pragmatic approach towards theory-building seems to underpin most management research, such a narrow application of political marketing research may hinder the discipline more than it gives it focus. Therefore, the issue of the research aims could lead to different 'discipline borders' for political marketing theories, that is, a narrow vs. broad view of the limits of research in political marketing.

Surveying current political marketing research, it becomes clear that most efforts are focused on a 'narrow' definition of political marketing, that is, one that is related to the description and application of political marketing strategies and instruments. This is connected to the multiple approach characteristic of political marketing research with its primary focus on instrumental/managerial marketing theory. Whilst this in itself is not a harmful development, the lack of more abstract and 'wider' theories of political marketing does make discussions with political scientists more limited. In fact, we would argue that wider theories of political marketing can actually help provide political marketing research with the intellectual rigour and legitimacy which will allow it to become a contributing factor to political theory itself (Henneberg, 2007).

Theme 5: theories cover what, how and especially why (and justify these choices)

'Good' theory consists of building blocks: 1) the *what*, the concepts or constructs and the variables that operationalise these; 2) the *how*, the interrelationships between the concepts and constructs; and 3) the *why*, the underlying rationale for the selection of specific factors and relationships (Whetten, 1989). The *why* issue is necessary for a comprehensive theory as it is arguably the explaining part (Weick, 1995). According to Hunt (1991), these explanatory models need to be pragmatic, intersubjectively certifiable and have empirical content. However, whether a theory needs to be judged by its application depends on the definition of theory itself; good theory can also be abstract and non-applied. Furthermore, rules for good theory-building include aspects of how the variables are defined: the focus is especially on the uniqueness of the variables, a clear understanding of the limits that each of the variables can explain, a logical way of deriving relationships between constructs, and the link between theory and empirical support (Wacker, 1998). Such theories (or concepts) cannot be justified by just selecting specific variables. It is important to explain *what* variables have been selected, *how* these have been selected and *why* they are believed to be connected.

Coming to the essence of building theory in political marketing, it is necessary to have a better and more precise definition of variables and constructs. Too often, political marketing research employs a very loose way of using conceptualisations without clearly spelling out the differences between constructs and their interactions with other constructs. Critical discussions such as the applicability of the value concept in political exchanges (Brennan, 2003) or of the meaning of market orientation for political actors (Ormrod, 2007) are rare. Furthermore, the *why* question that features so prominently in Weick's (1995) discussion of theorising is mostly absent from the literature on political marketing. A more conscious and reflective way of presenting the gestation process of political marketing theory development may actually increase the likelihood that other researchers will engage with these theories and develop them further.

Theme 6: theories contextualise as well as bridge levels

Theories and concepts need to be placed in a context; they need not attempt to be universal laws but should at least attempt to model specific contexts. Whetten (1989: 492) calls this the who/where/when questions, which are linked to providing a multi-level outlook. Macro- and micro-structures and their relationships need to be developed theoretically. Klein et al. (1999) have summarised the benefits of multi-level work: bridging theoretical gaps, integrating the focus of different research areas to provide richer explanations, and getting to grips with complexity to 'illuminate the context [macro level] surrounding individual-level processes [micro level]' (p. 243). However, barriers to such an outlook are the fact that especially in overarching knowledge fields, the macro- and micro-levels are often integrated. Furthermore, with regard to political marketing theory, a clash of interest exists between commercial marketing theory with its main focus on individual-level analyses, and political science with its main focus on structural perspectives.

Level issues in theory development are among the most difficult aspects. Political marketing research does not always provide a clear indication of the explanatory level it operates on. Individual actors such as candidates and professional political marketers are mixed with organisational levels such as parties and governments. The interaction between the macro- and micro-levels often remains obscure, and the party system level as a further macro-level has so far been excluded from political marketing research. However, as the structures of the party system may be an important contextual variable, it seems reasonable to expect more research that is linked to the aspect of the interplay of political marketing management by actors/organisations and the political party system itself (a relationship that is clearly bi-directional).

Theme 7: juxtaposition of theoretical and empirical plane

The last theme extends theory and concept development by integrating it with empirical data. A validation of theories and concepts needs to link the abstract process of theorising to the empirical plane by assessing the likelihood of providing support for hypotheses and structuring empirical phenomena. Consequently there exists a need to develop more stochastic models in contrast with deterministic explanations, and therefore any theory or concept of political marketing needs to be constantly compared with political experiences. However, the relationship between data and theory is a two-way interaction, with theories and concepts explaining and shaping the data, and with data testing the explanatory power of theories and concepts.

Empirical research, especially theory-testing projects, are still rare in political marketing research. Only through a strong empirical involvement can we achieve substantive theories (Cornelissen and Lock, 2005). However, mostly descriptive and qualitative approaches dominate the methodology agenda in political marketing research, and describing or categorising data do not fulfil theory development, although they can already contain an unconscious recognition of a theory as part of the process of assembling the data (Weick, 1995). What is missing in political marketing research are rigorous quantitative and especially comparative analyses that integrate theory and concept development with a deep understanding of data. Research on political voting behaviour in relation to political marketing instruments leads the way in this area (Newman, 2002), but other theory aspects of political marketing research need to follow.

Conclusion

Whilst political marketing management is a well-established focus of research, political marketing theories and concepts are not afforded the same importance. This is arguably a direct result of the widespread adoption of a narrow interpretation of the nature and scope of political marketing. Instead, this chapter argues that it is necessary to widen the focus to include questions regarding the impact of political marketing on society. This chapter has also proposed seven key themes that are central to the advancement of the field of political marketing. Common to them all is the need for a better understanding of the theoretical and conceptual foundation upon which political marketing research is based.

Discussion questions

- Think about your political system. Which of the two interpretations of political marketing is most prevalent?
- Now think about the characteristics of modern political marketing management. Which of the two interpretations of the nature and scope of political marketing do they fit best with?
- We advocate a broad interpretation of the nature and scope of political marketing; do you think that this is realistic given the current focus on political marketing management by politicians, political professionals and the media?

Key terms

Narrow interpretation (of political marketing)

Wide interpretation (of political marketing)

Further reading

Henneberg and O'Shaughnessy (2007): This chapter is based on some of the work published in Henneberg and O'Shaughnessy's (2007) article in the *Journal of Political Marketing*.

Henneberg (2008): This chapter is based on some of the work published in Henneberg's (2008) article in the *Journal of Political Marketing*.

References

Ackroyd, S. and Fleetwood, S. (2000) 'Realism in contemporary organisation and management studies', in S. Ackroyd and S. Fleetwood (eds), *Realist Perspectives on Management and Organisations*. London: Routledge, 3–25.

Bagozzi, R.P. (1975) 'Marketing as exchange', *Journal of Marketing*, 39 (Oct.): 32–9.

Baines, P. and Egan, J. (2001) 'Marketing and political campaigning: mutually exclusive or exclusively mutual?', *Qualitative Market Research*, 4 (1): 25–34.

Baines, P., Fill, C. and Page, K. (2011) *Marketing*. Oxford: Oxford University Press.

Bannon, D.P. (2005) 'Relationship marketing and the political process', *Journal of Political Marketing*, 4 (2): 85–102.

Brenkert, G.G. (2002) 'Ethical challenges of social marketing', *Journal of Public Policy & Marketing*, 21 (1): 14–25.

Brennan, R. (2003) 'Does political marketing need the concept of customer value?', paper presented at the Political Marketing Conference, London, September.

Burton, D. (2005) 'Marketing theory matters', *British Journal of Management*, 16: 5–18.

Butler, P. and Collins, N. (1999) 'A conceptual framework for political marketing', in B.I. Newman (ed.), *Handbook of Political Marketing*. Thousand Oaks, CA: Sage, 55–72.

Cornelissen, J.P. and Lock, A.R. (2000) 'The organizational relationship between marketing and public relations: exploring paradigmatic viewpoints', *Journal of Marketing Communications*, 6: 231–45.

Cornelissen, J. and Lock, A. (2005), 'The uses of marketing theory: constructs, research propositions, and managerial implications', *Marketing Theory*, 5 (2): 165–84.

Dean, D. and Croft, R. (2001) 'Friends and relations: long-term approaches to political campaigning', *European Journal of Marketing*, 35 (11): 1197–216.

Dermody, J. and Scullion, R. (2001) 'Delusions of grandeur? Marketing's contribution to "meaningful" Western political consumption', *European Journal of Marketing*, 35 (9/10): 1085–98.

Ford, D. and Håkansson, H. (2006) 'The idea of interaction', *The IMP Journal*, 1 (1): 4–27.

Grönroos, C. (1994) 'Quo vadis, marketing? Toward a relationship marketing paradigm', *Journal of Marketing Management*, 10: 347–60.

Harris, P. (2001) 'To spin or not to spin, that is the question: the emergence of modern political marketing', *The Marketing Review*, 2: 35–53.

Henneberg, S.C. (2002) 'The idea of political marketing', in S.C. Henneberg and N.J. O'Shaughnessy (eds), *The Idea of Political Marketing*, Wesport, CT: Praeger.

Henneberg, S.C. (2004) 'The views of an *advocatus dei*: political marketing and its critics', *Journal of Public Affairs*, 4 (3): 225–43.

Henneberg, S.C. (2006) 'Leading or following? A theoretical analysis of political marketing postures', *Journal of Political Marketing*, 5 (3): 29–46.

Henneberg, S.C. (2008) 'An epistemological perspective on political marketing', *Journal of Political Marketing*, 7 (2): 151–82.

Henneberg, S.C. and O'Shaughnessy, N.J. (2007) 'Theory and concept development in political marketing: issues and agenda', *Journal of Political Marketing*, 6 (2/3): 5–32.

Hunt, S.D. (1991) *Modern Marketing Theory: Critical Issues in the Philosophy of Marketing Science*. Cincinnati: Southwestern Publishing.

Klein, K.J., Tosi, H. and Cannella, A.A. (1999) 'Multilevel theory building: benefits, barriers, and new developments', *Academy of Management Review*, 24 (2): 243–8.

Mancini, P. and Swanson, D. (1996) 'Introduction', in P. Mancini and D. Swanson (eds), *Politics, Media and Modern Democracy*, Westport, CT: Praeger, 1–28.

Marland, A. (2003) 'Political marketing: the good, the bad, and the ugly', paper presented at the Political Marketing Conference, London, September.

Newman, B.I. (2002) 'Testing a predictive model of voter behavior on the 2000 U.S. presidential election', *Journal of Political Marketing*, 1 (2/3): 159–73.

Ormrod, R.P. (2007) 'Political market orientation and its commercial cousin: close family or distant relatives?', *Journal of Political Marketing*, 6 (2/3): 69–90.

Panebianco, A. (1988) *Political Parties' Organisation and Power*. Cambridge: Cambridge University Press.

Perloff, R.M. (1999) 'Elite, popular, and merchandised politics', in B.I. Newman (ed.), *Handbook of Political Marketing*. Thousand Oaks, CA: Sage.

Scammell, M. (1999) 'Political marketing: lessons for political science', *Political Studies*, 47: 718–39.

Wacker, J.G. (1998) 'A definition of theory: research guidelines for different theory-building research methods in operations management', *Journal of Operations Management*, 16: 361–85.

Weick, K.E. (1995) 'What theory is not, theorizing is', *Administrative Science Quarterly*, 40: 385–90.

Whetten, D.A. (1989) 'What constitutes a theoretical contribution?', *Academy of Management Review*, 14 (4): 490–5.

Wilkie, W.L. and Moore, E.S. (2003) 'Scholarly research in marketing: exploring the "4 eras" of thought development', *Journal of Public Policy & Marketing*, 22: 116–46.

Chapter 3 is developed from Henneberg, S.C. and O'Shaughnessy, N.J. (2007) 'Theory and concept development in political marketing: issues and an agenda', *Journal of Political Marketing*, 6 (2/3): 5–31, and Henneberg, S.C. (2008) 'An epistemological perspective on research in political marketing', *Journal of Political Marketing*, 7 (2): 151–82. Both reprinted by permission of Taylor & Francis (www.tandfonline.com).

4 The Triadic Interaction Model of Political Exchange

After reading this chapter, you should be able to:

- distinguish between the concept of exchange in commercial and political marketing theory
- distinguish between electoral, parliamentary and governmental interactions
- describe how the three interactions that make up the political exchange can be integrated into research in political marketing and political marketing management practice.

Introduction

Marketing theory is conceptually grounded in an understanding of exchanges and interactions between actors. With the broadening of the marketing concept into non-profit areas in the late 1960s and 1970s, non-traditional and social exchanges have joined commercial exchanges as being essential to the understanding of marketing as a research area and organisational practice. The underlying rationale for an exchange, irrespective of context, is the concept of reciprocated value, and social exchange theory is generally assumed to be fundamental to understanding this feature of marketing. Therefore, it is important for marketing theory to understand and incorporate the relevant underlying exchange structures and the corresponding aspects of value, power and (inter-) dependency in research and explanations of marketing phenomena. This is irrespective of whether the actors involved operate in the commercial or non-profit market.

Arguably one of the more unconventional arenas in which exchanges take place is the political marketplace. The characteristics of interactions between actors have been identified as one reason why the application of marketing theory to the sphere of politics, whilst legitimised by marketing scholars more than thirty years ago, remains difficult, complex and unresolved (Henneberg, 2002). The aim of this chapter is to demonstrate that exchanges as we know them from the commercial marketing literature do occur in the political marketplace, but that a successful **political marketing exchange** is dependent on the result of three **dyadic interactions** that enable value to be reciprocated. This chapter is therefore motivated by a desire to contribute to the wider marketing literature and goes some way to resolving some of the problems associated with the application of commercial marketing theory to the political marketing context (Lock and Harris, 1996).

This chapter begins with a discussion of the exchange concept in commercial marketing theory, after which we compare the characteristics of a commercial exchange to the specific characteristics of the political marketing exchange. We then propose a new conceptualisation of a marketing exchange that is developed with the political context in mind, consisting of a triadic constellation of three dyadic interactions. This redefines the exchange in the political marketing context by introducing interaction structures, which together constitute the basic exchange model of political marketing. Finally, we discuss the implications of the **triadic interaction** model of political marketing exchange.

The exchange concept in marketing theory

It has been argued that marketing is fundamentally an 'exchange' theory, grounded in and derived from social exchange theory. As Levy and Kotler (1969) famously put it: 'the crux of marketing lies in a general idea of exchange rather than the narrower thesis of market transactions' (1969: 57). Exchange became a central tenet during the 1950s in what Wilkie and Moore (2003) have described as the transition from the traditional approach of marketing to the modern school. Business exchanges were generally understood to be a subgroup of generic or social exchanges (Shaw and Jones, 2005), enabling ideas from social exchange theory to contribute to marketing theory (Granovetter, 1985). Consequently, second-level constructs of marketing were derived such as goal-seeking behaviour of the involved parties based on intended needs satisfaction (Houston and Gassenheimer, 1987) and mutual value as a foundation for exchanges to occur (Bagozzi, 1978). More recently, discussions surrounding 'value co-creation' (Cova et al., 2011) have questioned the role of the consumer in the production of value, especially in the information age (Ritzer and Jurgenson, 2010).

In Hunt's (1976) 'liberalized thesis of marketing', any interaction of at least two actors, each possessing something of value to the other actor and who are capable of exchanging and are able to either accept or reject such an exchange, can be the focus of marketing research. Such an exchange structure could potentially encompass most if not all human activities; for example, marketing has been applied to essentially social exchanges such as heterosexual partner-seeking behaviour (Murgolo-Poore et al., 2003). However, Bagozzi (1975, 1978) attempted to develop a more circumspect general exchange theory as underlying marketing, based on social actors, their interactions and situational variables. This was subsequently criticised as a mere conceptual framework (Ferrell and Parrachione, 1980) and the conceptual broadening of marketing was considered to have had a greater impact on marketing practice than on theoretical developments (Arndt, 1979). Building on Bagozzi's work, Hunt (1983) defined the explanation of exchange relationships as the crucial aspect of marketing theory and consequently as being a behavioural science. Specifically, an exchange can be described by the following dependent variables of what Hunt calls 'fundamental explananda' (1983: 13): the behaviour of the exchange partners, the exchange environment in which the interactions take place and the environmental consequences of the exchanges. However, these elements have been criticised recently by Hyman (2004) for pedagogic and practical reasons.

The exchange concept in marketing theory has also not been without criticism. Houston and Gassenheimer (1987) observe that it is still unclear whether or not marketing and exchange theory are one and the same, whether they are parallel theories, or whether one is a subset of the other and, if so, which is which? Furthermore, while marketing as exchange is based on individual agency, that is, two or more individual actors that are nevertheless bound together via interdependencies (Ford and Håkansson, 2006), this micro-level view has been opposed for being insufficient to analyse exchange structures (macro-level phenomena). An institutional political economy paradigm has been proposed (Arndt, 1983) and implemented (Pandya and Dholakia, 1992) to complement the micro-perspective of marketing. Another argument relates to the fact that marketing focuses on exchange outcomes whilst economic exchange theories also take inputs into account as part of the production process (Houston and Gassenheimer, 1987). However, as Shaw and Jones (2005) state in a review of marketing schools, exchange theory as a generic concept is now simply assumed to underpin marketing, although one may question whether exchange theory has fundamentally influenced mainstream marketing writing (Levy, 2002).

The exchange concept in political marketing research

Political marketing uses the conceptual foundation of marketing theory applied to political exchanges (Henneberg, 2002). Political marketing is part of the broadened scope of marketing introduced in the 1970s and 1980s that incorporated non-profit and social exchange phenomena in the marketing domain (Kotler, 1972). This also encompasses social marketing, that is, the use of concepts and tools from commercial marketing theory and practice to further social idea(l)s (Levy and Kotler, 1969). Therefore, the conceptual existence of political marketing as a marketing phenomenon is directly linked to the theoretical treatment of exchange phenomena by marketing theory (Kotler, 2005).

In order for marketing science to provide a rigorous conceptual framework in the political sphere, political marketing needs to be based on an understanding of the unique nature of political marketing exchanges and especially on their differences from commercial exchanges which inform on traditional marketing theory (Lock and Harris, 1996). At least one marketing theorist has argued that the political sphere should be excluded from the marketing domain because no value-exchange exists (Carman, 1973). However, Kotler (1972) explicitly includes political marketing exchanges to illustrate the scope of marketing, and Sheth (in Newman, 1994) argues that a core marketing concept, that of market orientation, is a *de facto* element of modern political practice.

It is worthy of note that non-profit and social marketing seem to be almost exclusively defined in terms of service exchanges; thus, a substitution under services marketing was also suggested (Butler and Harris, 2009). Non-profit and social marketing exchanges are arguably more complex as they are structurally different to the basic buyer–seller dyad that underpins commercial exchanges, irrespective of whether these exchanges are between organisations, or between organisations and consumers. Such differences have implications for the non-profit marketing management activities that are appropriate or even possible, as well as implications for the applicability of marketing concepts (Baines et al., 2003). In the political marketplace, the successful reciprocation of electoral support for sound government between voter and candidate is reliant on three elements. First, that the aggregated result of the election enables the candidate to represent the voter in the parliament. Second, that the successful conclusion of negotiations in the parliament with other elected representatives provides support for the offering. Finally, that environmental conditions allow governments to enact legislation to reciprocate the value linked to the initial electoral support.

Having identified the exchange as the underlying construct of marketing theory, when developing a *specific* theory of political marketing it is necessary to compare the similarities (or dissimilarities) of exchanges in the commercial and political domains. The often-implied equivalence of these exchanges, or at least the accepted adaptability of marketing concepts based on commercial exchanges (Ormrod and Henneberg, 2010), represents an underexposed aspect of contemporary political marketing thought (Scammell, 1999). Analysing the political marketing exchange situation and discussing its implications for marketing activities in the political sphere provides, using Enis's (1973) terminology, a 'deepening' of the concept of political marketing. This means not so much a focus on the content of the exchange(s), although this is also of importance, but primarily on the structure or description of the exchanges, that is, the morphology of the political market.

The dangers of a 'one-to-one' transfer of commercial marketing theory and tools to application in politics have long and often been noted, the best example being the misleading notion of 'selling politics like soap' (Baines et al., 2003). Bagozzi (1975) demonstrated the importance of understanding the qualitative difference between commercial exchanges and non-commercial exchanges in his example of social policy issues for the underlying marketing management activities. On the other hand, Egan (1999) has argued that exchanges that occur in political campaigns are more similar to traditional commercial exchanges than normally acknowledged in the literature. Whilst research generally agrees that there is a difference (Lock and Harris, 1996; Baines et al. 2003), very little theoretical work has been forthcoming that explicitly analyses the exchanges in the political context and describes the implications for political marketing theory and the practice of political marketing management (Henneberg, 2008). Too often the political marketing exchange is sidelined from discussions in political marketing research.

Nevertheless, several authors have put forward interpretations (often implicitly) of political marketing exchanges. In general, political marketing or the 'political market' is defined exclusively in relation to exchange processes that are related to electoral campaigns. This is very much in line with Schumpeter's theory of the political entrepreneur and other micro-economic market and rational choice-related models (Butler and Collins, 1996). Although a wide range of stakeholders have been identified as relevant actors in the political marketplace (Ormrod, 2007), the most common application of political marketing research is in the context of a campaign.

Kotler (1972) describes the exchange between political candidates and the voting public as characterised by an offering of 'honest government' in exchange for votes. In a further development, Kotler and Kotler (1999) analyse the political marketplace, but restrict themselves to candidate-centred exchange situations with multiple stakeholders (voters, media, party organisations, party contributors and other interest groups). However, the continuation of 'campaign-like' exchanges as part of governing has been noted under the construct of the 'permanent campaign' (Steger, 1999), but this is normally seen as a type of aberration. As part of the electoral or campaign focus of political marketing exchanges, it is common to emphasise the 'service-characteristics' of the exchange process and the offering (Butler and Collins, 1999; Scammell, 1999; O'Shaughnessy and Henneberg, 2002; Butler and Harris, 2009).

Exceptions to this exclusive focus on elections do, however, exist. Harrop (1990: 279) describes the political offering as 'governing' and makes a link with the 'monopoly franchise' of one government as the single service provider at a particular time. Similarly, Butler and Collins (1999) describe some structural aspects of the wider political marketing exchange, such as offering characteristics, the 'market' structures or value elements, although they do not characterise the exchange itself. Whilst Butler and Collins (1999) focus primarily on campaigns, they do allude to the fact that 'implementation' and value-delivery is an additional aspect. On the other hand, O'Cass (2009) considers value-delivery to be a more central element in discussions of political marketing. Henneberg (2002) provides a structural model of political marketing exchange, linking different political exchange spheres. Three different political exchange 'markets' and their interactions within the context of political marketing are analysed: an 'electoral market', a 'governmental market' and a 'political activism market'. Media and donors are seen as links between these three sub-markets whose players, nevertheless, also have direct exchange relationships between each other. However, Henneberg (2002) acknowledges that this analysis remains party- and candidate-centred in its orientation towards political marketing management.

In summary, research on political marketing, whilst concerned with exchange phenomena, does not take into account the complex linkages and interdependencies between actors and structures in political marketing exchanges. The problems of the adaptability of marketing concepts in politics manifest themselves in an almost exclusive research focus on interactions during political campaigns, leading to an understanding of these events as consisting of exchanges rather than discrete interactions in a wider political marketing exchange. In other words, while commercial exchanges are characterised by a closed dyadic system between sellers and buyers, we argue that political marketing exchanges are open and characterised by dyadic interactions. The existing research on political marketing is therefore of only limited conceptual rigour with regard to its ability to provide an underlying exchange construct for political marketing. In the following we discuss the relevant political interactions in the context of political marketing, using an interdependence view of interactions and the exchange that focuses on actors, activities and resources (Ford and Håkansson, 2006).

Electoral, parliamentary and governmental interactions

Commercial exchanges compared to political marketing exchanges

Current political marketing research is characterised by an assumption that interactions in the electoral market (between candidates or parties, on the one hand, and voters, on the other) are synonymous with the political marketing exchange and are complex and difficult to get to grips with. In addition to this, instrumental or mix analyses of political marketing focus mainly on the **electoral interaction** and from this derive implicit assumptions about the wider political marketing exchange (Henneberg and O'Shaughnessy, 2009). This is unsurprising given that the electoral interaction is the most visible interaction: elections are high-profile events with obvious long-term consequences. It is only if a candidate or party can successfully gain the support of a majority of voters that the candidate or party can be in a position to be represented in parliament (the parliamentary market) or in government (the governmental market). Thus the electoral interaction can be considered to be the initial 'proto-interaction' in a democratic context, irrespective of whether this represents the first time a new candidate or party stands for election or the first election in a newly democratised nation.

Commercial exchanges may depend to some extent on other direct and indirect exchanges or interactions (Ford and Håkansson, 2006) but are not essentially linked to them. However, political marketing exchanges are fundamentally different to commercial exchanges in that the former only make sense as part of a wider political marketing exchange system. Thus, interactions in the electoral market are directly dependent on interactions in the parliamentary and governmental markets (after the proto-interaction). In addition to this, the electoral interaction does not resemble most commercial buyer–seller exchanges as it is characterised by complexity, openness, opaqueness and the involvement of many and varied actors. The electoral interaction does not itself allow for a direct transformation of support (votes) into 'sound government', the exchange that underlies the political marketing concept (Baines et al., 2003). This was hinted at in Bauer et al. (1995) who stated that the political marketing exchange is in fact a systems-exchange. Therefore, a representation as a dyadic concept (analogously to buyers and sellers) does not fully capture the overarching political marketing exchange, and therefore does not provide a rigorous theoretical underpinning of theories of political marketing.

Thus the political marketing exchange is not 'closed' (or 'restricted', Bagozzi, 1975) after the electoral interaction; a closed exchange would imply a balanced reciprocity situation. Direct benefits for the voters are instead 'deferred' (except for more emotional benefits like having done a 'civic duty' by voting, or having voted for a 'winner') and the political marketing exchange is said to be 'open'. The concept of open exchanges mirrors Bagozzi's (1975) construct of generalised exchange, that is, those characterised by univocal reciprocity between at least three actors in a ring chain of interactions. Wortmann (1989) acknowledged that political marketing exchanges also encompass the spheres of parliamentary negotiations between coalition partners, and of the interactions between governments and citizens.

Furthermore, any future reciprocity is 'risky' as the provider (the party or candidate in government) is not bound by their promises. In fact, once elected, most systems in a representative democracy allow parliamentarians to decide according to their free will and independent of what they promised or what voters want them to do (Henneberg et al., 2009). Thus the indirect and deferred nature of political marketing exchanges can become unstable. For political marketing exchanges to work in equilibrium, all exchange partners need to accept the underlying mechanism (Houston and Gassenheimer, 1987), in this case referring to the legitimacy of the government, parliament and the democratic system itself through the eyes of citizens. Consequently, we propose a triadic interaction structure of generalised exchange (Bagozzi, 1975), consisting of three interlocking dyads represent-ing the electoral interaction, the **parliamentary interaction** and the **governmental interaction** (see Figure 4.1).

In the commercial sphere, buyers and sellers are negotiating and later exchanging well-defined 'private goods' which become the exclusive prop-erty of the exchange partner as part of the commercial exchange process. The characteristics of any offering in the political marketing exchange process are conversely represented by 'public good' characteristics. If implemented, the political offering relates to all citizens; none is excluded from the offering but also none can exclude themselves from it bar the rather extreme action of emigrating (Lock and Harris, 1996). The offering becomes 'general' in that it determines the political marketing exchange in one specific form for every citizen. In addition to this, there can be a considerable time lag between the electoral interaction and the reciprocation of value via the implementation of the offering as part of the governmental interaction (Wortmann, 1989).

However, it can be argued that voters offer not only their votes but also their involvement in political discourse, word-of-mouth and 'public opin-ion', and, in a material sense, their donations and volunteer help to political organisations/actors (Farrell and Wortmann, 1987) and that therefore the exchange is closed (by being directly reciprocated). Nevertheless, if the political marketing exchange in a narrow sense is about the realisation of political ideas and stands on issues, and the exchanged value consists of cultural guidance, social order and realisation of interests *via* policies, then this constitutes a systemic phenomenon beyond electoral interactions. Therefore, to understand the outcome of political marketing exchanges it is necessary to adopt a systemic view, embedding the dyadic electoral inter-action within parliamentary interactions and governmental interactions.

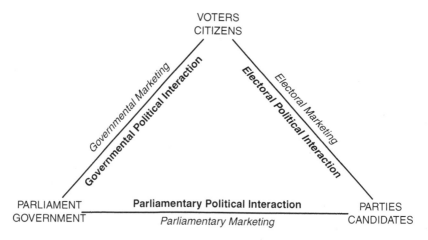

Figure 4.1   Triadic interaction model of political marketing (Henneberg and Ormrod, 2013)

Electoral, parliamentary and governmental interactions

Electoral interactions are between political actors, on the one hand, and voters, on the other. Political actors can be parties that are represented by candidates or 'lists' of candidates, or individual candidates that are embedded in a wider campaign-specific organisation. Irrespective of whether the organisation consists of active party members or campaign volunteers, the resource endowment and the agenda-setting function in the electoral interaction is skewed towards the political actor: voters are 'reactive' *vis-à-vis* candidates or parties. While this is in common with most business-to-consumer exchanges, it must be noted that business-to-business exchanges are embedded in complex value-creating systems, networks of business-to-business exchanges that facilitate (and ultimately determine) offerings and therefore exchanges. These business-to-business exchanges show collaborative and co-operative exchange structures between theoretically symmetrical exchange partners. Such auxiliary exchange networks between symmetrical actors (in terms of resources, power position, activity prerogative, etc.) are largely missing from the electoral interaction dyad of the political marketing exchange.

Electoral interactions are also asymmetric with regard to what is exchanged between the parties. In commercial exchanges, reciprocity exists based on value: both buyers and sellers receive something they perceive to be valuable in the context of satisfying their underlying needs and wants. Primarily this value is embedded in the benefits of an offering for the buyer and a reciprocal cash flow for the seller. With the exchange, the transaction is closed. Such exchanges are known as balanced reciprocity and imply intermediate levels of social distance of exchange partners. In such exchanges transactions are immediate, as is value exchange (Houston and Gassenheimer, 1987). Electoral interactions are different in that whilst voters provide direct benefits for the party or candidate by voting for them, this is not reciprocated as the parties/candidates only offer general promises of future activities (e.g. policy implementation or governmental actions).

As a result of this, the 'competition' regarding offerings in the political sphere draws essentially on Schumpeterian thoughts: it is about promises or ideas (Thurber, 1995) and 'truthful' representation according to some principles (Farrell and Wortmann, 1987). As such, politicians sell 'hope' (O'Shaughnessy, 1990) and voters invest 'hope' (Dermody and Scullion, 2001). It is therefore unsurprising that the electoral 'promise' is often conceptualised as a multifaceted offering construct in the political marketing literature. Political promises manifest themselves through party image or ideology, perceived candidate characteristics and specific policy stands (Wring, 2002). It has been argued that this offering construct can also be considered a 'brand' (Smith and French, 2009) which re-aggregates the different offering components into a bundle (Lock and Harris, 1996). However, all these interaction elements can be interpreted as being constructed via cultural signs and are therefore symbolic (and social) exchanges (Axford and Huggins, 2002). For politicians and candidates, this symbolism is an element of the political offering, whilst for the electorate, such symbolism represents the meaning attached by each voter to the act of voting for a particular party, candidate or cause (Moufahim and Lim, 2009).

Whilst commercial exchanges are concerned with obtaining offerings through individual decision-making, electoral interactions are based on 'cumulative' decision-making. Buyers' decisions are made individually or by a limited group such as a family or purchasing department, whereas political decisions are made by all voters who take part in an election. The cumulative decisions of voters are transformed (depending on the voting system) into seats in parliament. As such, the electoral interaction provides a mechanism for the transformation of the entirety of votes in an election into parliamentary power, expressed by a mandate allocated to a specific individual candidate or to a party. However, this may or may not allow a government to come into existence. Especially in party systems with a proportional representation-based voting system, governments are again the outcome of the interactions between parties and/or members of parliaments that are aimed at reciprocating the value provided by voters (support) in the electoral interaction.

As a consequence of this, the result of the electoral interaction of the political marketing exchange may be ambiguous and needs clarification through further interactions in parliament. Coalition negotiations, embedded in compromises on political issues and horse-trading regarding government posts, are the result. Members of the legislative assembly provide support for the policy positions of their political leadership in return for following a certain ideology or specific issue-stands (in the case of the governing parties), or a check-and-balance system for governmental information (in the case of the opposition parties). Both aspects provide the government as well as the policies that are to be implemented with legitimate powers by a majority of elected parliamentarians. Thus the parliamentary interaction of the political marketing exchange can dramatically qualify the electoral outcome, for example in the case of the 2005 German general election when the electorate's least favoured outcome was a grand coalition of the two largest parties, the Social Democrats and Christian Democrats. However, this is exactly what the parliamentary interaction resulted in, based on the limited (perceived) option set that was available to the parties because of the electoral outcome.

The ability to participate in the governmental interaction element of the political marketing exchange (the enactment of legislation to fulfil the promise offered in the electoral interaction) is dependent on success in both the electoral interaction (leading to participation in the legislative assembly) and the parliamentary interaction (leading to participation in government, either through a majority or by a negotiated solution in the case of minority governments). As Lock and Harris observe: '… we cannot treat government as a disinterested or exogenous component in an exchange perspective on political marketing...' (1996: 20). While the parliamentary interaction brings government into existence, such government has the remit (policy proposals) as well as the power (legitimacy and executive resources) to implement the service promises, which are the substance of the political sphere: that is, enacted politics (Buurma, 2001). This completes the political marketing exchange of value with the voters who supported the candidate or party, but also includes all other citizens.

Whilst the value which is derived from the candidate's or party's offering is now reciprocated with a majority of voters, the governmental interaction (and thus the political marketing exchange) permeates every social, cultural, economic and legal aspect of the life of all citizens. As such, the governmental interaction is distinct from both the electoral interactions and the parliamentary interactions, lending support to Harrop's (1990) conceptualisation of the political marketing exchange as a monopoly franchise. However, the governmental interaction can only be completed by involving citizens. As any service offering, the 'customer' is part of the offering characteristics. As such, those aspects of governmental interactions have a low social distance, that is, they exhibit 'generalised reciprocity' in which, in extreme cases, an exchange can be between a perpetual 'giver' and 'taker' (an extreme like the mother/child relationships) (Houston and Gassenheimer, 1987). However, the citizenry/electorate reciprocates directly (through fees for specific usage of executive services like toll roads) or indirectly (by providing tax revenue that is not bound specifically to spending intentions but provides the general resource generation function for governments) (Henneberg and O'Shaughnessy, 2009).

The political marketing exchange and political marketing research and practice

The electoral, parliamentary and governmental interactions are embedded within an overall structure of generalised political marketing exchange, consisting of limited mutually reciprocal interactions within a systemic closed chain (Ekeh, 1974). As such, no dyadic interaction is independent of the other interactions; they inform each other and form an interdependent exchange system that can only be fully understood in its entirety. The limited mutual reciprocity of the dyads (i.e. the fact that within each dyad only a certain amount of reciprocity exists) is framed by a dominant, uni-directional exchange logic (Ekeh, 1974) which links the electoral interaction with the parliamentary interaction and, subsequently, the governmental interaction, before flowing back into the electoral political sphere (clockwise circularity in Figure 4.1). This does not prevent each individual interaction dyad from showing some aspect of reciprocity, although it is insufficient to provide a 'balanced' exchange that, in itself, is closed.

The triadic structure of the political marketing exchange provides a more rigorous construct underlying political marketing theory with regard to understanding the 'political market' and its interactions than what the political market metaphor of 'buyers' and 'sellers' implies. A link between such a structural analysis and political marketing activities needs to be established. This is done by employing a structural or system typology of political marketing exchange interactions. Such a typology is based on the underlying structure of the social relations that make up both the dyadic interactions and, conversely, the basis of action. This is achieved from the managerial viewpoint of the party/candidates (and its flipside, the elected executive government) as the main actors of political marketing management.

By utilising a categorisation system developed by Biggart and Delbridge (2004), one can distinguish the following logic that political managers can base their activities on: an instrumental rationality (means-orientation) or a substantive rationality (ends-orientation). It can be argued that the managerial activities facilitating electoral interactions are guided by an instrumental rationality (achieving votes to further ones chances of getting into a position in which one has the means – a majority of mandates – to implement one's policies). However, parliamentary marketing (between parties/candidates and government) is primarily characterised by a substantive rationality, directed towards negotiations about policies themselves. This is similar to governmental marketing which shows an orientation towards ends (substantive rationality) by facilitating the enactment of offerings (policy implementation).

This actor-oriented logic can be juxtaposed within the typology by introducing a structural dimension. This refers to the social relations in which any dyadic exchange (in the political marketing exchange, the dyadic interactions), and therefore the individual orientation, is played out (Granovetter, 1985). The structures of the social relations can refer to particularistic ones that are targeted at particular interests, or universalistic ones aimed at a community as a whole. Particularistic structures are visible in the electoral interaction (in political marketing activities towards aligned voters), and in parliamentary interactions where party or candidate stances are safeguarded in negotiations. A universalistic structure of social relations is visible in electoral interactions with floating or unaligned voters as well as in governmental interactions. Thus the use of the Biggart and Delbridge (2004) typology provides an overview of differences of the three dyadic components of the political marketing exchange (see Table 4.1). Each of the dyadic interactions exhibits a specific and qualitatively distinct logic with associated norms, actor expectations and organisational structures.

Thus the challenge of a theory of political marketing is to align itself with the underlying structural characteristics of the political marketing exchange within which political marketing management is enacted. As has been shown above, while current research on political marketing focuses primarily on electoral phenomena, this causes a short-term view of the many and linked aspects of interactions in the political market. Due to the complexity of the underlying political marketing exchange, political marketing needs to be based on a qualitatively different foundation than that of striving towards a 'mutually beneficial exchange'. Accepting that the political marketing exchange is not synonymous with commercial buyer–seller exchanges but instead possesses a deferred and circular interaction structure has wide-ranging implications for political marketing research and practice.

Table 4.1   Typology of political exchange (structure adapted from Biggart and Delbridge, 2004)

	Structure of Social Relations	
Basis of Action	Particularistic	Universalistic
Instrumental Rationality	Electoral interactions (aligned voters)	Electoral interactions (floating/unaligned voters)
Substantive Rationality	Parliamentary interactions	Governmental interactions

Implications for research in political marketing

As outlined above, current research in political marketing has its primary focus on the electoral interactions. However, focusing research in such a way does not cover the exchange requirements of candidates and parties, and the strategic political marketing activities subsumed within the parliamentary and governmental interaction dyads. Whilst the three interaction dyads are distinct, they nevertheless depend on each other in order to facilitate the political marketing exchange of value, that is, support for sound government. As such, for a research agenda in political marketing, they need to be understood in context, taking network and system effects into account (Henneberg, 2008). Therefore, research into election campaigns needs to recognise that governmental interactions and parliamentary interactions play a decisive role in determining the nature and result of electoral interactions, and that discussions focusing on electoral exchanges need to be explicitly linked to the parliamentary interactions and governmental interactions, be they on the conceptual or on the empirical plane of analysis. In this context, all three political marketing-related interactions should be seen as an integrated system of symbolic actions (Dermody and Scullion, 2001). This has direct implications for aspects of political marketing management in that it could broaden the use of theories from commercial marketing, such as the resource-based view of the firm (O'Cass, 2009) or service-dominant logic (Butler and Harris, 2009), within the wider political marketing arena.

A triadic, interdependence-based view of political marketing exchange will also allow for the unravelling of certain areas of political marketing that have hitherto been critically discussed when analysed in isolation. For example, Foxall (1984) argues that a marketing orientation is unlikely to exist in a genuine and lasting way for governments (and in his view also for parties). He considers the example of government–citizen exchanges and comes to the conclusion that this is not a marketing exchange as the customer (citizen) is not independent in its actions; for example, a citizen cannot withhold taxes. However, when conceptualising the government–citizen relationship as an interaction integrated within a wider exchange system rather than as an isolated and closed dyadic exchange, therefore linking the governmental interaction to the parliamentary interaction and electoral interaction, it becomes clear that the direct (negative) feedback mechanism for citizens is not within the dyadic structure of the governmental interaction, but in the linked one of the electoral interaction. Citizens, in their capacity as voters, do react to governmental offerings by their voting behaviour and the subsequent electoral consequences. In this context more phenomenological approaches regarding how voters understand (and make sense of) the political marketing exchange system in its different facets could provide interesting juxtapositions of research based in political marketing theory with traditional political science research.

The extremely important issue of implementation, which is at the forefront of services marketing thinking, needs clearer analysis (Henneberg and O'Shaughnessy, 2009). Policy promises in the electoral interaction need to be converted into policy implementation in the governmental interaction via 'inter-organisational' parliamentary interactions based on negotiations which, to date, have not been analysed using political marketing constructs. This is arguably a central topic in future political marketing research given that the implementation of promises provides the overall exchange rationale for the political system of delivering 'value' to citizens.

The interaction structures, their characteristics and place in a triadic interaction model of political marketing exchange enables research in political marketing to embrace a more holistic picture of political marketing management activities and the relationship of these activities to the wider society (Henneberg et al., 2009). Adopting an interaction-based approach can be a step towards facilitating more reliable construct development by explicitly connecting systemic structures with research concepts that are derived from marketing theory and social exchange theory. Research on political marketing without a clear link between electoral, governmental and parliamentary marketing issues falls short of a rigorous application of exchange theory and therefore cannot constitute a conceptual system for the development of state-of-the-art political marketing theory.

Conclusion

Many marketing theorists are used to explanatory concepts that have been developed with dyadic and directly reciprocated exchange relationships in mind. Therefore, one is tempted to superimpose these on other, related exchanges (Egan, 1999), despite the fact that marketing theory has also adopted more complex, systemic orientations. Based on the exchange construct, non-commercial exchanges including social and political ones have become an accepted marketing *explanandum* since the broadening debate of marketing of the 1970s. Therefore, in order to build a theory of political marketing exchange needs to be developed beyond the simplistic assumption of it being synonymous with commercial exchange or by using metaphorical constructs like the 'political market' (Lock and Harris, 1996).

Certain aspects of the marketing analogies such as the service characteristics of the political offering only make full sense if understood as being triadic interactions rather than dyadic exchanges. Thus, the aspect of the presumptive effect of political services (Baines et al., 2003) only comes to the fore if the electoral interaction is not seen in isolation but as part of a wider political marketing exchange system. The triadic interaction structure of the political marketing exchange provides an initial attempt to develop a broadened concept on which further theory-building as well as empirical analysis in political marketing can be based. As such, many of the uncertainties regarding political marketing with regard to its fit with commercial marketing theory can be resolved by focusing on a broadened understanding of the specific exchange situation of politics.

Discussion questions

- At election time, you vote for the candidate or party of your choice. The question is, what do you want to get out of it – apart from lower taxes, what is the value that you will gain by entering into an electoral interaction with the candidate or party of your choice?
- Your candidate or party is represented in the parliament after the election and forms part of a coalition government. How will this affect the parliamentary interactions between your candidate or party and the coalition partner? Even though there is nothing you can do about it, what is the value that you get out of the parliamentary interaction?
- The state of the economy leaves the government with no choice but to pass legislation that raises taxes, which is *not* what you voted for. What is the value that you get out of the entire political marketing exchange? What can you do about it?

Key terms

Political marketing exchange	Electoral interactions
Dyadic interactions	Governmental interactions
Triadic interactions	Parliamentary interactions

Further reading

Henneberg and Ormrod (2013): This article forms the basis for the chapter.

Shaw and Jones (2005): This article traces the development of marketing as an academic discipline over the last hundred years from its focus on the activities that occurred within the marketing function to the three current alternative foci on management activities, consumer behaviour and marketing exchanges. Common to all three of the current approaches is the ability to explain non-profit and political marketing phenomena.

Schwartzkopf (2011): This article criticises the assumption that customers function as voters in a 'consumer democracy', where consumer demand can be equated with a vote for a specific offering. Schwartzkopf argues that market research tools such as consumer juries and focus groups have served to perpetuate this assumption to the detriment of both commercial and political marketing research and practice.

References

Arndt, J. (1979) 'Toward a concept of domesticated markets', *Journal of Marketing*, 43 (Fall): 69–75.

Arndt, J. (1983) 'The political economy paradigm: foundation for theory building in marketing', *Journal of Marketing*, 47 (Fall): 44–54.

Axford, B. and Huggins, R. (2002) 'Political marketing and the aestheticization of politics: modern politics and postmodern trends', in N.J. O'Shaughnessy and S.C. Henneberg (eds), *The Idea of Political Marketing*. Westport, CT: Praeger.

Bagozzi, R.P. (1975) 'Marketing as exchange', *Journal of Marketing*, 39 (October): 32–9.

Bagozzi, R.P. (1978) 'Marketing as exchange: a theory of transactions in the marketplace', *American Behavioral Scientist*, 21 (4): 535–56.

Baines, P.R., Brennan, R. and Egan, J. (2003) '"Market" classification and political campaigning: some strategic implications', *Journal of Political Marketing*, 2 (2): 47–66.

Bauer, H.H., Huber, F. and Herrmann, A. (1995) 'Politik-Marketing: Inhalt, Instrumente and Institutionen', *Der Markt*, 34: 115–24.

Biggart, N.W. and Delbridge, R. (2004) 'Systems of exchange', *Academy of Management Review*, 29 (1): 28–49.

Butler, P. and Collins, N. (1996) 'Strategic analysis in political markets', *European Journal of Marketing*, 30 (10/11): 25–36.

Butler, P. and Collins, N. (1999) 'A conceptual framework for political marketing', in B.I. Newman (ed.) *Handbook of Political Marketing*. Thousand Oaks, CA: Sage.

Butler, P. and Harris, P. (2009) 'Considerations on the evolution of political marketing theory', *Marketing Theory*, 9 (2): 149–64.

Buurma, H. (2001) 'Public policy marketing: marketing exchange in the public sector', *European Journal of Marketing*, 35 (11/12): 1287–302.

Carman, J.M. (1973) 'On the universality of marketing', *Journal of Contemporary Business*, 2 (Autumn): 142.

Cova, B., Dalli, D. and Zwick, D. (2011) 'Critical perspectives on consumers' role as "producers": broadening the debate on value co-creation in marketing processes', *Marketing Theory*, 11 (3): 231–41.

Dermody, J. and Scullion, R. (2001) 'Delusions of grandeur? Marketing's contribution to "meaningful" Western political consumption', *European Journal of Marketing*, 35 (9/10): 1085–98.

Egan, J. (1999) 'Political marketing: lessons from the mainstream', *Journal of Marketing Management*, 15: 495–503.

Ekeh, P.P. (1974) *Social Exchange Theory: The Two Traditions*. Cambridge, MA: Harvard University Press.

Enis, B.M. (1973) 'Deepening the concept of marketing', *Journal of Marketing*, 37 (October): 57–62.

Farrell, D.M. and Wortmann, M. (1987) 'Party strategies in the electoral market: political marketing in West Germany, Britain and Ireland', *European Journal of Political Research*, 15: 297–318.

Ferrell, O.C. and Perrachione, J.R. (1980) 'An inquiry into Bagozzi's Formal Theory of Marketing Exchanges', in C. Lamb Jr and P.M. Dunne (eds), *Theoretical Developments in Marketing*. Chicago: American Marketing Association.

Ford, D. and Håkansson, H. (2006) 'The idea of interaction', *The IMP Journal*, 1 (1): 4–27.

Foxall, G. (1984) 'Marketing's domain', *European Journal of Marketing*, 18 (1): 25–40.

Granovetter, M. (1985) 'Economic action and social structure: a theory of embeddedness', *American Journal of Sociology*, 91: 481–510.

Harrop, M. (1990) 'Political marketing', *Parliamentary Affairs*, 43: 277–91.

Henneberg, S.C. (2002) 'Understanding political marketing', in N.J. O'Shaughnessy and S.C. Henneberg (eds), *The Idea of Political Marketing*, Westport, CT: Praeger.

Henneberg, S.C. (2008) 'An epistemological perspective on research in political marketing', *Journal of Political Marketing*, 7 (2): 151–82.

Henneberg, S.C. and Ormrod, R.P. (2013) 'A triadic interaction model of political marketing exchange, *Marketing Theory*.

Henneberg, S.C. and O'Shaughnessy, N.J. (2009) 'Political relationship marketing: some macro/micro thoughts', *Journal of Marketing Management*, 25 (1/2): 5–29.

Henneberg, S.C., Scammell, M. and O'Shaughnessy, N.J. (2009) 'Political marketing management and theories of democracy, *Marketing Theory*, 9 (2): 165–88.

Houston, F.S. and Gassenheimer, J.B. (1987) 'Marketing and exchange', *Journal of Marketing*, 51 (Oct): 3–18.

Hunt, S.D. (1976) 'The nature and scope of marketing, *Journal of Marketing*, 40 (July): 17–28.

Hunt, S.D. (1983) 'General theories and the fundamental explananda of marketing', *Journal of Marketing*, 47 (Fall): 9–17.

Hyman, M.R. (2004) 'Revising the structural framework for marketing management', *Journal of Business Research*, 57: 923–32.

Kotler, P. (1972) 'A generic concept of marketing', *Journal of Marketing*, 36 (April): 46–54.

Kotler, P. (2005) 'The role played by the broadening of marketing movement in the history of marketing thought', *Journal of Public Policy & Marketing*, 24 (1): 114–16.

Kotler, P. and Kotler, N. (1999) 'Political marketing: generating effective candidates, campaigns, and causes', in B.I. Newman (ed.) *Handbook of Political Marketing*. Thousand Oaks, CA: Sage.

Levy, S.J. (2002) 'Revisiting the marketing domain', *European Journal of Marketing*, 36 (3): 299–304.

Levy, S.J. and Kotler, P. (1969) 'Beyond marketing: the furthering concept', *California Management Review*, 12 (2): 67–73.

Lock, A. and Harris, P. (1996) 'Political marketing – *vive la différence!*', *European Journal of Marketing*, 30 (10/11): 21–31.

Moufahim, M. and Lim, M. (2009) 'Towards a critical political marketing agenda?', *Journal of Marketing Management*, 25 (7/8): 763–76.

Murgolo-Poore, M.E., Pitt, L.F. and Berthon, P.R. (2003) 'Three theoretical perspective on one of marketing's most fundamental exchanges', *Marketing Theory*, 3 (2): 235–65.

Newman, B.I. (1994) *The Marketing of the President*. Thousand Oaks, CA: Sage.

O'Cass, A. (2009) 'A resource-based view of the political party and value creation for the voter-citizen: an integrated framework for political marketing', *Marketing Theory*, 9 (2): 189–208.

Ormrod, R.P. (2007) 'Political market orientation and its commercial cousin: close family or distant relatives?', *Journal of Political Marketing*, 6 (2/3): 69-90.

Ormrod, R.P. and Henneberg, S.C. (2010) 'Strategic political postures and political market orientation: towards an integrated construct of political marketing strategy', *Journal of Political Marketing*, 9 (4): 294–313.

O'Shaughnessy, N.J. (1990) *The Phenomenon of Political Marketing*. Basingstoke: Macmillan.

O'Shaughnessy, N.J. and Henneberg, S.C. (2002) 'Introduction: the idea of political marketing', in N.J. O'Shaughnessy and S.C. Henneberg (eds), *The Idea of Political Marketing*. Westport, CT: Praeger.

Pandya, A. and Dholakia, N. (1992) 'An institutional theory of exchange in marketing', *European Journal of Marketing*, 26 (12): 19–41.

Ritzer, G. and Jurgenson, N. (2010) 'Production, consumption, presumption: the nature of capitalism in the age of the digital "prosumer"', *Journal of Consumer Culture*, 10 (1): 13–36.

Scammell, M. (1999) 'Political marketing: lessons for political science', *Political Studies*, 47: 718–39.

Schwartzkopf, S. (2011) 'The consumer as "voter," "judge," and "jury": historical origins and political consequences of a marketing myth', *Journal of Macromarketing*, 31 (1): 8–18.

Shaw, E.H. and Jones, D.G.B. (2005) 'A history of schools of marketing thought', *Marketing Theory*, 5 (3): 239–81.

Sheth, J.N. (1994) 'Preface', in B.I. Newman, *The Marketing of the President*. Thousand Oaks, CA: Sage, ix–xii.

Smith, G. and French, A. (2009) 'The political brand: a consumer perspective', *Marketing Theory*, 9 (2): 209–26.

Steger, W.P. (1999) 'The permanent campaign: marketing from the hill', in B.I. Newman (ed.), *Handbook of Political Marketing*. London: Sage, 661–86.

Thurber, J.A. (1995) 'The transformation of American campaigns', in J.A. Thurber and C.J. Nelson (eds), *Campaigns and Elections American Style*. Boulder, CO: Westview, 1–13.

Wilkie, W. and Moore, E. (2003) 'Scholarly research in marketing: exploring the "4 eras" of thought development', *Journal of Public Policy & Marketing*, 22 (Fall): 116–46.

Wortmann, M. (1989) 'Political marketing: a modern party strategy', unpublished doctoral thesis, European University Institute, Florence.

Wring, D. (2002) 'Conceptualising political marketing: a framework for election-campaign analysis', in N.J. O'Shaughnessy and S.C. Henneberg (eds), *The Idea of Political Marketing*. Westport, CT: Praeger, 171–86.

5 Critical Perspectives on Political Marketing

After reading this chapter, you should be able to:

- list the criticisms levelled at political marketing and political marketing management by political science and marketing scholars
- distinguish between the theory of political marketing, the theory of political marketing management and political marketing management as an activity
- distinguish between normative and descriptive criticisms of political marketing.

Introduction

Political marketing as a research area and a practical activity often has to justify itself and defend itself against criticisms of its focus on the use of marketing concepts and instruments in the political sphere. It sometimes seems as if attempts to understand the way in which political actors strive to achieve mutually beneficial exchanges are automatically assumed to be part of some Machiavellian plot to take over the world (or at least the local council). Perceptions of political marketing as a research field have gradually improved over the last twenty years, but political scientists, whilst not hostile, are still uneasy (Savigny, 2008; Ormrod and Savigny, 2012).

The application of outdated concepts based on the managerial/instrumental approaches to marketing (e.g. Lloyd, 2005), the misapplication of others (Lees-Marshment, 2001) and a continuing empirical focus on post-hoc rationalisations of election campaigns have done nothing to improve this state of affairs. Few attempts have been made to develop state-of-the-art marketing theories and concepts to the political context (e.g. Ormrod and Henneberg, 2010; Ormrod and Savigny, 2012) or discuss the implications of political marketing for democracy (Henneberg et al., 2009). So whilst political marketers are gradually becoming more accepted as legitimate contributors to academic debate, there is still a long way to go.

The question of the applicability of marketing activities (and by association, research) to the political context is mostly raised by political scientists; however, researchers from marketing science have also voiced concerns as to the seemingly indiscriminate way in which 'marketing' is (mis)applied to the political context without an academically rigorous understanding of the implications of this (Henneberg, 2002). In the following we discuss several of the principal critical arguments raised by academics in the fields of marketing and political science against political marketing. There are two distinct groups of issues: criticisms of political marketing practice and criticisms of the political marketing research associated with such practice. In order to structure our discussion, we use a categorisation scheme derived from Henneberg (1995). We also explore the consequences of our results for political marketing theory and practice.

Categories of political marketing and political marketing management

Discussions concerning political marketing research and practice can suffer from a somewhat confusing understanding of different categories of political marketing. For the purpose of this chapter, a specific categorisation scheme is used (see Figure 5.1). It is possible to distinguish between three levels of involvement and two levels of focus (Henneberg, 2002). We understand the term **political marketing** to represent the theoretical and conceptual backbone upon which **political marketing management** activities are structured. Examples of these activities are developing the party's strategic political posture, deciding on the political market orientation profile of the party, election campaign management and analysing the results of political market research.

We can distinguish between two levels of theory, namely the theory of political marketing management and the theory of political marketing. The theory of political marketing management encompasses the academic interest in dealing with the operational management issues of political exchanges. It consists of a theoretical and analytical examination of managerial behaviour. Questions answered on this level of theory are, for example: What do political actors do to manage the political exchange? Which instruments and concepts are successful, and under what circumstances? However, this operational and managerial focus means that certain elements are not covered by the theory of political marketing management. One may ask: what about the wider impact of political

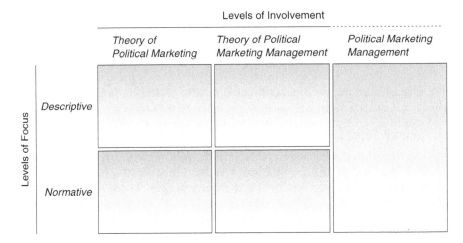

Figure 5.1   Categorisation scheme of political marketing and political marketing
management

marketing activities on democracy or the interplay with different party or electoral systems? What about the description and definition of different exchange
structures in political marketing? These and more fundamental questions, without direct managerial relevance, are covered by the theory of political marketing. Finally, it is also important to distinguish two levels of focus: the **descriptive**
focus (what parties do) and the **normative/prescriptive focus** (what parties
ought or *should* do). As these categories are widely used in marketing theory, a
detailed description can be omitted. Putting these categories together, the categorisation scheme allows a clear focus of criticism of political marketing.

Criticism of political marketing management and political marketing

The most common criticisms of the practice of political marketing management can be summarised by the following six statements:

1   Through the use of political marketing management, elections can in effect be
'bought' (also: only rich candidates can afford to run).
2   Political marketing management has transformed politics into being obsessed
with 'spin' and 'packaging' (also: politics has become devoid of content because of
political marketing).
3   Political marketing management has caused more populism in politics and a
'follower mentality' prevails, based on focus group results and perceived public
opinion (also: politics has become devoid of political leadership).

4 Parties and politicians that use political marketing management are using the wrong reference points/mindsets. Politics is essentially not about 'selling' but about something completely different.
5 Political marketing management is not compatible with how voters (should) make an informed voting decision (also: political marketing uses manipulative methods/smokescreens to betray voters).
6 Political marketing management activities cause campaigns to be negative.

On the level of the theory of political marketing as well as the theory of political marketing management, five more criticisms can be distinguished with regard to how researchers approach political marketing:

7 Research on political marketing is not focusing on politics but on ephemeral activities like communication tactics and campaigning.
8 All research into political marketing helps in the end to foster the adoption and application of (inherently bad) management practice and thinking in politics. This is not only true of normative research but also of purely descriptive research.
9 Research in political marketing is unsophisticated and does not utilise the leading edge political science and especially marketing theories available.
10 The political arena is not really part of the 'marketing domain' and should therefore not be researched using marketing concepts.
11 No theoretical and ethical framework exists that allows (value-)discussions about political marketing.

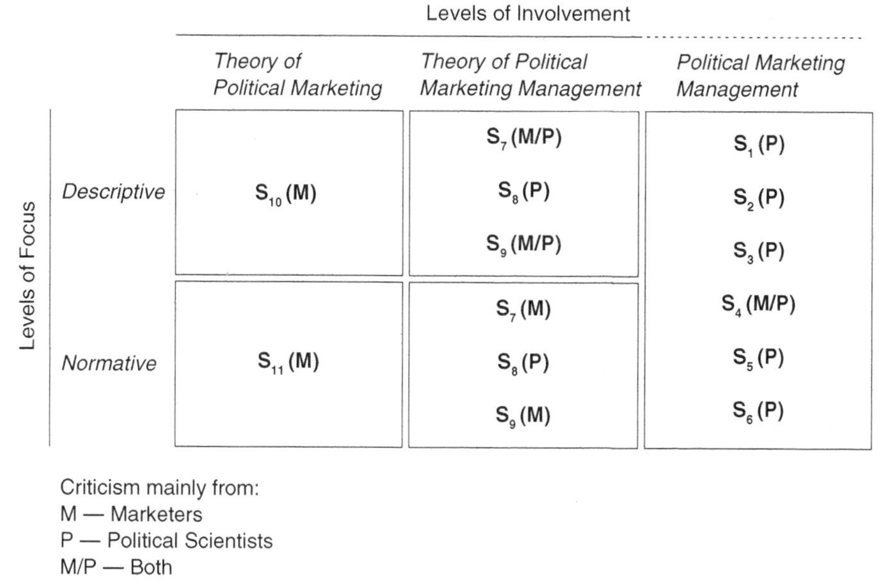

Levels of Involvement

	Theory of Political Marketing	Theory of Political Marketing Management	Political Marketing Management
Descriptive	S_{10} (M)	S_7 (M/P) S_8 (P) S_9 (M/P)	S_1 (P) S_2 (P) S_3 (P)
Normative	S_{11} (M)	S_7 (M) S_8 (P) S_9 (M)	S_4 (M/P) S_5 (P) S_6 (P)

Levels of Focus

Criticism mainly from:
M — Marketers
P — Political Scientists
M/P — Both

Figure 5.2 Criticisms of political marketing

If these statements are clustered into the categorisation scheme of political marketing (see Figure 5.2), a picture emerges of whether each of the critical statements is typically associated with a political scientist, a marketer, or is a concern of scholars from both academic traditions. Most criticisms regarding political marketing management come from political scientists, whilst few marketers find the use of marketing instruments and concepts in politics objectionable. The main problem voiced by scholars from the marketing tradition concerns the fundamental theoretical problems stated in Statements 10 and 11: whether or not commercial marketing concepts can and should be used to describe political behaviour (the 'domain' question). Marketers also focus on critical aspects of the theory of political marketing, that is, thinking about some underlying theoretical and conceptual elements of political marketing that affect and shape the theory of political marketing management as well as the epistemological position *vis à vis* its research object.

Statement 1: Elections can be bought

One of the most damning criticisms of the use of marketing instruments in the political arena is that democratic elections can now be 'bought'. The argument is that modern elections are won by the candidate or party with the most professional campaign. Activities include agenda-setting through political adverts and media manipulation, the planting of sound bites in the news media, the micro-targeting of communication instruments and focus on marginal seats. As this professionalism and access to the paid media come at a price, the party or candidate with more resources or better fund-raising capabilities over the period of high electoral competition wins, irrespective of the political argument (Wray, 1999).

Whilst it is certainly true that electoral campaigns have become progressively more expensive – President Obama spent hundreds of millions of dollars getting elected to the White House – the direct relationship between campaign spending and campaign success is arguably overstated. Looking at commercial campaigns in a for-profit market environment, a larger campaign budget does not necessarily correlate with commercial success (Berkowitz et al., 2001). Furthermore, whilst there are certainly examples where the big political spenders in the end win elections, there are also counter-examples: in the run-up to the 2001 general elections in the UK, the opposition Conservative Party spent £12,751,813 in comparison to the £10,945,119 spent by the incumbent Labour Party; despite this, the Conservative Party was defeated at the polls (31.7 per cent of the national vote compared to Labour's 40.9 per cent). Furthermore, the 18.3 per cent of the popular vote received by the Liberal Democrat Party, the third largest political party in the UK system, sounds extraordinary if one looks at their respective campaign spending: £1,361,377 (Electoral Commission, 2002). In addition, this statement would not be able to account for the sometimes considerable electoral volatility in party systems where the main source of funding is state-based and calculated as a result of a party's electoral success at the last election (e.g. as in Germany) (Seidle, 1991). While resource-acquisition is certainly a contentious issue on the political agenda (Jamieson, 1992), it is arguably more a discussion about funding sources in a democracy than about political marketing management itself.

Statement 2: Packaging without content

Political marketing management is commonly accused of having emptied political communication of content and party politics of deeply held political convictions; in Franklin's (1994: 9) words: 'Image has supplanted substance.' Instead, critics argue that political marketing emphasises the way in which political messages are packaged. Political arguments are reduced to spin and sound bites and framed according to imagery and symbolism rather than political content. Consequently, some image consultants have argued that politicians should become brand managers and prime ministers and governments should manage the nation as a brand (Smith, 2001).

From a marketing perspective it is possible to agree with this criticism to some extent. Politics is essentially about managing a service in the form of promises (public goods) to constituents (e.g. the electorate). The promises evoke expectations in the minds of the constituents that are measured against political activities once the political actor is in a position to influence the content of legislation in the parliamentary marketplace and subsequently implement these promises in the governmental marketplace (Henneberg and Ormrod, 2012). In a simplified way this means that if these expectations are not met by delivering certain political outcomes (e.g. tax cuts, political leadership, improving the international importance of a country), dissatisfaction follows (according to the confirmation/disconfirmation model of consumer behaviour) (Fournier and Mick, 1999).

If expectations are constantly not met and the constituents perceive most promises to be empty, a general disillusionment can follow. Whilst this disillusionment can manifest itself as falling turnout at elections, disillusionment also leads to other forms of behavioural change, such as withholding votes, resources and donations from parties and shifting these to other actors or out of the electoral market altogether (O'Shaughnessy and Wring, 1994). Some argue that the electorate forgets false promises and that after an election period the lies and disappointments of the previous campaign and the first year(s) of the government are not relevant for the voter decision-making process. However, this same electorate, when acting as consumers in the commercial marketplace, quickly shift brand loyalties when dissatisfied. It seems unlikely that relatively unsophisticated political marketing techniques have a much stronger influence on behaviour and attitudes than highly developed techniques from the commercial field. However, imagery and symbolism continue to be used to package political promises and messages with the aim of addressing the needs and wants of certain target audiences.

Spin and imagery are not modern phenomena but inherent in any attempt to convince and make an argument; rhetoric, the ancient practice of political communication, used exaggerations to emphasise a point but did not necessarily set out to deceive. It should also be remembered that spin depends on the media and therefore has to be seen in a dialectic relationship between different actors, each with their own agenda, although some critics assume that the '[m]edia are used routinely by politicians to set news agendas' (Franklin, 1994: 17). What differentiates spin from rhetoric is the professionalism and omnipresence of spin and political consultants (Johnson, 2002) and directors of communications such as Alastair Campbell for Tony Blair, Karl Rove for George Bush Jnr. and Bodo Hombach for Gerhardt Schröder. However, it is interesting to see that these communication and campaign specialists have now gained influence over the formulation of policy rather than just its communication, and some have even become politicians themselves (Newman, 2001). Whilst this raises questions regarding accountability, this professionalism has at least caused the political process to be much more efficient and effective.

Statement 3: Populism and no leadership

Political actors are often accused of pandering to crucial segments of the electorate such as opinion leaders and swing voters, or concentrating their energies on electoral areas with 'marginal seats' (Harris, 2001). In order to uncover the explicit needs and wants of these voters, political actors use market research techniques, especially focus groups. The outcome of this market research then determines policy, in marketing terms a market-driven offering development. This focus on the *vox populi* is often attributed to one of the core concepts in commercial marketing, customer orientation. However, it is often forgotten that being customer-oriented is not the same as being customer led (Slater and Narver, 1998, 1999).

It is the confusion that surrounds being customer (voter) leading versus being customer (voter) led that provides support for the 'marketing leads to populism' argument. Being voter led can be electorally successful in certain circumstances as a strategic posture and does echo the democratic notion of the representation of, and responsiveness to, a self-selected segment of the electorate. However, being led by voter opinion when developing policy is not an optimal strategy under other circumstances and neglects crucial aspects of a customer orientation as postulated in the commercial marketing literature. Without going into the details of the 'market orientation versus customer orientation' debate in commercial marketing theory and the related aspect of a social orientation (Liao et al., 2001), it can nevertheless be stated that an exclusively market-led approach in politics falls short of a voter orientation (Newman, 1999). In fact, the conscious integration of voter-led and voter-leading behaviour characterises successful political marketing management in terms of building long-term relationships (Ormrod and Henneberg, 2010). An element of leading complements an emphasis on following and satisfying customer needs and wants. Indeed, a political marketing management approach that is purely voter led is often bad politics and bad marketing as well. The irony is that leading and following can sometimes develop into a 'devil and the deep blue sea' phenomenon, as British Prime Minister Tony Blair discovered. Usually criticised as an opportunist who relied on focus group results for policy-making, Blair's leadership stance of siding with the US during the Second Iraq War is now characterised as being out of touch with the people and even members of his own party (Ritson, 2003).

Statement 4: Politics is about selling

Selling and marketing are not the same. As such, equating political marketing management activities with selling washing powder or cornflakes corrupts and devalues politics. The importance of democratic political decisions and their wide-ranging implications for the wellbeing of many people constitutes a completely different quality from picking up a box of cornflakes in a supermarket. This argument is based on a like-for-like equation of the political and the economic market. However, as already alluded to above, this is not a straightforward case. Whilst political offerings are dissimilar to commercial offerings, an analogy with services is not totally unreasonable. Many characteristics are similar: for example, both political and commercial offerings are promise and experience based, non-tangible, perishable and partly public goods (O'Shaughnessy and Henneberg, 2002). Furthermore, constituents like voters or grass-roots supporters are not really customers but more resemble clients and so the analogy of politics with a professional service, say a lawyer or an accountant, seems a more reasonable one (Henneberg, 2002). Services marketing, which is heavily committed to building trust and commitment in a relational exchange, can therefore be a guiding concept for political marketing management.

Another and more fundamental issue of the selling politics argument has to do with the question of whether or not marketing management practices or concepts are applicable in non-economic exchanges. Non-profit and social marketing (e.g. cause-related marketing, health management, sports or arts marketing, to name only a few) have developed into sub-disciplines of marketing, but not without discussions about the boundaries of marketing as a research field. This fundamental discussion will be addressed in Statement 10.

Statement 5: The electorate votes differently

This argument is grounded in understanding how voters make sense of political issues and their subsequent choice behaviour. This choice can consist of forming a political opinion or triggering certain political behaviours and is most salient during election campaigns. The argument against political marketing management insists that the electorate needs to be able to gain access to political information and facts in order to form a rational opinion on which they can base their voting decision. However, nowadays voters do not get the information about important political issues that they need as political marketing management activities focus political campaigns on personal characteristics, empty arguments, images, catch-phrases and sound bites. These stimuli do not generally consist of the 'right' kind of political information for voters to be able to form an informed opinion. The voter's opinion remains a one-dimensional image of the shallow political discussions fostered by political marketing management.

These arguments are clearly inspired by political theory and a prescriptive understanding of how democracy ought to work and how voters are supposed to make up their mind (Brennan and Lomasky, 1993). However, the assumption that voters (could) decide in a rational way and that they (could) form opinions in a 'power and dominance-free' environment is certainly based on a fallacy. Such deontological abstraction might serve some purpose in underpinning micro-economic theory (in political science, for example, embraced by the economic school of voting behaviour). To derive normative considerations on how a political discourse ought to look and what kind of information should or should not be part of political campaigns using a rational choice approach is simply not realistic (O'Shaughnessy, 2002). Any voting behaviour theory based on rational choice shows only part of the complex human processes of deciding and acting. Consumer behaviour theory, although indebted to micro-economic models, has accepted this and there have been attempts to integrate the findings of consumption studies with those of voting behaviour theories (Newman and Sheth, 1987; Bartle and Griffiths, 2002).

In its essence, the voting decision is a very complex and difficult process. Therefore, non-rational elements or decision shortcuts such as the reliance on heuristics and decision cues help voters to make up their minds (Newman, 2001). This could mean using the perceived personal characteristics of the main candidate as an indication of the attractiveness of a political party and its offering. Such reasoning does not constitute a demeaning of politics but is an expression of the coping strategies innate in human beings. Political marketing management accepts these shortcomings and uses them to develop an appropriate communication strategy. Therefore, any arguments against political marketing on normative grounds of an optimal decision-making process need to be qualified. More appropriate and realistic voter behaviour theories (i.e. better description and less prescription) can, however, provide the basis for a criticism of certain political marketing management phenomena.

Statement 6: Campaigns have become personal and negative

With the advent of political marketing management, political discourse and especially political campaigns have become increasingly negative. Negative campaigning can be concerned with political issues or highlight the failure of an incumbent to fulfil their electoral promise but, more often than not, direct and personal attacks on political opponents (their character, their biography, their personal relationships and so on) become the focal point of political discussions. Political marketing has changed political culture away from issues and towards persons; with this, political discourse has entered the arena of show business and character assassinations. Negative campaigns also create counter-campaigns, and so political discourse disintegrates into a mud-slinging contest. Worse, there is the fear that these methods actually work and that negative campaigns can win elections.

When assessing negative campaigns it is important to deconstruct the argument into two aspects: a focus on persons, on the one hand, and a focus on the negative content of the communication, on the other. In line with the service characteristics of the political offering, the importance of those who deliver the service for assessing the (anticipated) quality of a service does not come as a surprise. In services marketing, 'people' are an additional instrument in the marketing mix of the 7Ps (Zeithaml and Bitner, 2003). As the service is intangible, the contact and delivery personnel (as well as the tangible elements of the delivery channel) become an important cue in forming expectations about the service and, indeed, also satisfaction/experience judgements. The mere content of a political programme does not say everything about a party; for voters it is also important if they believe that the politicians have the necessary characteristics (e.g. leadership, expertise, emotional balance, pragmatism, international standing) to implement the programme and deliver on their promises (Popkin, 1994). The political offering needs to be seen as an amalgamation of different elements, like the programme and personal characteristics, and it is therefore beneficial if political marketing management (as well as media coverage) takes these different elements into consideration (Axford and Huggins, 2002).

Negative content in political discourse is often condemned in general, but it is possible to construct a defence. Comparative advertising can help voters and other decision makers to clearly see the difference between alternative political offerings, and it allows political parties and candidates to emphasise those elements that differentiate the political party or candidate from the competition. This is especially relevant as more information – negative or not – can enhance voters' understanding of the political market in times when many parties compete in the political centre (Banker, 1992). In fact, it has been shown that negative advertisements are more issue-oriented than positive ones (Kaid, 1999). On the other hand, character assassinations, constant personal attacks (founded or unfounded) and the routine scrutinising of opponents' private lives (sometimes going back decades) is unquestionably an unsavoury aspect, but not one necessarily unique to political marketing management, as sports and movie celebrities will testify. However, the political culture and the structure of the party system can foster or dampen this tendency (Holtz-Bacha and Kaid, 1995); for example, in countries with a party-oriented system, negative campaigns might be less prevalent. A strong political culture can also counteract interest in the private lives of politicians, but the tendencies of increasing emphasis on the 'people' aspect of (political) service delivery might have an impact on the political culture and the degree of privacy that politicians are allowed.

The research: the theory of political marketing (management)

Statement 7: Too much communication focus

Research on political marketing has often been criticised for being overly focused on one aspect of marketing theory, communication as part of an election campaign. Political campaigns and political marketing activities are often exclusively defined through their communication content and the media vehicles that are employed (Franklin and Richardson, 2002). This narrow focus means that many aspects of marketing theory are neglected and that the focus is purely operational and mainly on a small number of marketing instruments. The oversimplification of political marketing research arguably constitutes an impoverishment of the sub-discipline, an oversimplification which has the potential to restrict the development of research. Strategic aspects of political marketing management, other marketing instruments and the underlying functions of political marketing management have been neglected as research foci (Henneberg, 2002). Too much of the emphasis of current research appears to be channelled towards comparative campaign studies, looking at different countries, describing how political marketing (management) instruments are used and the content of campaign communication, without synthesis or conceptual work appearing alongside.

Whilst this state is lamentable and the criticism is somewhat justified, the emphasis in research on campaigns and communication mirrors the emphasis of political marketing management itself. It seems that the practitioners share the reductionist approach towards marketing. Political marketing management, in most cases, does not focus extensively on strategic issues and also has a very narrow view with regard to the underlying tactical functions of political marketing management (Henneberg, 2002). This becomes more understandable when one looks at the background of political marketing managers or consultants: more often than not they are trained in advertising or communication and have worked as commercial campaign managers.

Statement 8: Research insinuates management practice

Research on political marketing management helps to spread management practice and ethics in the political sphere. It encourages the use of such marketing instruments and concepts and redefines the way everyone thinks about politics. This 'imperialism' of management theories crowds out other ways of thinking about politics. This is not just true for the research that helps optimise political marketing management tools and concepts, but also for purely descriptive research. Thus, a radical argument contends that one should either abstain from research grounded in marketing theory or at the very most use it with circumspection.

That such objections are still voiced demonstrates a high level of critical vigour and that (political) marketing theory has not yet been able to convince its opponents that research into the activities of political actors can gain considerable insight using political marketing concepts without harming its research object. Three issues can be addressed with regard to the various objections to marketing in politics: first, it is often stated that political actors use instruments and concepts that are influenced by marketing. Therefore, marketing theory is uniquely positioned as a research tool in order to make sense of these phenomena and to interpret them in an appropriate way. Second, much research that is published in the field of political marketing uses marketing theories only tangentially or inappropriately (see Statement 9) and is still steeped in political science and communication studies methodology. Therefore, the influence of marketing theory in describing politics as well as prescribing political marketing management instruments is still small and should not be overestimated. The practice of political marketing management seems to be far ahead of any catching-up efforts by academics. Finally, the compatibility of the 'professionalisation' of politics with political science concepts of democracy itself is a very interesting subject for the theory of political marketing. This has not been addressed sufficiently so far by political scientists and marketing theorists (see Collins and Butler, 2003, for an exception). General discussions on the appropriateness and domain of non-profit marketing (see Statement 10) are not enough to resolve this underlying ethical issue. Statement 11 will touch upon this problem again.

Statement 9: Non-sophisticated research

Marketers, especially, often voice the concern that political marketing research is not sophisticated enough. Two (linked) aspects of this critical argument can be distinguished: one is concerned with the lack of a connection between research in political marketing and the forefront of mainstream marketing theory, whilst the other concern focuses on the static nature of research in political marketing.

Although research at the level of the theory of political marketing (management) is still somewhat in its infancy (most research in this area did not start before the beginning of the 1990s, taking O'Shaughnessy, 1990, and Harrop, 1990 as the seminal 'kick-off' sources), it seems to be strangely decoupled from several major trends that have dominated marketing theory during this time. For example, the discussions around market orientation as well as relational and network marketing and the advancements of the 'Nordic school' of marketing in the area of services marketing have had little impact on political marketing scholars. Sometimes it seems (polemically speaking) as if political marketing theory consists of not much more than an analysis of the 4Ps (with emphasis on Promotion) of the political marketing mix, an outdated concept in commercial marketing research and practice. The fact that mainstream marketing theory itself has now advanced from this concept towards relationship-based approaches (Grönroos, 1997) makes the limited use of marketing concepts by political marketing researchers even more worrying.

Furthermore, and this addresses the second point of the 'non-sophistication' argument, a tendency to 'reinvent the wheel' with regard to research content has been observed. Although progress has been made by adding to the research agenda on political marketing, articles that fundamentally do nothing else but till the same ground over and over again still prevail. Many descriptive pieces on campaigning in different countries are based on anecdotal evidence and are without new conceptual developments and a clear impetus for further research.

Statement 10: Not a marketing domain

A fundamental criticism of political marketing concerns whether or not it has a place within the domain of marketing in its broadest sense. This issue clearly hinges around the theory of political marketing and as a criticism, if accepted, would mean that the research community in political marketing is actually 'barking up the wrong tree'. The domain discussion, that of defining the 'nature and scope of marketing' (Hunt, 1976: 17), was one of the focal points of discourse in marketing theory in the 1960s and 1970s and linked to the clarification of the exchange paradigm in marketing. Broadening the concept of marketing beyond classical product-based for-profit organisations (Kotler and Levy, 1969) meant incorporating services organisations and non-profit organisations. The inclusion of non-profit or social marketing was grounded in a wide definition of the marketing domain, which was not universally accepted and is to some extent still occasionally contested. The use of marketing theories and concepts to explain and frame research on political issues in a non-profit marketplace (i.e. shaped by competitive but non-economic exchanges) can be rejected for theoretical reasons when using the narrow definition of marketing, which limits marketing to economically moti-vated exchanges in which values can be directly quantified through an exchange price. However, in the last two decades, social marketing has gained importance with regard to practice and research and it is now generally accepted as being part of the marketing domain. The wide definition of marketing has prevailed in marketing textbooks and the proliferation of social marketing studies in all kind of varieties (e.g. church marketing, arts marketing, sports marketing, cause-related market-ing) shows that such a conceptual grounding in marketing theory has become accepted (Cornelissen, 2002).

Statement 11: Value discussions are not grounded

Marketing management in the political sphere needs to be judged and supervised from a moral and ethical point of view, especially with regard to possible (positive or negative) ramifications for democratic practices. The tendency towards professionalisation and political management, of increased populism and voter-led behaviour by political actors, and of expensive and negative campaigning make it inevitable that the influence of marketing on the functioning of the political system needs to be assessed and also judged. The widespread use of political marketing management has the potential to change the way our democracy works (Collins and Butler, 2003). To understand these implications, it is necessary for value discussions to have a theoretical and ethical framework that can make sense of political marketing management (O'Shaughnessy, 2002). It is the conjecture of Statement 11 that we are currently lacking such a framework, and therefore political marketing has no normative instrument or yardstick of its own to assess our *explanandum* in question. Many value discussions do not take into consideration the specific stance of political marketing and its underlying conceptual tenets. Therefore, it is difficult for researchers to judge the value of political marketing through more common (deontologi-cal) theories of democracy, which see any political marketing management activity as an alien (exogenous) element to politics. Unsurprisingly, these researchers are somewhat loaded against the use of political marketing (management).

It is remarkable that many marketers have identified this as one of the main research shortcomings of political marketing. There seems to be an understanding in the research community that genuine ethical and norma-tive research on political marketing has been neglected, especially by mar-keting theorists (O'Shaughnessy, 2002). It therefore seems valid to shift the responsibility for some of the shortcomings with regard to discussions about political marketing (e.g. Statements 8 and 9) onto the level of the theory of political marketing and hope for more involvement in normative discussion *within* political marketing research.

So what now? Conclusion and research propositions

The discussion has dealt with eleven statements, all critical of political marketing on a practical as well as research level. To conclude this discussion, whilst the shortcomings of political marketing management (Statements 1–6) cannot all be accepted, more fundamental criticism with regard to political marketing research shows some structural shortcomings: not enough rigid and conceptually grounded research has been carried out, especially with regard to the holistic nature of political marketing and its ethical implications.

However, it has to be said that each of the eleven statements merits further discussion and that there are undoubtedly many more valid criticisms of political marketing which have not been touched upon in this chapter. Thus, the argument above will, we hope, stimulate further discourse by representatives from other disciplines. Political marketing is still something of an 'academic parvenu' (O'Shaughnessy and Henneberg, 2002: xiv). Fundamental conceptual issues are still unresolved. For example, it is still not clear what impact using marketing and managerial concepts has in and on politics (Harris, 2001). The assumption that there is a distinction between policy-making, on the one hand, and the management of government/politics, on the other, is seen as somewhat unrealistic (Collins and Butler, 2003) but the interactions and repercussions are more often than not implied rather than analysed.

Therefore, critics of political marketing should lose their sometimes exaggerated fear of the impact of political marketing as well as the grounding of their critique in normative reasoning. A better understanding of political marketing theory through more conceptual discussions as well as the laying of the foundations for an ethical debate are needed; similar considerations in the area of social marketing could lead the way (Brenkert, 2002). For example, questions could focus on how far political marketing shifts political systems towards plebiscitary democracy, and why this has not happened (yet?). To make sure that political marketing research is innovative, more conceptual rigour is needed, fostered by a link with newest developments in marketing theory and political science. It has to be said that marketers have not always been rigorous when conducting political marketing research and can therefore be held responsible for some of the shortcomings exposed in Statements 7 to 11.

Discussion questions

- Think about the criticisms primarily raised by political scientists. Do you think that these criticisms are justified?
- Now think about the criticisms primarily raised by marketing scholars. Do you think that these criticisms are justified?
- What can researchers of political marketing do to answer these criticisms? What about political marketing practitioners?

Key terms

Political marketing   Descriptive focus
Political marketing   Normative/prescriptive focus
management

Further reading

Collins and Butler (2003): The article criticises the assumption that market research into public opinion naturally produces the optimal basis for policy decisions in representative democracies. It concludes by stating that political discourse and citizen engagement in the political process is superior to a simple responsiveness to voters when considering the implications of policy for society as a whole.

Henneberg (2004): This chapter is an updated version of Henneberg's article.

Lloyd (2005): The article discusses how the 'product' and the 'marketing mix' are understood in the political marketing literature, and argues that it is necessary to develop both to suit the political context. Lloyd proposes her own definition of the political product and suggests ways in which the commercial marketing mix can be developed to suit the political context.

References

Axford, B. and Huggins, R. (2002) 'Political marketing and the aestheticization of politics: modern politics and postmodern trends', in N.J. O'Shaughnessy and S.C. Henneberg (eds), *The Idea of Political Marketing*. Westport, CT: Praeger, 187–208.

Banker, S. (1992) 'The ethics of political marketing practices, the rhetorical perspective', *Journal of Business Ethics*, 11: 843–8.

Bartle, J. and Griffiths, D. (2002) 'Social-psychological, economic and marketing models of voting behaviour compared', in N.J. O'Shaughnessy and S.C. Henneberg (eds), *The Idea of Political Marketing*, Westport, CT: Praeger, 19–38.

Berkowitz, D., Allaway, A. and D'Souza, G. (2001) 'The impact of differential lag effects on the allocation of advertising budgets across media', *Journal of Advertising Research*, 41 (2): 27–36.

Brenkert, G.G. (2002) 'Ethical challenges of social marketing', *Journal of Public Policy & Marketing*, 21 (1): 14–25.

Brennan, G. and Lomasky, L. (1993) *Democracy and Decision*. Cambridge: Cambridge University Press.

Collins, N. and Butler, P. (2003) 'When marketing models clash with democracy', *Journal of Public Affairs*, 3 (1): 52–62.

Cornelissen, J.P. (2002) 'Metaphorical reasoning and knowledge generation: the case of political marketing', *Journal of Political Marketing*, 1 (1): 193–208.

Electoral Commission (2002) 'Election 2001: campaign spending', Report, November.

Fournier, S. and Mick, D.G. (1999) 'Rediscovering satisfaction,' *Journal of Marketing*, 63: 5–23.

Franklin, B. (1994) *Packaging Politics*. London: Edward Arnold.

Franklin, B. and Richardson, J.E. (2002) 'Priming the parish pump: political marketing and news management in local political communications networks', *Journal of Political Marketing*, 1 (1): 117–47.

Grönroos, C. (1997) 'From marketing mix to relationship marketing – towards a paradigm shift in marketing', *Management Decision*, 35 (4): 322–39.

Harris, P. (2001) 'Machiavelli, political marketing and reinventing government', *European Journal of Marketing*, 35 (9): 1136–54.

Harrop, M. (1990) 'Political marketing', *Parliamentary Affairs*, 43: 277–91.

Henneberg, S.C. (1995) 'A theoretical approach to categorising research in political marketing', paper presented at the PSA Elections, Public Opinion and Parties Conference, London, 15–17 September.

Henneberg, S.C. (2002) 'Understanding political marketing', in N.J. O'Shaughnessy and S.C. Henneberg (eds), *The Idea of Political Marketing*, Westport, CT: Praeger, 93–170.

Henneberg, S.C. (2004) 'The views of an *advocatus dei*: political marketing and its critics', *Journal of Public Affairs*, 4: 225–43.

Henneberg, S.C. and Ormrod, R.P. (2012) 'The triadic interaction model of political marketing exchange', *Marketing Theory*.

Henneberg, S.C., Scammell, M. and O'Shaughnessy, N.J. (2009) 'Political marketing management and theories of democracy', *Marketing Theory*, 9 (2): 165–88.

Holtz-Bacha, C. and Kaid, L.L. (1995) 'A comparative perspective on political advertising', in L.L. Kaid and C. Holtz-Bacha (eds), *Political Advertising in Western Democracies*, Thousand Oaks, CA: Sage, 8–18.

Hunt, S.D. (1976) 'The nature and scope of marketing', *Journal of Marketing*, 40: 17–28.

Jamieson, K.H. (1992) *Packaging the Presidency*. New York: Oxford University Press.

Johnson, D.W. (2002) 'Perspectives on political consulting', *Journal of Political Marketing*, 1 (1): 7–21.

Kaid, L.L. (1999) 'Political advertising', in B.I. Newman (ed.), *Handbook of Political Marketing*, Thousand Oaks, CA: Sage, 423–38.

Kotler, P. and Levy, S.J. (1969) 'Broadening the concept of marketing', *Journal of Marketing*, 33: 10–5.

Lees-Marshment, J. (2001) *Political Marketing and British Political Parties*. Manchester: Manchester University Press.

Liao, M.-N., Foreman, S. and Sargeant, A. (2001) 'Market versus societal orientation in the nonprofit context', *International Journal of Nonprofit and Voluntary Sector Marketing*, 6 (3): 254–68.

Lloyd, J. (2005) 'Square peg, round hole? Can marketing-based concepts have a useful role in the political arena?, *Journal of Non-profit and Public Sector Marketing*, 14 (1/2): 27–46.

Newman, B.I. (1999) *The Mass Marketing of Politics*. Thousand Oaks, CA: Sage.

Newman, B.I. (2001) 'Image-manufacturing in the USA: recent US presidential elections and beyond', *European Journal of Marketing*, 35 (9): 966–70.

Newman, B.I. and Sheth, J.N. (1987) *A Theory of Political Choice Behavior*. New York: Praeger.

Ormrod, R.P. and Henneberg, S.C. (2010) 'Strategic political postures and political market orientation: towards an integrated concept of political marketing strategy', *Journal of Political Marketing*, 9 (4): 294–313.

Ormrod, R.P. and Savigny, H. (2012) 'Political market orientation: a framework for understanding relationship structures in political parties', *Party Politics*, 18 (4): 487–502.

O'Shaughnessy, N.J. (1990) *The Phenomenon of Political Marketing*. Basingstoke: Macmillan.

O'Shaughnessy, N.J. (2002) 'Toward an ethical framework for political marketing', *Psychology & Marketing*, 19 (12): 1079–95.

O'Shaughnessy, N.J. and Henneberg, S.C. (2002) 'Introduction', in N.J. O'Shaughnessy and S.C. Henneberg (eds), *The Idea of Political Marketing*. Westport, CT: Praeger, xi–xx.

O'Shaughnessy, N.J. and Wring, D. (1994) 'Political marketing in Britain', in H. Tam (ed.), *Marketing, Competition and the Public Sector*. Harlow: Longman, 246–70.

Popkin, S.L. (1994) *The Reasoning Voter*. Chicago: University of Chicago Press.

Ritson, M. (2003) 'We lost our say over war when Labour deprioritised marketing', *Marketing* (UK), 20 March.

Savigny, H. (2008) *The Problem of Political Marketing*. London: Continuum.

Seidle, F.L. (1991) *Comparative Issues in Party and Election Finance*. Toronto: Dundurn.

Slater, S.F. and Narver, J.C. (1998) 'Customer-led and market-oriented: let's not confuse the two', *Strategic Management Journal*, 19: 1001–6.

Slater, S.F. and Narver, J.C. (1999) 'Market-oriented is more than being customer-led', *Strategic Management Journal*, 20: 1165–8.

Smith, G. (2001) 'The 2001 General Election: factors influencing the brand image of political parties and their leaders', *Journal of Marketing Management*, 17: 989–1006.

Wray, J.H. (1999) 'Money and politics', in B.I. Newman (ed.), *Handbook of Political Marketing*. Thousand Oaks, CA: Sage, 741–58.

Zeithaml, V.A. and Bitner, M.J. (2003) *Services Marketing*. New York: McGraw-Hill.

Chapter 5 is developed from Henneberg, S.C. (2004), 'The views of an *advocatus dei*: political marketing and its critics', *Journal of Public affairs*, 4 (3): 225–243. Reprinted by permission of John Wiley & Sons.

6 Political Marketing and Theories of Democracy

After reading this chapter, you should be able to:

- describe the differences between the sales-based, instrumental/ managerial-based and relationship-based schools of thought in political marketing
- identify which of the three schools of political marketing thought is most common in your political system
- relate the three schools of political marketing to the *competitive elitist* and *deliberative* types of democracy
- discuss whether political marketing *should* be linked to specific theories of democracy.

Uneasy partners: political marketing and politics

Political marketing means many things to many people. In general, it is a term more often used in academia and practice in Europe than in the US (Scammell, 1999). The distinction between political marketing, political marketing management and political communication is not always clear and often obscured by overlapping interpretations. However, what is clear is that political marketing often evokes negative feelings and is assumed to be harmful for politics and democratic systems; while political scientists mostly focus on ethical aspects of political marketing management practice, that is, questioning the use of political marketing instruments during election campaigning, marketing theorists are more concerned with shortcomings in the theory of political marketing. Especially the lack of a clear and consistent position of political marketing regarding both political practice and democratic fundamentals are factors which hold back the research area of political marketing (Henneberg and O'Shaughnessy, 2007).

In general, the merging of the two worlds of commercial marketing and political science makes academics anxious, especially political scientists who fear that politics will be transformed from what should rightly be a quest for a common vision of the just, noble and good into the private and often irrational whimsy of consumerism. Political marketing, it is argued, encourages voters to judge politicians in terms of the selfish rewards of consumer purchases (Bauman, 2005); equally it may undermine the courage necessary for political leadership (Klein, 2006). However, on the other hand, political marketing has been discussed in a more positive light, with Bannon (2005) arguing that a relationship-building approach of political marketing could well provide the basis for more meaningful interactions between voters and political institutions. Furthermore, political marketing should not be judged against ideal and impossible standards of a perfectly informed, knowledgeable and participating electorate, but rather against the real world of relatively low interest and knowledge in politics. This 'realist' strand of research claims that marketing of some sort may be valuable, even essential, for encouraging voter interest and involvement (Scammell, 2003).

However, as O'Shaughnessy (1990: 6) put it, 'The answer to the ethical question [regarding political marketing] depends on the views of democracy we hold.' Therefore, we argue that a critique of political marketing needs to be underpinned by a clear understanding of the conceptual complexity of the phenomenon in question as well as by a rigorous analysis of the yardstick that is employed. The vast majority of literature in political marketing and political science does not engage with the theoretical foundations of political marketing but remains concerned with specific applications and tools (Henneberg, 2008). This chapter is concerned with a discussion of different aspects of political marketing with regard to key concepts of democracy, with the aim of investigating the compatibility or incompatibility between them. Specifically, we are interested in whether the current 'dominant paradigm' of (political) marketing is commensurable with theories of democracy.

First, we briefly discuss the status of political marketing with regards to politics, and then analyse the characteristics of three distinct schools of political marketing that are derived from alternative theoretical vantage points. We then discuss two different normative concepts of democracy which will enable us to link political marketing with the democratic theories in a categorisation scheme. Finally, we synthesise our findings and their consequences and discuss implications for research in the area of political marketing.

The 'status' of political marketing in politics

Political marketing as an academic discipline 'works' on two levels: first, it consists of explanatory constructs for political marketing management activities as used by political actors in practice; second, it represents an exchange or interaction-based research lens to explain the political sphere *per se* (Henneberg and O'Shaughnessy, 2007). However, research in this area also ought to be concerned with the general 'fit' of the concepts of political marketing in relation to the research phenomenon in question (Lock and Harris, 1996). More specifically, political marketing research needs to be concerned with issues of democracy in general and its commensurability with political marketing management activities and underlying concepts, such as market orientation (Ormrod, 2007). This goes beyond more specific questions about the applicability of political marketing management activities in politics, such as whether it is ethical to focus only on 'floating voters' in a targeted election strategy (Baines et al., 2002).

The point of departure of this argument is the fundamental question regarding the integrity of political marketing (O'Shaughnessy, 2002). When posing the question in this way, there is somehow not enough clarity regarding the constructs concerned: what do we mean by 'democracy', and what exactly is 'political marketing' in this context? Thus, this question quickly disintegrates into more complex sub-questions once the two main components are examined. Political marketing and its theoretical and conceptual foundations, following commercial marketing theory, are not a monolithic bloc of unambiguous definitions, clear aims and aligned activities, but comprise many different 'schools' (Wilkie and Moore, 2003). Below, we focus on three distinct concepts of marketing in politics which span the space of possible options: 'selling-oriented', 'instrument-mix-oriented' and 'relationship-building' concepts of political marketing which are also informed by societal marketing considerations. Thus, the initial conceptual question about the relationship between political marketing and democracy needs to be related to each of these concepts of political marketing.

Moving to the second core component, that of democracy, it is equally clear that, conceptually, this too is a contested and fragmented construct (Cunningham, 2002). To judge the 'affinity' of political marketing against a democratic 'yardstick', one needs to consider which of the many expressions and principles of democracy are used; are we talking about the ideals of deliberative democracy or the norms of realist models? Again, for the purpose of our argument, we will focus on just two influential schools of democracy to illustrate our points: the 'competitive elitist' approach and the 'deliberative' concept of democracy.

Our analysis is therefore grounded in two parsimonious categorisation schemes (one of political marketing concepts, and one of theories of democracies) and their interrelations (Hunt, 1983). Such an analysis will allow us to provide a discussion of the concepts of political marketing and the activities of political marketing management. Furthermore, it also provides alternative benchmarks through the explicit use of a set of normative 'versions' of democracy (Henneberg and O'Shaughnessy, 2007).

Concepts of political marketing

Political marketing (PM) provides a theoretical umbrella for different applications of marketing concepts within the political sphere. No singular approach to PM exists, in line with the multifaceted nature of commercial schools of marketing. Sheth et al. (1988) identified twelve different schools of marketing, many of which were inspired by social exchange theory, microeconomical theory or institutional political economy. However, since then several other conceptual schools of commercial marketing have come to the forefront of academic research or practical application: for example, the relationship and network marketing approaches to organisational interactions (Shaw and Jones, 2005). Although commercial marketing theory is dominated by the 'instrumental' or 'managerial' paradigm, it has been questioned if this instrumental/managerial school of marketing is in line with the richness of social exchange theory underlying marketing thought (Grönroos, 1994). Furthermore, it has been argued that this school is incommensurable with core marketing concepts such as customer orientation, that it is simplistic and that it is merely a pedagogic tool (Grönroos, 2006).

As in the case of marketing theory, a similar variety of approaches exist in political marketing. This is represented in the extant literature by analyses of communication-based campaigning approaches (Newman, 1994; Harris et al., 2005), by strategic positioning approaches (Henneberg, 2006), or by concepts based on the organisational attitudes and behaviours in their relationship with external and internal political stakeholders (Ormrod, 2007). However, only a few categorisation attempts exist which provide a comparison of alternative political marketing approaches.

In order to link political marketing and democratic theory we have to be precise about the characteristics of PM as represented by different, often incompatible, concepts. We select and define three distinct schools of PM that cover the spectrum and richness of marketing approaches to politics:

- sales-based school of PM
- instrumental/managerial (IM) school of PM
- relationship-based school of PM.

These three overarching schools have been chosen because 1) they provide examples of 'ideal types' of PM, 2) they are based on state-of-the-art research discussions, and 3) they constitute the dominating paradigms in PM research and practice.

The *sales-based school of PM* is most often equated with a traditional, ideology-oriented approach to politics (Henneberg, 2002). The political offering is derived from solid political convictions, often characterised by an alignment with certain interests within dominant or social cleavages, such as class, ethnicity and region (Lipset and Rokkan, 1966). A 'market-leading' perspective and a predominantly tactical use of political marketing management instruments characterises this approach (Henneberg, 2006). Sales-based PM is often considered to be the 'first age' of political marketing, exemplified by the use of party political broadcasts, slogans, posters, and (in America) the thirty-second spot replacing the rally and the speaker meeting (O'Shaughnessy, 1990). It has been argued that this meant that political *marketing management* mattered more than political *marketing* (Wring, 2005). Examples of sales-based PM are now often found in primary-issue parties, typically Green parties or regional parties, such as the Welsh Plaid Cymru Party. The German Green Party campaigns offer an illustrative example, focusing on policies which are derived from a belief in environmental sustainability, while at the same time using selected management tools and concepts from PM (Blühdorn and Szarka, 2004).

The *IM school of PM* is generally accepted to be the 'normal paradigm' of current research in political marketing. Activities and strategies from the sphere of PM are used in a sophisticated way to convince voters of the value of the political offering, adapt the offering to target segment preferences and implement political marketing campaigns effectively and efficiently through the coordinated use of a multitude of tools and concepts from PM (Wring, 2005). This is in line with 'market-led' approaches of strategic marketing (Slater and Narver, 1998), or a 'following' mentality as a radical interpretation of a voter orientation (Henneberg, 2006). Tony Blair's first UK general election campaign represents an example of such 'focus group' driven campaigning (Wring, 2006). An instrumental approach can mean a focus on short-term expediency with emphasis on responding to tracking polls and public opinions. The IM school of PM describes an amalgam of techniques and a formulaic approach to the managerial implementation of the marketing concept (Johansen, 2005).

Recently, a *relationship-based approach to PM* has been advocated (Bannon, 2005). This is inspired by societal marketing considerations (Kang and James, 2007), which have also been advocated in the political sphere (Henneberg, 2002). The emphasis is on long-term interactions and exchanges that benefit all relevant actors as well as society, that is, direct as well as indirect stakeholder interests are considered (Laczniak and Murphy, 2006). Value considerations are linked to an acknowledgement of the (inter-)dependency of all involved interaction and exchange partners and are therefore grounded in mutual benefits as well as societal needs, based on delivering on promises and a voter- and citizen-inclusive approach to policy implementation (Johansen, 2005). To compare these three distinct schools we select some pivotal characteristics which are used to describe typical and therefore to some extent generic aspects of each school, and cover elements of the strategy on which each school of PM is based, the envisaged characteristics of the underlying political interactions of each school and the specific activity patterns associated with each school of PM (see Table 6.1). In the following discussion, we will focus particularly on the differences between these alternative schools of PM, rather than the similarities.

Table 6.1 Schools of political marketing

		Sales-based PM	IM-based PM	Relationship-based PM
Strategy Dimensions	*Rationale of PM*	Ideology	Needs and wants of target voters	Needs and wants of society
	Target voter segment(s)	Aligned voters	Floating voters and/or swing seats	Core and periphery voters
	Targeting strategy	Undifferentiated	Differentiated	Differentiated/Micro
	Importance of PM for party/candidates	Peripheral; tactical activity management	Central; tactical/strategic activity management	Central; strategic policy development/implementation; strategic/tactical activity management
Interaction Dimensions	*Communication*	One-way	Mediated one-way	Dialogue
	Value construct	Conviction-based promises	Needs-based promises	Mediated needs-based promises
	Temporal orientation	Short-term	Short-term, electoral	Long-term, electoral and governmental
Activity Dimensions	*Main PM activities*	Communication	Communication, offering development, activity co-ordination, intelligence management	Policy and value strategy development, promises implementation, micro-activity management, relationship management
	Main PM instruments	Push marketing instruments	Push and pull marketing instruments	Relationship building instruments
	Campaign orientation	Election	Election, resource-generation	Election, government, resource generation, implementation

With regard to the *strategic dimensions*, the rationale for the three schools of PM differ: whilst the sales-based school is focused on ideology, the IM school is focused on a deep understanding of primary stakeholders, specifically the needs and wants of target voters. The relationship-based school enhances this perspective in line with a wider societal orientation which also incorporates the interests of stakeholders that are not direct electoral interaction partners, and assesses the trade-offs between short-term and long-term effects of the party's offering. Whilst this implies that the relationship-based school adopts a differentiated targeting approach covering core and periphery actors, the IM-based school focuses pragmatically on those decisive voter segments which need to be convinced in order to achieve the organisational aims, the 'floating or indecisive voters' or 'swing seats'. An undifferentiated targeting of voters who are aligned with the core offering is to be expected for those parties adopting the sales-based approach to PM. Consequently, these parties only use PM in a limited fashion as a tactical tool for achieving party aims, whilst PM is central to the IM-based and relationship-based approaches, especially the latter which perceives PM strategy to be the guiding principle of offering creation, stakeholder interaction and service delivery in politics (Henneberg, 2006).

The *interaction dimensions* of PM are concerned with the nature of the interactions between the party and its key interaction partners. Here we consider the nature of communication between the party and the key interaction partners, on which aspects value considerations are based and what time perspective underpins the three schools of PM. The sales-based school of PM is characterised by a uni-directional and episodic communication, focusing on election campaigns. This is in line with the conviction-based nature of the political offering. The IM school of PM shows some similarities to the sales-based school, although the underlying value concept derives its content from the current needs of specific groups of voters or the prevailing public opinion. On the other hand, the relationship-based school of PM emphasises the long-term perspective. A dialogue with changing agenda-setting functions between different interaction partners is envisaged, with a societally mediated value concept as its foundation (Scammell, 1999).

The relationship-based PM is based on the comprehensive and 'permanent' use of marketing activities, including policy development, communication and implementation, and long-term relationship and stakeholder management. This contrasts with the more limited *activity dimension* set of the other two approaches: whilst the IM-based school focuses specifically on communication, intelligence gathering and market-based policy development, the sales-based school of PM predominantly uses communication activities, specifically deployed in a push-marketing setting for election campaigns (Bannon, 2005).

Concepts of democracy

The previous discussion has outlined the differences between the three schools of PM. In the following section we are concerned with how these schools of PM intersect theoretically with democracy. 'Democracy', in practice and theory, does not exist as a single universally agreed model (Lijphart, 1984). Held's (1996) influential categorisation identified six broad groups of democracy: Direct, Republican, Elitist, New Left, Participatory and New Right. These concepts of democracy differ with respect to the emphasis placed on the core ideas of participation, liberty, equality, leadership and the democratic process. In order to provide a clear and parsimonious discussion, we focus on **competitive elitism** (Schumpeter, 1942) and **deliberative democracy** (Habermas, 1996). This will enable us to shed conceptual light on the relative importance of political marketing to these concepts of democracy and to assess how the demands of democracy are met or threatened by the three schools of political marketing outlined above.

Deliberative democracy and competitive elitism cover widely different normative beliefs about the essence of democracy and how democracy ought to function. Each arises out of particular intellectual traditions and spawns its own set of internal arguments (Held, 1996). The prime reasons for our selection of these two conceptions are that they represent the broad spectrum of contemporary debate in democratic theory. Competitive elitism, by common consent, has been an extraordinarily influential model in Western democratic theory (Scammell, 2000). Its insistent realism (critics would say pessimism) has provided the touchstone for arguments about the nature of democracy for more than fifty years. Modern theories of participatory democracy emerged in part as a reaction against competitive elitism; of the various types of participatory democracy, deliberative democracy is the most influential in political communication research. Habermas's idea of the public sphere, a core concept of deliberative democracy, 'ballooned into the new God-term' of critical analysis over the course of the 1990s (Gitlin, 1998: 168).

Competitive elitism

The conception of democratic competitive elitism is based on elite theory which has a long heritage in political thought, from Plato's *The Republic* and Machiavelli's *The Prince*, through to early-twentieth-century 'Italian school' descendants, notably Mosca, Pareto and Michels (Blaug and Schwarzmantel, 2001). Its most durable claim is the inevitable stratification of society between rulers and the ruled. Elite theory is often disliked because of its profound pessimism about democratic possibilities, and rejection of the grander liberal and socialist ideals of freedom, equality, popular sovereignty and the realisation of human potential. The elitists' answer relies on 'realism': history and social science demonstrate the presence of a ruling class in all political organisms (Dunleavy and O'Leary, 1987). Furthermore, recognition of this unavoidable fact is essential for the establishment of the normatively desirable, namely that governing *should* be in the hands of those most fit to rule. Schumpeter's (1942) *Capitalism, Socialism and Democracy* remains the most influential account of *democratic* elitism. Schumpeter begins from a rejection of what he calls the 'classical doctrine of democracy', in which elected representatives realise the common good by carrying out the will of the people. His chief criticisms centre on 'the will of the people' and the 'common good': he argued that the classics had overestimated the possibilities of both. There was no such thing as the common good to which all people could agree by force of rational argument. Questions of principle were irreconcilable 'because ultimate values – our conceptions of what life and society should be – are beyond the range of mere logic' (Schumpeter, 1942: 251). He also disparaged the very idea of the will of the people: if it was to command respect, it required a level of knowledge and rational ability in individual human beings that simply did not exist among the masses. In reality the will of the people was little more than '...an indeterminate bundle of vague impulses loosely playing about given slogans and mistaken impressions' (Schumpeter, 1942: 253).

Schumpeter (1942) reverses the order of classical liberal theory in which the people elect representatives who then give effect to the will of the people. The role of the people is to produce a government that takes it upon itself to establish the common good. Democracy becomes an arrangement for arriving at political decisions, in which leaders acquire the power to decide by means of a competitive struggle for people's votes. Democracy, in short, is reduced to a method for the periodic and peaceful transfer of government between two or more groups of leaders. The most that can be expected of democracy is that it may choose the most competent leaders and provide mechanisms for controlling their excesses. According to Schumpeter (1942) this greatly improves the theory of the democratic process, emphasising the importance of leadership, which was neglected in classic theory. It states also that the method of competition for leadership is crucial to democracy: the process must be generally accepted as fair, if not perfect. Schumpeter's durability resides primarily in two factors: first, the considerable body of evidence which continues to show that despite apparent improvements in education, large minorities of the population (about one third in the USA) have little interest in or knowledge of politics (Bennett, 1988). Second, he compels attention to the quality of the electoral systems and processes. As Shapiro (2002) notes, theorists are often discomforted by the competitive elitist tendency to reduce democracy to procedures, yet these are vital for structuring power relations and limiting interference with individual and/or group pursuit of their versions of the good life. Norris's (2004) study of some three dozen parliamentary and presidential elections concurs: the detail of 'electoral systems may appear unduly technical and dry' but matter significantly for 'basic issues of political representation and accountability, for patterns of participation and party competition, and for the effective health of democratic institutions around the world' (Norris, 2004: 264).

Deliberative democracy

Contrasting with this view, deliberative democracy emerged as a distinc
tive strand of the New Left backlash against Schumpeter's (1942) pessi-
mistic portrait of democratic possibilities. Led by Pateman's (1970)
seminal work, the New Left argued that the Schumpeter-influenced
'contemporary model' of liberal democracy was excessively afraid of the
dangers of popular active participation. Whilst expressing some concern
with voter apathy, they offered no account for it, and instead located the
major threat to modern democracy in 'mediocrity and the danger that it
might destroy its own leaders' (Pateman, 1970: 10–11). Pateman argued
that the Schumpeterian legacy had abandoned a central democratic tenet:
the insistence on participation. For the New Left, the concept of participation is clearly differentiated from the far more limited pluralist concerns to
increase voter engagement with politics. Pateman argues that the plural-
ists' concern is essentially with stability: that is, participation is necessary
only to the extent that it is sufficient to ensure the legitimacy and stability
of the democratic system as a whole. For participationists, however, participation is itself a goal. Democratic politics, properly conceived, is about
the self-development of citizens, fostering concern for collective problems
and enabling the development of an active and knowledgeable citizenry.
Participationists dispute the 'realist' assumptions of elite theory; they
accept that the actual levels of knowledge and participation are low, but
dispute that they must always be low and that such low levels are compatible with genuine democracy.

The stress on participation as deliberative communication or dialogue is
the main contribution of deliberative democracy. Deliberative democracy
'represents an exciting development in political theory' (Bohman and Rehg,
1997: ix): it reclaims the classic idea that democratic government should
embody the will of the people. In essence, deliberative democracy holds that
legitimate lawmaking results from the public deliberation of citizens. It
rejects Schumpeter's (1942) view that there is no such thing as a common
will, and that the public is not capable of rationality. On the contrary, deliberative theorists argue that democratic legitimacy depends precisely on a
rational consensus of public opinion (see Table 6.2).

Habermas's conception of deliberative democracy, inspired by Rousseau's
republicanism, is the best known of these theories (Calhoun, 1992). For
Habermas, citizen status should mean more than the protection of private
rights and periodical voting opportunities. It demands a commitment to
democratic processes that ensures that the people are the authors of the laws
that govern them: in short, a healthy public sphere with a 'guarantee of an
inclusive opinion and will-formation in which free and equal citizens reach
an understanding on which goals and norms lie in the equal interest of all'
(Habermas, 1996: 22).

Table 6.2 Schools of theories of democracy

	Competitive Elitism Democracy	Deliberative/Participatory Democracy
Starting point	Structure of a stratified society Political preference incompatibility	Changeable structure Unified will of people exists/can exist
Context	Limited voter knowledge/interest in politics Political instability	Voter rationality/knowledge can be created
Focus	Process/method focus to produce government and imbue legitimacy	'Gestalt' perspective on political discourse framework Sovereignty of the people realised through deliberation in the public sphere
Main instruments	Political leadership by elite	Communication and dialogue by public (healthy public sphere)
Outcomes	Competent leadership Legitimate/fair process Stability	Political participation by citizens Knowledgeable citizenry

Habermas's (1996) version of deliberative democracy, that the public is in continuous, rational, deliberation about its own governance, has had a huge impact on political communication scholarship (Scammell, 2000). This is not surprising because, unusually for democratic theory, it places communication (via Habermas's, 1996, conception of the public sphere) at its core. Its power stems both from its critique of the failures of existing democratic practice, characterised by declining participation and increasing public dissatisfaction with the formal institutions of politics, and from its sheer optimism that given conducive conditions, a genuine mass participatory democracy is possible. Barber's (2003) *Strong Democracy*, with its menu of initiatives to encourage public debate, is arguably the most important practically oriented intervention in favour of deliberative democracy. Barber contrasts his model of strong democracy to what he calls the 'thin' democracy of Schumpeter-influenced liberalism, which actively encourages little or no participation from citizens between formal elections.

Relationships between PM and democracy

It now remains to be seen how the three distinct schools of political marketing relate to the two selected theories of democracy. The following provides a juxtaposition of them (progressing from a discussion of the **sales-based school of PM**, followed by the IM-based and relationship-based schools) to facilitate an assessment of their relationship with regard to each other, with specific focus on the current 'normal paradigm' of political marketing, the IM-based school.

Political marketing and competitive elitism

Schumpeter is often considered the theoretical forerunner of political marketing, although as often as not he is cited without any acknowledgement of the elitist underpinnings of his ideas (O'Shaughnessy, 1990). His attraction for political marketing scholars is that he is among the first and most important political theorists to argue that elections were analogous to sales in commercial markets (Street, 2003). The need for political salesmanship stemmed both from the logic of competition and from the passive and largely uninterested state of the electorate which needed mobilizing into voting. The economic logic of markets demands that producers compete to sell their wares; the reality of uninterested voters demands that politicians find ways to attract attention and mobilise support. Thus, famously for Schumpeter, what he called the 'psycho-technics' of electioneering (advertising, slogans, rallies, stirring music and suchlike) were not corruptions of democratic politics but were essential if the process was to work at all.

Conceptually, Schumpeter's approach fits closely to the sales-based school of political marketing. In both approaches, the party offering is essentially top-down, designed according to 'producer' convictions and then 'sold' through the tactical use of marketing instruments. Schumpeter's view reflected the mid-war period of ideologically polarised political choice, class and social bloc-based politics and limited affluence and consumer choice. The sales-based approach to PM was effectively the only one available for mass markets (Henneberg, 2002).

However, it is clear that competitive elitism must be less comfortable with the tenets of the IM-based school of political marketing. It is precisely a concern of modern competitive elite theorists that populist demands of mass-mediated democracy have potentially destructive effects upon political leadership (Scammell, 2000). While a voter-oriented 'follower' mentality may be hailed as bringing in more consultative democratic aspects (Lilleker, 2005), pressures of media and the proliferating opinion polls on virtually all aspects of our lives effectively squeeze the discretionary power of leaders to set the political agenda. Gergen, a White House adviser to Nixon, Ford, Reagan and Clinton, notes the escalation of poll-led politics:

> All modern presidents have polled heavily – Haldeman [for Nixon] put three different pollsters in the field at a time and secretly paid for a fourth to keep an eye on the others – but no one before Clinton has taken a poll to determine whether he should tell the truth publicly (the Lewinsky case) or to use American ground troops (Kosovo). (2000: 331)

According to Gergen (2000), Clinton spent nearly ten times as much on polling in his first year in office as his predecessor spent in two years.

The great concern of modern elitists is that IM-based political marketing encourages a shift in criteria for selecting candidates for office, away from intra-organisational success and competence towards the media-focused qualities of personality, likeability and attractiveness. IM-based PM may be seen as an understandable response to increasing media power, but nonetheless it ratchets up the threats to leadership as image comes to dominate, competent but media-awkward candidates are sidelined in favour of media-friendly candidates, and the political offering is increasingly cautious and determined by the results of polls and focus groups. The shoehorning of politicians into poll-driven strategic moulds has been a recurring complaint of commentators who witness politicians turning into on-message robots day after day. Klein (2006) denounces political marketing consultants precisely for draining the authentic, human qualities out of the politicians they serve: 'They've put democracy in a Styrofoam cage. And the politicians – who tend to see caution as an aphrodisiac – have gone along' (Klein, 2006: 240).

Thus, IM-based political marketing may ultimately harm democracy by fostering weak and follower-type leaders, or, just as damagingly, a politics devoid of the idea of common interest altogether. Leaders, in the classic Schumpeterian formulation, should take it upon themselves to determine the common interest. Yet an IM-based approach to political marketing segments electorates and concentrates resources on the targets and niches required for victory (Smith and Hirst, 2001). This may lead, as in the hands of a strategic marketer as effective as Karl Rove, George W. Bush's infamous architect, to a politics of national polarisation. Worse still, IM-based PM revives traditional fears about the depth of attachment to democratic ideals among ordinary citizens and their vulnerability to skilful manipulation. The people's choice might well be for 'the politics of demagogic xenophobia, as witnessed by popular support for radical right-wing movements in contemporary Europe' (Blaug and Schwartzmantel, 2001: 261).

With regard to relationship-based PM, competitive elitism also shows some concerns. These are derived from the involvement of citizens not so much in the process of democracy but also in the content of the offering creation and delivery, that is, the fundamentals of policy development and implementation. Modern competitive elitists are not convinced that deliberation produces 'better' democracy, in the sense of fostering consensus on fundamental conceptions of the common good. As Shapiro (2002) argues, 'there is no obvious reason to think that deliberation will bring people together' (Shapiro, 2002: 238). Moreover, even if deliberative consensus were achievable, it is not necessarily desirable and may lead to the suppression of difference: '...the competition of ideas – argument rather than deliberation' is the vital ingredient of democratic liberty (Shapiro, 2002: 239). Thus, to the extent that relationships and interdependencies preclude competition they will not foster liberty.

It is arguable that the relationship-based school of political marketing is inherently problematic for a democratic orientation focusing on the need for meritocratic leaders to derive clear and decisive actions out of incompatible preferences. Furthermore, the theory of political elitism is sceptical that meaningful relationships with citizens based on political interactions are realistic. Even by increasing the numbers of citizens who are interested and informed, and therefore interested in political relationships, the majority, or certainly a large minority, will (want to) stay ignorant and potentially easily manipulated. Democratic elitism's main concern is therefore with the role of leadership (specifically that it must be protected and safeguarded) as well as the political competitive process (it must be fair, open and designed to produce the best leaders). Neither aspect is self-evidently a main concern of the relationship-based school of political marketing.

Political marketing and deliberative democracy

Authentic public deliberation requires spaces protected from manipulation and self-interested promotion in which citizens may engage as equals in the discussion of matters of common concern. It is not so much that political salesmanship should not exist; rather, that it should not displace or dominate the discussion of private individuals coming together to form the public. However, it is arguable whether such an unmanipulated ideal public sphere ever has or ever could exist (Schudson, 1995). Nonetheless, it is the driving concern of deliberative democrats to increase protected spaces for citizen-to-citizen communication through, for example, neighbourhood assemblies, televised town hall meetings and mediated civic communications initiatives (Barber, 2003).

It would seem clear that the sales-based school of political marketing, as a vehicle for one-sided, uni-directional rhetoric, may be a threat to deliberative ideals; it offers at best competitive debate, which, while essential for electoral politics, is corrupting if it dominates the public sphere. After all, the ideal public sphere is precisely the place where private citizens create public opinion and hold critical authority over their governments and would-be leaders.

Proponents of deliberative democracy must also be deeply suspicious of the dominant current practice exemplified by the IM-based school of political marketing. Their concerns are the mirror image of the competitive elitists' anxiety. Where the prime fear of the competitive elitist is for weak leadership, the prime fear of the deliberative democrat is for a populist democracy that effectively bypasses public deliberation altogether. Polls and focus groups express opinion of sorts, but that opinion may be anything: a reflex, a prejudice, even a totally invented view. Polls do not necessarily correspond to thoughtful, considered opinion (Frankovich, 2005). The danger of politics that follows polls, focus groups and casually expressed voter opinions is that it may in the context of a deliberative democracy compound prejudice, elevate it to policy and neglect the fora of truly public deliberated opinion. The clever and unprincipled power-seeker may ride to office on waves of prejudice, and as such they will not be the meritocratic leader that competitive elitism seeks, but neither are they necessarily weak, and all the worse for democracy if strong.

Of the three schools of political marketing discussed here it would seem that only the relationship-based school of political marketing with a societal orientation has any potential for compatibility with the ideal construct of a deliberative democracy. This derives from the relationship-based school's insistence on the maintenance of relationships with real people, rather than a purely poll-driven assessment of preferences (Henneberg and O'Shaughnessy, 2009). Relationship marketing inherently invites dialogue, even if not necessarily the ideal deliberation of the public sphere. It emphasises the need to pay attention to the core (supporters and members) as well the periphery of target floating voters and other societal stakeholders, and thus provides incentives to develop political interest and engagement on an enduring basis. A truly deliberative democrat (but also a convinced political relationship marketer) must look with scepticism at the proliferating claims of parties to be 'listening'. The 'Big Conversation', which British Prime Minister Tony Blair launched in 2003, was claimed to be the biggest consultation exercise ever with voters but was quickly dismissed as a gimmick and is now largely forgotten. However, the political drive for increased connection with voters does present opportunities for mechanisms of relationship-building. Trippi's (2004) heralded open-source campaign for Howard Dean in 2004 (the 'Blog for America' campaign enabled citizens to place any message without censorship, and enlist to volunteer or to donate, with 40,000 people per day visiting this site) was high-risk and ultimately short-lived, but remains a high-profile and influential model of reciprocity between a candidate and supporters (Trayner, 2006). A polity constructed as part of ongoing relationship-building, for example, using regular referenda, citizens' juries or internet-based interactions, could bring forth a genre of political marketing which focuses on the goals of information, persuasion and reciprocity, rather than attack and defence. The positive aspects of dis-intermediarisation which are attributed to such internet-based PM would overlap with requirements of a deliberative democratic setting (Collins and Butler, 2003).

It is likely that the proponents of deliberative democracy have not fully grasped how flexible political marketing can be and how effective it can become when used as a tool to counteract elitist hegemony. Political marketing is not just confined to party campaigns. Marketing techniques, concepts and methodologies are being increasingly adopted by pressure groups such as the 'Stop the War Coalition' in the United Kingdom. Whilst the first big demonstration to be held against the Iraq War in 2003 was a mass of discordant images, an anarchy of amateur poster designs with the total effect of confusion, the more recent demonstrations have become almost corporate in tone. This is exemplified by hordes of individual demonstrators carrying the posters designed by David Gentleman with a unitary, cohesive anti-war brand symbolism (spots of bright red ink on a white background with the black slogan 'Stop the War'). If a complete critique is to be developed of the three schools of PM, it must be recognised that it is no longer the exclusive monopoly of elite groups such as parties, and that in the age of the internet even the powerless can turn to marketing.

However, it may be that competitive elitism is the more useful of the two democratic theories to political marketing theory. Its emphasis on the competitive nature of the struggle of votes regards marketing as essential to the democratic process and not an alien import. Its concern with process directs attention to the need for incentives and disincentives to practise a democratically more wholesome political marketing. It tells us that the rules matter. Commercial marketing has been persuaded to take societal issues seriously, through a mixture of enlightened self-interest and externally imposed regulation. Political marketing theory and practice should follow suit.

Summary, conclusions and implications

The relationship between PM and democracy encompasses the important issue of how to ensure that in liberal democracies the 'political competition' is enacted appropriately when measured against some normative ideals. As our argument has outlined, this relationship is multifaceted and ambiguous. Different conceptual implementations of political marketing can be 'tested' against different theories of democracy. Our comparison of democratic theory and alternative schools of PM has shown that whilst the sales-based school of political marketing is to some extent compatible with a Schumpeterian approach of competitive elitism, the ideal of a deliberative democracy shows more affinity with the relationship-based school of political marketing. What becomes clear is that the IM-based school of political marketing, the political marketing approach most clearly associated with the current normal paradigm of marketing theory (Wilkie and Moore, 2003), shows the least overlap with the conceptual demands of either theory of democracy. This has considerable implications for the development of political marketing theory and underlines the need for alternative and critical concept and method development in political marketing (Henneberg and O'Shaughnessy, 2007).

A clear implication of our analysis is that political marketing needs to engage with theories of democracy in order to provide itself with legitimacy. Whilst political marketing may arguably be 'conceptually neutral', its application and practice is not and needs to include a normative aim. For example, political relationship marketing, if pursued by politicians and political parties, could succeed in moving politics further towards the forms of deliberative democracy. The concepts, techniques and technologies inherent in the idea of political marketing that are based on societal marketing considerations could be used to foster a true relationship between party, politician and their publics, reinventing traditional methods of political communication such as direct mail, to inform as well as persuade, to listen as well as consult (Johansen, 2005). There are of course some good examples of exactly this, such as the 3000 constituents engaged in an internet dialogue with the British Liberal Democrat MP Stephen Webb (*Sunday Times*, 13 March 2005) or the Proposition Movement in California, a phenomenon that dates from the progressive era of a century ago.

In fact, the rise of such phenomena as bloggers, the idea of 'net roots' and the cacophony of democratic noise emanating from the internet has persuaded some at least that we are on the edge of a new era of deliberative or consultative democracy (Collins and Butler, 2003). The resulting change in the balance of power between policy producer (political parties and politicians as well as the media) and policy consumer (citizens), together with the empowerment of self-authorship, has some potential impact on the future possibilities for a deliberative democracy which can be channelled via relational marketing practices.

For its critics, the idea of 'political marketing' will be perennially suspect in relation to 'democracy', similar to the concept of marketing in the public sector in general (Collins and Butler, 2003). Partly this is because of the negative resonances of the label 'political marketing' which would appear to merge a significant activity, namely politics, with a seemingly trivial and inherently insignificant one, namely marketing. The inference is that political marketing represents the ideology of consumerism applied to politics, and thus connects to broader fears about consumerism and consumer culture. Whilst we do not want to be apologists of political marketing, that is, we see our argument as an 'ordering attempt', not as an 'order' (Tadajewski, 2006), we argue that the critics' view takes into account neither the subtleties of different interpretations of political marketing nor of different ideals of liberal democracy. Whilst some of the concerns against political marketing can be dismissed as amounting to mere prejudice (Henneberg, 2004), others are credible, for example the costs inherent in a marketing conceptualisation of politics mean that politicians and parties, particularly in America, are mortgaged to powerful vested interests (Harris and Lock, 2005). This would be a potential vindication of the Schumpeterian case; the gratification of sectarian interest is then seen as inherent in the practice of political marketing. Cost is a mighty factor in campaigning, and this raises fears of public opinion becoming a commodity to be manufactured, bought or sold, the commoditisation of opinion which becomes dysfunctional to the collective interest.

If political marketing is defined to embrace the isolated use of sophisticated instruments, such as the generation of public imagery of George Bush on the flight deck of the USS Abraham Lincoln and aspects of the so-called permanent campaign (Nimmo, 1999), then the critique that political marketing is enhancing an illusion of participation becomes more credible. However, we argue that there are other definitions of political marketing and that we cannot choose between the desirability or appropriateness of these alternatives without explicating the democratic yardstick we use. What emerges clearly out of our exploration is that types of marketing have implications, conducive and corrupting, for ideal types. We have examined only two models of democracy; but for both of these we find that the IM-based school of political marketing which dominates current political marketing theory is the least appropriate in terms of conceptual overlap with the theories of democracy.

Thus, we are left with two alternative narratives, which represent different assessments of the present and different ideas about future possibilities. The one, based on rhetoric of technology-driven empowerment, meaningful relationships, a societal orientation and inspired by ideals of deliberative democracy, would portray a benign future constituted by a more inclusive democracy and enhanced by the application of relational political marketing tools, technologies and concepts. The alternative is to argue for the acceptance of the elitist model, either from the perspective that it represents a genuinely more workable model of democracy or from the cynical resignation of the disillusioned idealist. It may therefore be that political marketing emerges almost naturally out of political competition, and is shaped by the structure of this competition. This would mean a preference for the sales-based school of political marketing, including a strategic posture of leading the electorate (Henneberg, 2006). In either case, the status accorded to political marketing is critical to the description of future scenarios of a desired democracy. Furthermore, for any of these two narratives to happen, the dominant paradigm in political marketing needs to change.

Further research on this issue is necessary. In fact, the development of a critical theory of political marketing, which takes an exchange perspective seriously and adapts it to the political sphere, is an important stepping-stone for further concept development in this area. This would include an understanding of the contingencies of the interplay of different aspects of political marketing and normative theories of democracy, and therefore constitute a 'marketing systems' approach (Shaw and Jones, 2005). As Dann et al. (2007) have pointed out, the current agenda is in need of comparative research about both the *effectiveness* and the *relevance* of political marketing. Whilst we were only able to focus on two interpretations of the democratic ideal, it is necessary to relate political marketing theory as well as practice to the contemporary discussions in political science and democratic theory. This includes discussions (and empirical analyses) of the ethical dimensions of the interplay of political marketing and theories of democracy, aspects which we have only 'framed' through our argument but not extensively touched upon (Laczniak and Murphy, 2006). Teleological (outcome-related) and deontological (means or duty-related) considerations are possible foundations for such political marketing ethics (Crane and Desmond, 2002). Furthermore, political marketing research needs to take the concerns of political scientists seriously and develop alternative approaches to political marketing which are complementary to the dominant IM-based school of political marketing.

Discussion questions

- Which of the three schools of political marketing do the parties in your system follow? Which of the two forms of democracy is your political system?
- When thinking about the type (school) of political marketing that each party adopts, how does each party 'fit' with the type of democracy?
- What is the relationship between the political marketing carried out by political actors on the one hand and theories of democracy on the other?

Key Terms

Competitive elitism
Deliberative democracy
Sales-based school of political
marketing
Instrumental/

managerial-based school
of political marketing
Relationship-based school
of political
marketing

Further reading

Collins and Butler (2003): The article criticises the assumption that market research into public opinion naturally produces the optimal basis for policy decisions in representative democracies. It concludes by stating that political discourse and citizen engagement in the political process is superior to a simple responsiveness to voters when considering the implications of policy for society as a whole.

Henneberg et al. (2009): This article forms the basis of this chapter.

Scammell (1999): This article was one of the first to discuss the unique contribution that political marketing – as distinct from political communication or campaign studies – could provide to understanding the strategic behaviour of political parties. The article was especially influential as it was written by a leading British political scientist and was published in a political science journal.

References

Baines, P.R., Harris, P. and Lewis, B.R. (2002) 'The political marketing planning process: improving image and message in strategic target areas', *Marketing Intelligence & Planning*, 20 (1): 6–14.

Bannon, D.P. (2005) 'Relationship marketing and the political process', *Journal of Political Marketing*, 4 (2): 85–102.

Barber, B. (2003) *Strong Democracy*. Berkeley, CA: University of California Press.

Bauman, Z. (2005) *Liquid Life*. Cambridge: Polity.

Bennett, S. (1988) 'Know-nothings revisited: the meaning of political ignorance today', *Social Science Quarterly*, 69 (2): 476–90.

Blaug, R. and Schwarzmantel, J. (2001) *Democracy: A Reader*. Edinburgh: Edinburgh University Press.

Blühdorn, I. and Szarka, J. (2004) 'Managing strategic positioning choices: a reappraisal of the development paths of the French and German Green Parties', *Journal of Contemporary European Studies*, 12 (3): 303–19.

Bohman, J. and Rehg, W. (1997) *Deliberative Democracy: Essays on Reason and Politics*. Cambridge, MA: MIT Press.

Calhoun, C. (1992) *Habermas and the Public Sphere*. Cambridge, MA: MIT Press.

Collins, N. and Butler, P. (2003) 'When marketing models clash with democracy', *Journal of Public Affairs*, 3 (1): 52–62.

Crane, A. and Desmond, J. (2002) 'Societal marketing and morality', *European Journal of Marketing*, 36 (5/6): 548–69.

Cunningham, F. (2002) *Theories of Democracy*. London: Routledge.

Dann, D., Harris, P., Mort, G.S., Fry M.-L. and Binney, W. (2007) 'Reigniting the fire: a contemporary research agenda for social, political and non-profit marketing', *Journal of Public Affairs*, 7 (3): 291–304.

Dunleavy, P. and O'Leary, B. (1987) *Theories of the State*. Basingstoke: Macmillan.

Frankovich, K.A. (2005) 'Reporting "the polls" in 2004', *Public Opinion Quarterly*, 69 (5): 682–97.

Gergen, D. (2000) *Eyewitness to Power: the Essence of Leadership: Nixon to Clinton*. New York: Touchstone.

Gitlin, T. (1998) 'Public sphere or public sphericules?', in T. Liebes and J. Curran (eds), *Media, Ritual, and Identity*. London: Routledge, 168–174.

Grönroos, C. (1994) 'Quo vadis, marketing? Towards a relationship marketing paradigm', *Journal of Marketing Management*, 10: 347–60.

Grönroos, C. (2006) 'Adopting a service logic for marketing', *Marketing Theory*, 6 (3): 317–33.

Habermas, J. (1996) 'Three normative models of democracy', in S. Benhabib (ed.) *Democracy and Difference: Contesting the Boundaries of the Political*. Princeton, NJ: Princeton University Press, 67–95.

Harris, P. and Lock, A. (2005) 'Political marketing funding and expenditure in the UK General Election campaign 2005', *Journal of Marketing Management*, 21: 1117–33.

Harris, P., Fury, D. and Lock, A. (2005) 'The evolution of a campaign: tracking press coverage and party press releases through the 2001 UK General Election', *Journal of Public Affairs*, 5: 99–111.

Held, D. (1996) *Models of Democracy*. Cambridge: Polity.

Henneberg, S.C. (2002) 'Understanding political marketing', in N.J. O'Shaughnessy and S.C. Henneberg (eds), *The Idea of Political Marketing*. Westport, CT: Praeger, 93–170.

Henneberg, S.C. (2004) 'Political marketing theory: hendiadyoin or oxymoron?', University of Bath working paper 2004.01.

Henneberg S.C. (2006) 'Leading or following? A theoretical analysis of political marketing postures', *Journal of Political Marketing*, 5 (3): 29–46.

Henneberg, S.C. (2008) 'An epistemological perspective on research in political marketing', *Journal of Political Marketing*, 7 (2): 151–82.

Henneberg, S.C. and O'Shaughnessy, N. (2007) 'Theory and concept development in political marketing: issues and an agenda', *Journal of Political Marketing*, 6 (2/3): 5–32.

Henneberg, S.C. and O'Shaughnessy, N. (2009) 'Political relationship marketing: some micro/macro thoughts', *Journal of Marketing Management*, 25 (1/2): 5–29.

Henneberg, S.C., Scammell, M. and O'Shaughnessy, N.J. (2009), 'Political marketing management and theories of democracy', *Marketing Theory*, 9 (2), pp. 165–88.

Hunt, S.D. (1983) 'General theories and the fundamental explananda of marketing', *Journal of Marketing*, 47 (Fall): 9–17.

Johansen, H.P.M. (2005) 'Political marketing: more than persuasive techniques, an organizational perspective', *Journal of Political Marketing*, 4 (4): 85–105.

Kang, G.-D. and James, J. (2007) 'Revisiting the concept of a societal orientation: conceptualization and delineation', *Journal of Business Ethics*, 73: 301–18.

Klein, J. (2006) *Politics Lost*. New York: Doubleday.

Laczniak, G.R. and Murphy, P.E. (2006) 'Normative perspectives for ethical and socially responsible marketing', *Journal of Macromarketing*, 26 (2): 154–77.

Lijphart, A. (1984) *Democracies: Patterns of Majoritarian and Consensus Government in Twenty-one Countries*. New Haven, CT: Yale University Press.

Lilleker, D.G. (2005) 'The cause of an emerging democratic deficit in Britain?', *Journal of Nonprofit & Public Sector Marketing*, 14 (1/2): 5–26.

Lipset, S.M. and Rokkan, S. (1966) 'Cleavage structure, party systems, and voter alignments: an introduction', in S.M. Lipset and S. Kokkan (eds), *Party Systems and Voter Alignments*. New York: Free Press.

Lock, A. and Harris P. (1996) 'Political marketing – *vive la différence!*', *European Journal of Marketing*, 30 (10/11): 14–24.

Newman, B.I. (1994) *The Marketing of the President*. Thousand Oaks, CA: Sage.

Nimmo, D. (1999) 'The permanent campaign: marketing as a governing tool', in B.I. Newman (ed.), *Handbook of Political Marketing*. Thousand Oaks, CA: Sage, 73–88.

Norris, P. (2004) *Electoral Engineering: Voting Rules and Political Behavior*, Cambridge: Cambridge University Press.

Ormrod R.P. (2007) 'Political market orientation and its commercial cousin: close family or distant relatives?', *Journal of Political Marketing*, 6 (2/3): 69–90.

O'Shaughnessy N.J. (1990) *The Phenomenon of Political Marketing*. Basingstoke: Macmillan.

O'Shaughnessy, N.J. (2002) 'The marketing of political marketing', in N.J. O'Shaughnessy and S.C. Henneberg (eds), *The Idea of Political Marketing*. Westport, CT: Praeger, 209–20.

Pateman, C. (1970) *Democracy and Participation*. Cambridge: Cambridge University Press.

Scammell, M. (1999) 'Political marketing: lessons for political science', *Political Studies*, 47: 718–39.

Scammell, M. (2000) 'Media and democracy: an introduction Part II', in M. Scammell and H. Semetko (eds), *Media, Journalism and Democracy: A Reader*. Aldershot: Dartmouth-Ashgate, xx–xlix.

Scammell, M. (2003) 'Citizen consumers: towards a new marketing of politics?', in J. Corner and D. Pels (eds), *Media and the Restyling of Politics*. London: Sage, 117–37.

Schudson, M. (1995) 'Was there ever a public sphere?', in M. Schudson, *The Power of News*. Boston: Harvard University Press, 189–203.

Schumpeter, J. (1942) *Capitalism, Socialism and Democracy*. London: George Allen & Unwin.

Shapiro, I. (2002) 'The state of democratic theory', in I. Katznelson and H. Milner (eds), *Political Science: State of the Discipline*. New York: W.W. Norton.

Shaw, E.H. and Jones, D.G.B. (2005) 'A history of schools of marketing thought', *Marketing Theory*, 5 (3): 239–81.

Sheth, J.N., Gardner, D.M. and Garrett, D.E. (1988) *Marketing Theory: Evolution and Evaluation*. New York: Wiley.

Slater, S.F. and Narver, J.C. (1998) 'Customer-led and market-oriented: let's not confuse the two', *Strategic Management Journal*, 19: 1001–6.

Smith, G. and Hirst, A. (2001) 'Strategic political segmentation – a new approach for a new era of political marketing', *European Journal of Marketing*, 35 (9): 1058–73.

Street, J. (2003) 'The celebrity politician: political style and popular culture', in J. Corner and D. Pels (eds), *Media and the Restyling of Politics*. London: Sage, 85–98.

Tadajewski, M. (2006) 'The ordering of marketing theory: the influence of McCarthyism and the Cold War', *Marketing Theory*, 6 (2): 163–99.

Trayner, G. (2006) 'Open source thinking: from passive consumers to active creators', Annual Conference of the Market Research Society, London.

Trippi, J. (2004) *The Revolution Will Not Be Televised*. New York: HarperCollins.

Wilkie, W. and Moore, E. (2003) 'Scholarly research in marketing: exploring the "4 eras" of thought development', *Journal of Public Policy & Marketing*, 22 (Fall): 116–46.

Wring, D. (2005) *The Politics of Marketing the Labour Party*. Houndsmill: Palgrave.

Wring, D. (2006) 'Focus group follies? Qualitative research and British Labour Party strategy', *Journal of Political Marketing*, 5 (4): 77–97.

The Ethics of Political Marketing

After reading this chapter, you should be able to:

- identify the ethical perspective adopted by political actors
- justify or criticise political decisions from alternative ethical perspectives
- discuss the ethicality of political advertisements from alternative ethical perspectives.

Introduction

Ethics are our own personal 'codes of conduct' that rest on the values that we live by. Even the simplest personal decision often has an ethical component. Trust, an ethical concept, underpins most human activity and is therefore an important concept in marketing. Without trust there would be no commerce, no socialisation and no community. In private life, ethics can be summarised as a regard for the sensitivities, rights and feelings of others. The fact that we live in a community where an ethical perspective is relevant to understanding human behaviour can be seen in social marketing campaigns. For example, anti-smoking campaigns stress the consequences for others – such as children and other members of the family – rather than the consequences for the individual. All political decisions have ethical consequences, for example, how do we use the wealth of our country? Should the government raise taxes in order to create jobs, or should the government lower taxes and let the free market take care of the rest? For a political party to be seen as lacking in ethics provokes a public outcry; look at any political scandal and this will be clear.

Everyone has an opinion on the ethics of political marketing, and it is often an unflattering one, as political marketing is known to the majority as 'spin'. Irrespective of name, political marketing has become associated in the public eye with the idea of manipulation and is one of those things that it is fashionable to worry about. Numerous political advertisement watchers in the American press testify that this is a matter of public concern. One area of anxiety, for example, is the idea that opinion is being 'bought' by the richest rather than the best, and this offends democratic notions. That there are ethical problems associated with political marketing is thus not in doubt. But what are the ethical problems – and whose ethics are we concerned with? Are the ethical problems worthy of serious attention, and even legislation? What if the wrong ethical problems are defined, and the wrong solutions embraced?

Ethical theory will not answer these questions, but it might help to clarify them, illuminating those areas where there should be real worry and offering reassurance when anxieties have been unnecessary, replacing a vague moral view of political marketing with more focused concerns organised within a coherent structure. The aim of this chapter is to review some of the principal contemporary and classical ethical theories of interest to political marketing, as summarised by O'Shaughnessy (1995): that is, **Kantian, utilitarian, contractarian, communitarian, objective relativism** and **cultural relativism**. Our question in this chapter is 'Can these ethical theories discriminate usefully among the mass of criticisms of political marketing, and offer enlightenment as to where the common interests are really being served and where anxieties should truly lie?'

The deontological (Kantian) approach

Although ancient Greece did not actually have a direct a word for 'duty' *per se*, the language possessed a term that referred to the imperative – the thing one must do; but in English the word means 'connected with duty'. Immanuel Kant (1724–1804) argued that action should flow from elemental principles that are both the moral basis for the action and the universal principles upon which all should act. This is actually an argument for moral absolutism, for the basing of all actions on rules to which all reasonable people should seek to conform: it is a non-negotiable morality formulated as an antidote to the potential dominance of all our lives by pleasure-seeking behaviour. How society actually arrives at these rules is left rather vague by Kant, and he appears to believe that they can be formulated by a process of reasoning alone.

The problem with the Kantian approach is that it is insensitive to context, defining the limits of what is permissible with no regard to circumstance; but in questions of political ethics – in ethics generally – context is all-important. Even duplicity can on occasion be justified, and the Kantian imperative is therefore of limited value in formulating an ethical basis for the conduct of political marketing. For example, if one were seeking to formulate such rules, the layperson might immediately suggest an agreement to ban negative advertising. As will be seen, even negativity has its articulate defenders on the grounds that the character of a politician is a legitimate element of the political offering.

Yet the criticism of political marketing sometimes seems rather Kantian, grounded as it sometimes is in normative models or ideals of democratic behaviour (Jamieson, 1992; Franklin, 1994). An example of this would be the normative model of voting decision-making based on objective information and full deliberation. For the convinced Kantian, any deviation from this would be unacceptable once it had been endorsed as universal law. Yet voters are not in the end particularly rational decision- makers, but respond to gut feelings and emotion. They cannot follow this model because of the intrinsic complexity of the decision-making task; therefore they use the cognitive shortcuts and cues provided by political advertising, journalism, etc. in order to facilitate a decision (Sniderman et al., 1993).

The consequentialist tradition

Consequentialism as an ethical approach emphasises that the results of an action should be used as the criteria for evaluating their ethical base. The question here is what is the consequence of a particular action, and is it ethical? In the political context this question can be applied to whether political marketing is an ethical activity; is the result of applying marketing to politics good government? This leaves us with another question: what is good government – is it responsiveness to public opinion? In this case there might be some vindication of the marketing conceptualisation of politics.

Utilitarianism is one form of this tradition, with its claim that the truth of ethics can be objectively established via rational means, and Benthamite-derived utilitarianism was popularly expressed by J.S. Mill (1806–73) as that which provides the greatest good for the greatest number. There are different forms of utilitarianism; for example, *act utilitarianism* claims that actions are justified by their contribution to the increase in welfare, whereas *rule utilitarianism* would seek out a set of rules that would lead to the maximising of welfare. Another form of utilitarianism is *motive utilitarianism*, where the worth of a particular motive is the issue, although this may be ascribed to a different system of ethics called 'teleological ethics', which incorporate the virtue of the motive, the argument being that there is a critical distinction between intentional and unintentional consequences.

There is, however, vagueness about how to operationalise these precepts: how is the worth of these motives evaluated, and what is 'welfare'? It raises as many questions as it solves. Both utilitarianism and the deontological approach can be reconciled by an argument that says the moral base on which one takes a particular action should be universal (that is, valid for all), and yet at the same time one must be guided by the consequences of that action for others (Hare, 1981). Yet utilitarian perspectives are possibly the richest field of ethical critique of political marketing. In particular:

- Issues may be prioritised for reasons other than their contribution to welfare: a political consulting firm may perceive political issues to be marketable commodities, and therefore select and market issues based on the criteria of their dramatic appeal. Important but perhaps less value-symbolic issues may be bypassed as a result.
- The marketing of issues based on dramatic appeal may be divisive, with deliberately polarising issues selected as the best marketing strategy. As Ansolabhere and Iyengar (1995) suggest in the case of negative advertising, an optimising strategy may be to deliberately seek to freeze out the political centre from any political participation. Motive utilitarians would certainly condemn this.
- Decisions may be made with no reference to the long term, because marketing considerations may mean maximising popularity in opinion polls without considering other consequences. Issues that are not dramatic get neglected until it is too late. Although it is reasonable to assume that the mass electorate knows where its own interests lie, on issues that have an inevitable though distant future impact, such as energy consumption and the environment, the electorate may be irresponsible.
- Political marketing methodologies also tempt people to use communication to fill the space vacated by ideas and ideology (Sherman, 1987): communications are substitutes for action, creating a world of professional campaigners and amateur statesmen.
- A 'fix-it' mentality is created, with pressure for instant, media-friendly solutions to elaborate problems. These are utilitarian-derived criticisms, because the claim is that only addressing an issue after it becomes necessary to address the issue leads to worse government and therefore a failure to achieve the greatest good for the greatest number.

Another criticism of the use of marketing in politics is that the costs of marketing create the need for significant campaign finances. In the USA, laws designed to curb expenditures on advertising have led to the creation of political action committees (PACs), ostensibly autonomous groups that function as the collector and administrator of campaign funds from citizens and professional groups. The favour is returned by benevolent legislation, and this can be seen as undermining the efficiency of government in terms of its ability to deliver the best for the most. The risk of losing contributions from groups whose concerns are seldom identical with those of the majority of voters can make it difficult for elected representatives to pass legislation that is best for the majority of voters. The US National Rifle Association and the tobacco industry are cases in point, where the political struggle against them has had to be carried out in the courts since the funds they provide are essential to successful campaigns.

Yet it would be unfair to state that the use of marketing tools and concepts in politics was by definition bad, as the use of marketing in politics can also be defended in utilitarian terms. First, marketing can increase the amount of information available to the public from which to make an informed decision (Ansolabhere and Iyengar, 1995) and can provide alternative perspectives on a particular issue (Banker, 1992). Banker (1992) provides an example where polling revealed that an incumbent candidate (Senator Denton) was perceived as rich and aloof. As a result of this, Denton's rival focused in a negatively styled advertising campaign on the incumbent's use of official monies to pay country club membership and on his anti-social security vote. In this context, the negative advertising can be justified in that it led to a more informed contest. Second, basing marketing priorities on the results of opinion research with voters can introduce legitimate public concerns into the election that might otherwise have been missed, because no issue can be successfully marketed without meeting some form of voter need. To argue otherwise assumes that the electorate is naïve and can be influenced by a simple stimulus–response model of political communication (Kraus and Davis, 1976).

Flanagan (1996) makes several significant criticisms of the Kantian and utilitarian philosophical approaches. Both Kantianism and utilitarianism are vague; from Banker's (1992) example of Senator Denton, Kantian and utilitarian arguments can be used to justify negative advertising campaigns, a style of campaigning that is usually considered to be a harmful by-product of using marketing in the political sphere. The key problem is therefore that abstract concepts need to be made concrete in coherent, workable rules that can guide actions, and the respective theoretical variables of duty and happiness need grounding in more precise values to give direction. Kantians have trouble articulating the categorical obligations – 'duty' – in a detailed way, whilst utilitarians are constantly debating the meaning of what the various philosophical 'goods' are, and how these goods can be ordered to maximise the greatest good overall.

The contract view of ethics

Utilitarianism has had many critics from its very beginnings as a coherent philosophy. For example, Rawls (1972) points out how the emphasis on the greatest good for the greatest number could lead to the sacrifice of individual liberty; indeed, communism itself can be justified on utilitarian arguments, for the 'dictatorship of the proletariat' represents precisely that. Thus an important source of criticism has been human rights perspectives, because the pressures of crude majoritarianism can sometimes be seen as overriding the liberty of the individual. Theories of rights were thus developed to protect the autonomy of the individual; Rawls regards the right to equal liberty as being the basis of all other freedoms and rights. But ethics involve both rights and duties – there is a social contract in operation between individuals, institutions and society. These contractarian perspectives argue that a bargain is struck between individuals, institutions and society for the benefit of all, an exchange that includes the acceptance of some restrictions on individual liberty.

There are of course important limitations to this perspective – what, for example, happens when rights of one group conflict with the rights of another group? If one can imagine such an invisible contract, then clearly some of the things political marketers do would be illegitimate in the sense that they would violate exchanges based on rights and duties. One area where this clearly emerges would be that of manipulated imagery in political marketing, such as the controversial George W. Bush subliminal television advertisement that flashed 'DemocRATS' at the boundary of perception. This is an instance of obvious manipulation but, more generally, political marketing may appear to give permission to be rather more generally evasive. If, for example, the entire area of spin control is admitted into the domain of political marketing – although there are arguments for saying that spin belongs to a separate conceptual realm – then the ethical critics of political marketing must be heeded.

Another potential problem from the contractarian perspective is the criticism that politicians are ceasing to try to enlist the direct physical participation of citizens in politics, as there is no real incentive for them to do so now that marketing can perform the persuasion task. By being active members of political organisations, people engage in self-persuasion and justify their actions retrospectively. As such, the argument is that marketing makes active membership of political organisations redundant, and the lack of active participation in politics today makes for a superficial commitment of support that is quickly lost. Perhaps more worryingly from a political perspective is that this development weakens the direct link between governors and governed.

Another area of potential interest to contractarians is the changing nature of the individual's relationship with the state. Perhaps there will be a loss of dignity if governments come to be seen as just big service organisations, and an erosion of loyalties and ties between governments and the governed is a consequence of citizens being taught at the aggregate level to be consumers in everything we do. Political marketing may be viewed as facilitating this tendency towards teaching people to think of themselves as political consumers. This may be another point at which we can discuss negative advertising, presenting it as a form of contractual violation. In fact, the ethical argument over negative advertising is a complex one and does not have any easy solution. As Banker (1992) proposes, the argument and the form of the argument need to be distinguished from one another: 'an individual "negative" political ad is an argument, at least implicitly. As an argument it may be reasonable or unreasonable. That does not mean that all "negative" ads, the argument form, should be discouraged.' However, the effect of negative advertising is to reinforce partisanship and remove the political centre: this may be the effect, and it is arguably sometimes the intent as well. It is this aspect contractarians might object to on the grounds that negative advertising may represent a deliberate seeking of the self-disenfranchisement of large numbers of people, thus undermining the very idea of democracy.

Communitarianism and virtue ethics

Communitarianism places virtue within the context of a parochial social setting. Virtues are traits and they are formed by a long process, underpinned by emotionally driven conviction (MacIntyre, 1981). Ethical traditions and sensitivities are seen as arising out of community. Aristotle argued that virtue was not a rule book, but a skill whose art lay in negotiating circumstance (Soloman, 1993). Yet these propositions are rather vague as a source of potential ethical guidance. Certainly it is true that some of the practices of political marketing are more acceptable to some cultures than to others. If virtue is what the community teaches, it is apparent that different communities teach different things, as will be clear from the very mixed reception that was initially given to the export of American political marketing techniques to different countries. Tradition legitimates, and the American tradition is to place an almost non-negotiable value on freedom of speech. It is this value of freedom of speech that has stood in the way of legislative attempts to, for example, control expenditure on campaign advertising.

It may be argued that other countries value freedom of expression less, and social integration more – there is a trade-off. The origins of political marketing and some of its associated practices, such as negative advertising, do in fact go back a long way in America, because they arise out of the particular value that culture has traditionally placed on the idea of liberty. The first negative campaign using modern media appeared fully formed in the California gubernatorial campaign of 1936 (Mitchell, 1992) in which Upton Sinclair was the unfortunate victim, while the first advertising agencies were enlisted in 1916 (O'Shaughnessy, 1990). A second, related, tradition is the value Americans place on market freedoms: the state should not tell people how to spend their money, and this includes more generous freedom than elsewhere to spend it on political involvement – as is the case, for example, with political action committees. Cultures with greater traditional intolerance of market freedoms have also tended to restrict the access of finance to politics more.

Community tradition is one locus for virtue ethics, but it is not the only one, as some philosophers have criticised community both for conservatism and excessive belief in the merit and possibility of communal consensus. Organisations are also viewed as relevant communities, with the relationships between different roles in the organisational community generating mutual obligations. These philosophers reject notions of hard and fast rules, as the key thing is to sponsor a cultural climate supportive of ethical behaviour: 'if the cultural climate is not openly supportive of ethical behavior, the motivational climate for ethical conduct will be missing' (O'Shaughnessy, 1995). More rules are not seen as particularly illuminating, and value is placed on developing skills to weigh up conflicting interests. As with the moral theories described above, attention has been focused on significant aspects of moral life whilst perhaps obscuring some of the salient features of morality and the problem of finding, at the real level, a particular solution to a particular moral dilemma. There is still a need to know what are the key moral issues today and what magnitude of importance is attached to them.

Motivation to comply

For the seventeenth-century philosopher Benedict de Spinoza, any system of ethics must be internalised and not just verbally endorsed. The key is motivation. Under the deontological (Kantian) position and utilitarianism, motivation arises from the appeal of reason and from a wish to behave in an ethically sound way. Contractarians perceive motivation as elevated self-interest, whilst communitarians see motivation as the emotions arising out of community-based custom, value and tradition. However, David Hume (1711–1776) spoke of the necessity of having an emotional base to ethical conduct. Others, such as the economist Frank (1988), endorsed essentially the same view, that ethics cannot be apprehended at the level of reason alone, but need emotional commitment, because emotions engender, energise and direct responses; otherwise 'short-termism' will rule. Frank (1988) claims that, in the long run, ethical conduct builds up trust and is linked to success. In fact it is a fallacy to divorce emotion from reason as completely as is so often done because it is only through emotion that we can convert decision into action or choose among the competing claims presented by reason. Indoctrination and social conditioning are more relevant here than abstract knowledge; as Aristotle wrote, you get a virtuous adult by training a child to do the right thing.

For those who would seek a way forward on the ethics of political marketing, the question is whether to anchor those ethics in reason, for example, enlightened self-interest, or find some way of getting politicians to adopt this emotional adherence to ethical values. It is not, however, easy to think of a way of achieving this, because unethical behaviour has sometimes been rewarded. Self-interest is probably a much stronger argument. However, arguably, any tendency to moral drift in American politics is held in check by the fact that negative or dishonest political advertisements can backfire. First, they can incite a counter-attack from opponents, who now have access to instant rebuttal facilities via the internet. Second, all political marketing may be subject to arbitration by the independent mass media. The media can fix a maligned interpretation on a text that is quite different from that which the party or candidate intended, the classic example being when the Canadian press accused the Tory Party of attacking a facial deformity of the Liberal leader Jean Chretien. Whether or not this was intentional on the part of the Tories, for most voters their only exposure to the advertisements was through the interpretative framework attached by television, and it suddenly became 'politically incorrect to be a Tory' (Whyte, 1994). In fact the Tories, previously the largest party in Canada, were left with just two seats.

   The system in which political marketing occurs may perhaps be seen as possessing an in-built self-corrective mechanism in which extremes of unethical behaviour, or even as in the Chretien case the mere suspicion of them, will be punished. For a political marketing text (such as an advertisement) stands in its own right as an autonomous political event with independent political consequences; it is not merely a conduit of persuasive information from encoder to decoder. The fact that harshly negative advertising is such a volatile weapon thus brings its own restraints. For example, a 1996 candidate for the Alabama Supreme Court, Harold See, was subject to one of the most vicious negative campaigns of recent years (Johnson, 1997). Commercials featured a skunk morphing into Harold See's face, and there were claims (strongly disputed) that he had abandoned his wife and children years before. However, See still won; a negative advertisement is as much a statement about the values of the attacker as it is about the values of the defender, and extremes have a tendency to alienate. Yet, as Johnson (1997) remarks, 'when other capable and civic-minded citizens contemplate the ridicule and vilification endured by See and his family, many will conclude that running for office today is not worth the price'.

Objective relativism

Objective relativists such as Putnam (1981) claim that the right ethical decision is relative to circumstance. This is a position that might provide some justification for the ethos, and many of the practices, of political marketing, because there is a credible argument that it has been propelled forward by circumstance, for in common with all voluntary civic activities, the willingness of people to be actively involved as citizen activists has been in sharp decline in America and Europe (Richardson, 1995). This coerced privatisation of hitherto public activity serves to create a need for persuasion to be electronic, and purchased. Put simply, it is difficult to persuade people to become volunteers. Moreover, with voting behaviour no longer driven by inherited class loyalties to the extent that it once was (a phenomenon of dissolving class barriers), the task of persuasion is greater because partisanship is less. In addition, there has been a significant decline in the willingness of

US media to cover politics as competition for ratings becomes more intense and entertainment values become ever more dominant on television. According to some authorities, television news has reduced its purely political coverage by as much as 60 per cent since 1995. Consequently, it is suggested that circumstance actively means resorting to marketing methods where the media does not live up to its traditional responsibilities.

Banker (1992) has argued:

> when considering whether a particular communication act was ethical the situation must be considered. Political campaigns are a competitive situation; there is just one winner. It is ridiculous to expect the same standards to apply to such a situation as apply to polite social discourse.

Any context prescribes specific rituals and rhetoric, and a political context is ultimately about the leadership and future direction of the nation and therefore may merit higher levels of rhetorical aggression than are legitimated by other communications situations, including commercial ones. Banker (1992: 846) would also include in this the *ad hominem* attacks that make the critics of political marketing so indignant: 'an election campaign is not just about what issues candidates favour and oppose, it is also, by its very nature, concerned with who we elect – the motives and character of the man or woman who will lead us'. Perceived character is an integral part of the political offering that is exchanged for votes. It is important because any publicly visible individual is perceived as symbolising values of one kind or another, and in practice it is difficult to create a separation between *character* and *issue* and declare the one off-limits to public curiosity. These points are valuable in that they provide a justification for the negative advertising that abounds in modern election campaigns, but they are of course not an entirely satisfactory answer to the critics of political negativity.

Cultural relativism

Cultural relativism resolves ethical conflicts between one culture and another by accepting that ethical standards are relative to culture (O'Shaughnessy, 1990). However, whilst accepting that legitimate intellectual and moral differences and traditions exist, not least in regard to the differing values placed on the needs of individualism versus the demands of community, cultural relativism becomes more difficult to accept once one gets down to the level of individual practices (e.g. the institutionalised bribery and 'kleptocracy' rife in certain political systems). At its worst, cultural relativism is simply an excuse to suspend the operation of judgement. As O'Shaughnessy (1995) argues:

> There is evidence from both anthropology and history demonstrating the essential
> ethical similarities among different cultures. In accepting ethical relativism, we
> put up a rival standard, namely, universal ethical tolerance as the absolute virtue.
> To make ethical tolerance the absolute virtue means treating public wellbeing,
> honesty and justice as of secondary concern. This cannot be acceptable.

In a sense, to tolerate all is in fact to believe in nothing.

For the extreme cultural relativist, political marketing in the USA might indeed present no problems at all, although these philosophers might balk at its export to countries with no such tradition on the grounds that it represents an alien cultural graft. However, there may be some merit in permitting elements of the cultural relativist critique to creep into the ethical analysis of political marketing. The different political traditions of different countries must be seen as embodying different value systems but contain an internal coherence, so that to change one variable in any particular political system (US or otherwise) is to change the interrelationships of all its internal components. Thus elements that might be objectionable on an individual basis, like the role of money in US politics, may be justified as a structured part of the overall workable pattern of US politics. The transfer of a marketplace ethos, that is, conceptualisation and techniques, applies to many areas of American life, where in other countries commercialisation might be perceived as some kind of devaluation.

The use of money to purchase political persuasion is part of the US political system, with money seen as a legitimate expression of power, although it is often difficult for even the richest in the land to merely buy political office. For example, Michael Huffington lost $20 million in his bid to become a senator for California (*Daily Telegraph*, 7 June 2000), and as for another multimillionaire 'the more he spent, the more obscure he got' (*Daily Telegraph*, 9 June 2000). Another US tradition is to recognise that power in a democracy is not only a function of the numbers of those who have a particular stance on an issue, but also a function of those who feel most intensely about that issue. In a sense this represents elements of a stakeholder approach to social ownership of US politics, an approach that is also manifest in the power of political action committees in the US political system.

Yet it is possible that a cultural relativist with an educated knowledge of US history would claim to see coherence here with other aspects of US life and tradition. The amounts spent on the campaign trail are exceptional, but the practices that are used are not. Another ideological trajectory for the cultural relativist to follow would be that of postmodernism, claiming that political marketing was just another category of postmodernist culture, reflecting and reinforcing its core themes. Such a critic would be troubled less by the notion that political marketing has tended to lead the political agenda into a focus on symbolic goals and the serial creation of meaning. Thus Axford and Huggins (2002) see political marketing as part of a broad postmodernist culture of signs and symbols, a phenomenon of dissolving class barriers where people lose their traditional anchors. They take the example of Forza Italia as an extreme case of this, a media-created party that seemed to answer a huge appetite for change, a party people were comfortable with. They see political marketing as simply part of a world of serial symbolism and media saturated imagery, whose self-referentiality is captured in a scene from *Murphy Brown*, where she watches Dan Quayle criticising her giving birth outside wedlock.

Conclusion

The application of ethical frameworks does not generate any final answers, as no ethical debate is ever final; ethical questions can only ever be taken further, not answered. What the ethical debate does seek to achieve is further clarification of the nature of the moral issues associated with political marketing, and some sort of ordering among them as a magnitude of priorities. However, the overall direction of the ethical critique is clear, that it is an error to state that political marketing in general (and negative advertising and spin in particular) is by definition a bad thing. What is morally questionable is not so much the genre and its derivatives, but the individual cases where negative campaigns become toxic, legislative seats are bought and video images are merely fabricated.

Despite this, utilitarians, objective relativists, cultural relativists and communitarians would place the balance in favour of political marketing as it sharpens debate (utilitarian), arises out of cultural–political tradition (cultural relativist), is legitimated by competitive context (objective relativist), and the nature of the postmodern condition enforces it (cultural relativist), as it is a response to, rather than a cause of, the social and economic phenomena of these times. Freedom of speech, including economic speech, would be an argument of particular interest to communitarians. Against these, however, there are certain strong contractualist arguments: where the generation of imagery can be a substitute for political action and for the direct civic participation of citizens, the contract-violation criticisms cannot be dismissed as merely trivial. As can be seen, there is no final resting place for the ethical debates surrounding the uses – and abuses – of political marketing.

Discussion questions

- Find a negative advertisement from an election campaign on the internet. Taking each ethical approach in turn, try to justify the advertisement. Then try to criticise the advertisement using each of the ethical approaches.
- What other elements of political life can be judged using ethical approaches?
- Look at the web sites of the major political parties in your country. What are their main policy positions? Are these ethically justifiable? Remember to think about the different ethical approaches.

Key terms

Kantianism (deontological ethics)

Utilitarianism

Contractualism

Communitarianism

Objective relativism

Cultural relativism

Further reading

Banker (1992): This article focuses on negative advertising and the impact it has on voter opinions about the practice of political marketing. Banker argues that instead of causing voter apathy, negative advertising can have a positive effect when it is used to increase the amount of knowledge available to voters with which to make an informed voting decision.

Henneberg et al. (2009): This article identifies three main 'schools of thought' in current political marketing research and practice, and demonstrates the extent to which each school is compatible with the political science theories of participatory democracy and competitive elitism. Henneberg et al. conclude that whilst all three schools of political marketing are compatible with the two democratic traditions, the school that is least compatible is, ironically, that which forms the foundation of most of the current research into political marketing.

O'Shaughnessy (2002): This chapter is based on O'Shaughnessy's article.

References

Ansolabhere, S. and Iyengar, S. (1995) *Going Negative*. New York: The Free Press.

Axford, B. and Huggins, R. (2002) 'Political marketing and the aestheticization of politics: modern politics and postmodern trends', in N.J. O'Shaughnessy and S.C. Henneberg (eds), *The Idea of Political Marketing*. Westport, CT: Praeger, 187–208.

Banker, S. (1992) 'The ethics of political marketing practices: the rhetorical perspective', *Journal of Business Ethics*, 11: 843–8.

Flanagan, O. (1996) *Mind, Morals, and the Meaning of Life*. New York: Oxford University Press.

Frank, R. (1988) *Passions Within Reason*. New York: W.W. Norton.

Franklin, R. (1994) *Packaging Politics*. London: Edward Arnold.

Hare, R.M. (1981) *Moral Thinking*. Oxford: Clarendon Press.

Henneberg, S.C., Scammell, M. and O'Shaughnessy, N.J. (2009) 'Political marketing management and theories of democracy', *Marketing Theory*, 9 (2): 165–88.

Jamieson, K.H. (1992) *Dirty Politics*. Oxford: Oxford University Press.

Johnson, D. (1997) 'Political communication in the information age', paper presented at the Wissenchaftszentrum Berlin/Bertelsmann Stiftung, February.

Kraus, S. and Davis, D. (1976) *The Effects of Mass Communication on Political Behavior*. University Park, PA: Pennsylvania State University Press.

MacIntyre, A. (1981) *After Virtue*. London: Duckworth.

Mitchell, G. (1992) *The Campaign of the Century*. New York: Random House.

O'Shaughnessy, J. (1995) *Competitive Marketing: A Strategic Approach*. London: Routledge.

O'Shaughnessy, N.J. (1990) *The Phenomenon of Political Marketing*. New York: Macmillan.

O'Shaughnessy, N.J. (2002) 'Towards an ethical framework for political marketing', *Psychology and Marketing*, 19 (12): 1079–94.

Putnam, H. (1981) *Reason, Truth and History*. Cambridge: Cambridge University Press.

Rawls, J. (1972) *A Theory of Justice*. Oxford: Oxford University Press.

Richardson, J. (1995) 'Interest groups: challenges to political parties', *West European Politics*, 18: 116–39.

Sherman, A. (1987) 'The ad man cometh', *Guardian*, 6 May.

Sniderman, P.M., Body, R.A. and Tetlock, P.E. (1993) *Reasoning and Choice: Explorations in Political Psychology*. Cambridge: Cambridge University Press.

Soloman, R.C. (1993) 'Corporate roles, personal virtues: an Aristotelian approach to business ethics', in E.R. Winkler and J.R. Coombs (eds), *Applied Ethics: a Reader*. Oxford: Basil Blackwell.

Whyte, K. (1994) 'The face that sank a thousand Tories', *Saturday Night* (Canada), p. 14.

Chapter 7 is developed from O'Shaughnessy, N.J. (2002) 'Toward an ethical framework for political marketing', *Psychology & Marketing*, 19 (12): 1079–94. Reprinted by permission of John Wiley & Sons.

Part 2

Conceptual Issues in Political Marketing

8 Political Relationship Marketing

After reading this chapter, you should be able to:

- identify the characteristics of relationship marketing in the commercial and political spheres
- distinguish between political marketing at the macro-level and at the micro-level
- discuss the major issues that affect the ability of a relationship marketing approach to contribute to our understanding of the political sphere.

Introduction

Marketing theory concerns itself more and more with network phenomena as part of the new dominant logic of marketing (Vargo and Lusch, 2004). Within a network context, exchange is not seen as happening between two actors but as being part of complex and ongoing interactions. Building on this, there has been a shift in emphasis in marketing away from a product-based, instrumental or dyadic view and towards an emphasis on **relationships** and the co-creation of value within service-centred models of exchange. Based on this, relationship marketing has become central to marketing theory in the last decades; not only in business-to-business settings but also for business-to-consumer interactions (Bagozzi, 1995).

However, relationship marketing and the theoretical and conceptual implications for social and non-profit marketing are still somewhat under-explored (Hastings, 2003), especially in the field of political marketing (Bannon, 2005). This is strange given the possibility of a beneficial connection between what we will call **political relationship marketing** (PRM) and the development and legitimacy of political actors (as in parties, candidates, single-interest groups, governments), but also for the overall liberal party system itself (O'Shaughnessy, 1990; Newman, 1999). The aim of this chapter is therefore to provide an argument for the development of a rigorous conceptual framework of PRM by discussing existing, as well as potential, applications of relationship marketing within the political sphere. To achieve this we will distinguish between two perspectives on political relationship marketing: a **micro-perspective** that is concerned with specific entity and exchange-oriented aspects of PRM, and a **macro-perspective** concerned with the interplay with the wider political structures and the overall political system.

Relationship marketing: a new horizon for political marketing?

Political marketing theory has neglected issues around relationship management so far (Bannon, 2005), and so theoretical studies on political marketing are still crowded out by more applied and comparative studies about political campaigns and the use of marketing tools and instruments in politics (Scammell, 1999). As such, this mirrors the managerial and the instrumental schools of marketing theory that focus on tools such as the marketing mix and the 4Ps framework. The marketing mix was developed in the 1960s and is usually exemplified through McCarthy's (1960) 4Ps framework. Whilst the marketing mix and the 4P framework lend themselves perfectly to managerial application (Grönroos, 1994), they do not fulfil the essential elements of a reliable marketing concept or categorisation scheme and only partly fit within the commercial marketing concept of a customer orientation. Thus, the managerial school has come under considerable criticism for practical reasons since the 1980s because of its reliance on simple (albeit pedagogic) concepts and its misunderstanding or reinterpretation of some original sources.

Implicitly, theories emanating from the managerial and instrumental schools perceive the exchange as characterised by one-off transactions between active sellers and passive customers. In business-to-business as well as in business-to-consumer marketing all these elements are representative of only a small number of marketing management activities and exchange situations (Ford et al., 2003). A more realistic (and intellectually rigorous) approach is to understand exchanges as occurring within and between networks of actors with indirect and direct interactions being relevant. Customers, be they consumers or other businesses, become heavily involved in the exchange process and even in the value-creation process in cooperative and collaborative ways (Vargo and Lusch, 2004). This leads to multiple transactions occurring over an extended period of time, forming relationships of stable interaction patterns. Activities are dependent on relationships in addition to those between the other actors that are directly involved; cooperation and collaboration become more important than opposing positions.

Many of the characteristics of relationships formed the main argument against the hitherto leading paradigm of marketing theory. Consequently, schools and methodologies that tackle these issues, the so-called relational marketing theories, became more influential in marketing theory development, especially as part of the new dominant logic of marketing (Vargo and Lusch, 2004). What is important for the purpose of our argument is the fact that there is considerable conceptual and methodological diversity within and outside the leading paradigm in marketing theory, which makes the discipline vibrant (and just a little chaotic) (Arndt, 1985). If we look at theory-building in political marketing, a different picture emerges. Not surprisingly, academic interest in political marketing takes the leading (managerial/instrumental) paradigms of its mother-discipline for the purpose of theory-building (Peattie and Peattie, 2003) and mirrors the approaches adopted in marketing textbooks. Therefore, analyses of political marketing instruments (Newman, 1994; Lloyd, 2003) and managerial applications of these political marketing instruments (Butler and Collins, 1996; Newman, 1999; Smith, 2001) dominate the literature. This is fostered by the fact that political marketing management practice leads the way. The momentum of the research agenda is set by new (managerial) developments in the political marketplace (Baines et al., 2003). This also means that the literature is characterised more by description than prescription (Henneberg, 2004).

While this seems to be normal for any young discipline, it may cause the development of political marketing research to slow down and stagnate at some point; our opinion is that political marketing is presently at this point. Most of the current research on political marketing does not utilise state-of-the-art marketing theory. Furthermore, political marketing theory has neglected to incorporate major developments in commercial marketing theory as part of the leading political marketing management paradigm, e.g. market-orientation (Ormrod, 2007) and resource-based theories of the firm (Hunt and Lambe, 2000). Therefore, it is time for political marketing to embrace a 'second wave of research' fuelled by the adoption of new marketing theory perspectives. We have chosen the relationship marketing theory as the foundation of this chapter because of the importance of relationships within social and political exchanges. Although political marketing was initially transaction-oriented (O'Shaughnessy, 1990), it has been suggested that relationship marketing will help research and analyse the phenomenon of political marketing (Bannon, 2005). This is in line with Dermody and Scullion's (2001) reinterpretation of political marketing as a process of signification and representation.

Towards political relationship marketing

Building and maintaining long-term trust- and commitment-based relationships is an interesting proposition for political actors. Political parties and candidates, and also voters and citizens, perceive political exchanges not merely as isolated transactions (like the episode of actually voting for a party or a candidate) but as an enduring social process of interactivity within which they live their daily lives (Sniderman et al., 1993). This implies that understanding the character and the mutuality of the political exchange process is central to understanding the character of the market orientation of political actors. Analogously with traditional economic activity, it has been argued that political actors are moving away from a focus on instrumental (transactional) exchanges and towards a focus on building value-laden relationships and marketing networks in the form of social contracts with citizens (Newman, 1999).

Despite a twenty-year history of research in the commercial marketing literature, research into PRM is virtually non-existent. One of the few studies was carried out by Dean and Croft (2001) who used a relational **stakeholder** model adapted from Christopher et al. (1991) to the political sphere. Whilst this provided a better understanding of the complexities of political exchange processes and hinted at a wider framing of political marketing definitions, the essence of these relationships was not discussed. While as yet there is no explicit conceptual foundation of PRM, there are nevertheless many examples of political marketing management which follow the relationship marketing premise. It is these examples, historical and contemporary, that we will use to build an initial understanding of the construct of PRM in order to facilitate future conceptual development.

Macro-/micro-perspectives of political relationship marketing

This section reviews the ways in which PRM has been used in practice and examines why PRM in theory might impact and transform politics (the macro-perspective), and reviews both current practice and earlier history where anticipatory elements of PRM have been visible (the micro-perspective). Broadly speaking, we review practice which falls far short of a holistic PRM approach but in some ways foreshadows it. We further make the case for PRM at the theoretical and applied levels and outline key contributions that PRM could make to the literature. We then assess the potential transforming contribution that PRM could achieve if applied seriously, with numerous tactical and strategic ideas to give the concept political flesh and blood. The suggestion is that PRM is intrinsically a valuable approach that has the potential to reduce the alienation of voters and replace crude manipulation with something that is less superficial.

Macro-issues of political relationship marketing

At one level, the proposition of PRM is common sense: to use a commercial analogy, we are more likely to get repeat purchases if we think of marketing as a search for customers (i.e. interaction partners) rather than simply selling goods and services. Key elements in PRM are seen as the fulfilment of a promise (something that political parties find notoriously difficult) and, related to this, trust. The political party or candidate must establish (earn) an image of trustworthiness as a basis for PRM. In the case of politics, the short-term, electoral orientation of politicians makes this issue even more acute. Politicians are more likely to think in terms of popular election pledges such as tax cuts than seeking lasting relationships with citizens or members of their own party.

In transactional marketing the price sensitivity of customers is often high: the electoral equivalent of price competition is an economic bribe or promising a popular response to an emotional hot topic such as the immigration scare of the type perpetuated by the Tories in the UK general election of 2005. In contrast:

> A firm pursuing a relationship marketing strategy, on the other hand, has created more value for its customers than that which is provided by the core product alone. Such a firm develops over time more and tighter ties with its customers ... Relationship Marketing makes customers less price sensitive.
>
> (Grönroos, 1994: 11)

Grönroos (1994) claims that organisations have the opportunity to provide customers with various kinds of added value: technological, information, knowledge, social and so on. Similarly in politics the PRM approach offers social involvement, chances to contribute to policy and participation in public events. These attractions of PRM are not merely intuitive but well grounded in psychology. Humans are cognitive misers so that the creation of explicit and lasting relationships becomes highly desirable:

> Research has shown that consumers process information rapidly and protect their memories from being inundated with unwanted information by erecting perceptual barriers. One study has revealed that, on a typical day, approximately 550 advertisements are directed at consumers, yet they pay attention to less than 1% of these.
>
> (de Chernatony, 1993: 71)

Modern elections are about small numbers of swing voters concentrated in certain (geographical or socio-demographical) areas. Some 10 per cent of UK voters in 2005 did not know which way they would vote late on in the election campaign, and one third of those who did were still not absolutely certain (O'Shaughnessy, 2006). It could therefore be argued that the election lay in the hands of just one million undecided voters resident in 100 constituencies. It follows that seeking a relationship with this group, investing time and resources over a period of several years, is the only insurance policy political actors have against political 'consumerism'. In the

US, President Bush only won by a small margin twice (Thomas et al., 2004). Seen in this light, the promise of adopting a PRM approach is significant. It may make a marginal difference, but elections are all about margins.

Another issue of PRM relates to the nature of the exchange offering. Too often political parties have appealed exclusively to economic criteria and therefore created political consumers and not new loyalists; notions of a rational voter lead merely to temporary support and not the creation of converts. Allegiance is merely borrowed and people will desert the party for a more convincing monetary bribe. Because of this, PRM has to be about values as well as issues. Elections seem to be becoming more value-oriented, and liberal intellectuals ignore their salience in voter decision processes at their peril (O'Shaughnessy, 2004). The last US presidential election in 2004, though planned as a campaign structured round political and personality themes, became in the end a referendum on values. Bush demonstrated a strong belief system and clear value judgements; in fact, a Manichean world view of absolute right and absolute wrong.

One aspect of this value orientation is the characteristics of the political actor, at the extreme alternately seducing and frightening segments of the electorate (Britt, 2005). It is this kind of intimacy that a PRM approach would certainly seek to embody. The internet (which is still exempt from candidate-endorsement rules in many countries) could be employed as the private voice, its negative imagery removed from public (mainstream) media. Contrast George Bush's initial suburban-safe, airbrushed 2004 campaign television advertising with this video on his campaign website:

> A woman, sitting at a keyboard, seeks information about Senator John Kerry on the Internet. She unearths all sorts of scandalizing titbits. 'More special interest money than any other senator. How much?' she says. The answer flashes on the screen: $640,000. 'Ooh, for what?' she says, typing out 'Paybacks?' and then reading aloud from the screen, she says, 'Millions from executives at HMOs, telecoms, drug companies.'
>
> (O'Shaughnessy, 2004: 168)

So what would be the contribution of PRM if it were completely and comprehensively implemented as a governing ideology of political organisations? Much of course depends on the quality and imagination of the implementation, but, properly done, PRM could stabilise a party's core support, reduce the number of swing voters and the volatility of the party system, make politics less overtly cynical and manipulative and deepen democracy by increasing a plebiscitary element (Scammell, 1999). The main thrust of a PRM approach would be greater involvement: voters would be consulted more often (and not only for election purposes), party members turned into stakeholders, the nation would become better informed and be asked for its ideas on policy as well as have its responses to new political suggestions intelligently regarded. An energised, aware public that could self-mobilise would become relevant to governing elites both as actor and reactor. This could include elements of involvement in governmental political marketing, the policy delivery and implementation process that is an often forgotten interaction in the political marketing exchange.

The bonds of intimacy and solidarity that PRM aspires to bring about can be created in several ways, such as giving people confidential information and the kind of detail they would seldom get from the press. Such solidarity can also be achieved by fostering a sense of political ownership: technology can enable a move to greater internal party democracy via the inclusion of non-party members in policy development (Heidar and Saglie, 2003). The plebiscitary internal party democracy could be extended towards the mass public, but it is its potential for motivating party members that is critical. Party members can vote for policies and participate in policy forums and online electronic debates could be held (Hudson, 2005). This need for involvement and influence is a commonly felt need: a society where we 'bowl alone' will always have a latent appetite for that social intimacy that the postmodern social order lacks (Bauman, 2000) This possibility of intimate dialogue with voters is historically unique.

PRM allied to internet technology can broaden not only a party's membership base, but also the range of creative and policy inputs feeding into it. There are great possibilities here; for example, to test-market a party's advertising or policy suggestions. It can invite in the creative talents of the people, for example, in the construct of a party slogan. The response could be stronger than anticipated: thus www.moveon.org, a cyber-pressure group, sponsored an anti-Bush advertising contest and found 1500 commercials on its website: the two comparing Bush to Hitler received national publicity (O'Shaughnessy, 2004). Not all innovations work; in one episode, the Republican internet invitation to make a pro-Bush poster was swamped with anti-Bush material.

PRM can also make it possible for an unfunded candidate or minority party to achieve a wide exposure. The Democratic nomination bid of Howard Dean pioneered political uses of the internet; the key to Dean's campaign was the new forms of direct involvement and participation that the internet permitted (Rosenthal, 2003). The campaign was the opposite of the 'traditional' approach, seeking volunteers and donations from website conversations. 'Blog for America' permitted visitors to post any message they wanted and received 40,000 hits per day, and by November 2003 there were half a million email addresses on the Dean database, while the campaign had raised $5 million in the last days of September alone; his campaign in Tennessee was 'so virtual ... it does not even appear to have a telephone' (O'Shaughnessy, 2004: 170). Clearly, such a campaign anticipates a PRM approach even though it does not technically constitute one. The claim is that the public are keen to express their views once requested to do so. British Liberal Democrat Steve Webb, who gained the Channel 4 politics award for best use of new technology to encourage political participation, had a dialogue with approximately 3000 constituents by text and email, and the response had been 'hugely positive', with one constituent apparently claiming it was the 'nearest thing to democracy' he had encountered (O'Shaughnessy, 2006).

Micro-issues of political relationship marketing

In this section we will discuss the actual and potential application of PRM to politics today and in the past. Parties and politicians do not tend to recognise any of the things they do as PRM, but some of what they do anticipates the PRM approach and some of what they do parodies it. There appears to be no authentic, comprehensive application or general managerial concept of relationship marketing extant in politics, that is, the integration of tactics within a strategy that derives from intellectual recognition or ideological acceptance.

In both the US and the UK, the expenditures on targeted marketing relative to other forms of political marketing are now colossal. This cannot really be said to amount to PRM, but the tactical understanding behind it will inevitably drive parties towards adopting PRM since it embodies the recognition that electoral success lies less in communicating to an undifferentiated mass electorate than in the depth of engagement with specific target groups within that mass. The British Conservative Party sent prime-ministerial candidate Michael Howard's pre-recorded messages via telephone, and newsletters were targeted via voter interest.

The British Labour Party manufactured DVDs for marginal seats, which featured local celebration and dynamic, caring Labour Party candidates. Labour intended to communicate directly to its own disaffected supporters seven times in the later stages of the 2005 general election. Seats with majorities of fewer than 5000 voters (i.e. so-called 'marginal' seats) received personalised letters and phone calls from the party's call centre in Gosforth, Tyneside (O'Shaughessy, 2006). Meanwhile the Conservative election machine was in the process of contacting 2.5 million key voters. In the US presidential elections, the targeting of political television advertising was precise; for example, there were half a million airings that only appeared in three to six states. Thus 60 per cent of voters were excluded from any exposure to political television commercials (Henneberg and O'Shaughnessy, 2007).

The PRM approach seeks the intimacy of the targeted medium with its associated accents of emotion and no compromise. Echoes of this were seen in the US election cycle (nomination/presidential cycle 2003–2004), where candidates sought to speak to a select coterie by mail or internet in a more uncompromising voice as a way of securing their loyalty. With PRM, this kind of private voice can be taken much further to a micro-targeted and therefore highly differentiated level. A dual private and public strategy was pursued by US primary candidates. Parties' and candidates' ability to target has now become much more refined. Political agents mix in data on consumer and credit history purchases with geo-demographic software, telephone canvassing and electoral rolls to target individual voters and turn them into prospects. The theory is that a habitual drinker of Coors beer (for example) is more likely to vote Republican (Elliott, 2005). Such political database marketing ideally lends itself to the logical extension to PRM, although parties and candidates rarely recognise this.

PRM has a history and a prehistory. In the past, parties and candidates have carried out tactical manoeuvres which could be seen as PRM and would be the kind of measures that the PRM approach would result in. However, these do not add up to a PRM approach, and sometimes they seem to be a caricature of it. Frequently, political operatives get it wrong: the idea of having a deep relationship with voters may be applied clumsily, or back-fire because of crude tactical implementation. In fact, there is a long prehistory to the 'technology' of PRM practice, particularly targeted direct mail: an early user was Father Charles Coughlin in the 1930s (Warren, 1996). The Republican Party reinvented it in the post-Watergate era when it was compelled to seek a mass participation membership, and since then political direct mail has become a feature of political life in the United States. There are of course other historical precedents such as the handwritten address by Margaret Bonfield in 1924 or the 1950 Tory personalised letter to opinion formers; by 1981 Britain's new SDP party was creating computer-generated direct mail while the first recorded use of email for campaigning was by Jerry Brown in 1993 (Jackson, 2005).

This said, a 'direct-mail relationship' is not the only primordial form of PRM. In earlier times some parties perceived the importance of creating relationships with key cadres by mixing politics with entertainment and socialisation. In his book *Selling God*, Moore (1994) concluded that the popularity of religion in that supermarket of churches, the United States, was facilitated by faith entrepreneurs who understood the need to mix entertainment with religion. A similar situation existed in the political sphere, where early examples include the British Conservative Party's Primrose League, established in the late nineteenth century in memory of Benjamin Disraeli, and more recently the Young Conservatives of the 1950s. The latter organisation was ostensibly a mass political movement which catered to its members' social needs; entertainment took centre stage and it quickly became known as a 'marriage bureau'.

The tactics of PRM were thus discernible, but they remained ideas without an explicit place in the wider political strategy. By the 1980s, some US politicians used several types of media in an attempt to create a permanent relationship with other stakeholders that would pay dividends at election time. In the words of one Congressman:

> I am not only a news maker, but a news man – perhaps the most widely read journalist in my district. I have a radio show, a television programme, and a news column with a circulation larger than that of most of the weekly newspapers in my district.

(O'Shaughnessy, 1990: 70)

By the late 1990s, internet technology had given rise to a new kind of political intensity, the precursor of PRM:

> campaign contributions can be solicited; policy papers posted for voter inspection; interactive chat lines established, so that the campaign can respond to questions from voters; volunteers recruited; candidate schedules publicised; and press releases and other announcements posted.
>
> (Johnson, 1997: 18)

Other methods such as the 'town meetings' held by the British Conservative Party tried to connect with voters, but these were merely tactical devices, whilst the British Labour Party's model of credit card participation had the same limitations as single-issue group membership, that is, no real participation in policy discussions and a high membership turnover (Richardson, 1995). The practice is to appear to be getting closer to the people or hearing them or communicating with them, such as the British Conservative Party's mantra 'Are you thinking what we're thinking?' in the UK 2005 general election (Ormrod and Henneberg, 2006). But these moves are seldom more than opportunistic; a concept of achieving greater intimacy is just another electoral trigger device rather than part of some wider political strategy that might have informed and directed it. This continues today, as politicians still use online technology as a means of monologue rather than dialogue.

So how can the concept of PRM be applied in practice? The answer to this question is a matter of creativity and of evolving imaginative ideas that enable PRM to facilitate a more involved and responsive politics. It is also a question of understanding the potential of various technologies, especially the online media, to enhance the creation of special relationships between parties, their members and their broader stakeholders. For example, Jackson (2005) provides a laundry list of 'what to do' to make online newsletters more effective, and things to avoid (self-promotion, campaign commercials, email attachments). These are also the methods that lead towards a truer realisation of the PRM concept; for example the possession of a fast feedback facility and its processing. This also raises possibilities of PRM as the pathway to a better (in the sense of more responsive) form of (party) democracy. But the content of online newsletters risks becoming simply a rehash of press releases, or at best a digest of a range of sources (Jackson, 2005). Adopting a PRM approach to creating an online newsletter would mean emphasising topicality and relevance to the target group and speaking to them in their own language.

Thus for all of this to be effective, PRM needs to begin with a core segmentation strategy (Smith and Hirst, 2001), as its effectiveness is governed by its ability to target the culture of a specific subgroup. However, the broader targets of PRM fall into four groups: first, the party's core supporters and activists; second, the party's national members; third, the party's loyal voter base; and fourth, voters in general and their various sub-segments. These are different groups with different needs, and whilst they all require PRM, they do not require the same relationship strategies. Creative ways are needed to motivate and involve the activists, who are the foot soldiers of any campaign. They must be distinguished – as in the case of the structure of pressure groups (Richardson, 1995) – from the inactive party members, whose function is to give money (and whose loyalty, as New Labour found, is always tenuous; single-issue groups can lose most of their members in the space of a single year) (Richardson, 1995). Incidentally, it is worth recalling that for Jaques Ellul, the French theoretician of propaganda, membership was essential for successful persuasion: enlist someone in a cause, get them to perform some task, and they are the more convinced (Ellul, 1973).

Voters in general are also an important target of PRM: they can be segmented almost infinitely, with each subgroup sent regular updates about what the party is doing for their specific group or community. The idea is of more than 'instrumental' exchange – it is the notion of mutual dependency and trust. Such tactics might achieve the ends of PRM, but its operational effectiveness is dependent on a party or candidate's ability to optimise the information sent to each segment, and to the amount of detail a political actor can accumulate about people. The party can then maintain the relationship by continually updating the members of the segment with relevant and timely news (Smith and Saunders, 1990; Smith and Hirst, 2001). But segmentation approaches can also be used to attract crucial younger generations by fashioning appeals and modes of involvement that cater to their needs and wants. Currently, segmentation opportunities by relationship 'type' are not widely exploited by parties, despite the fact that their affinities and memberships are not monolithic.

Thus the need is to identify ways in which parties can imagine and implement PRM tactics. In short, by listening as well as initiating, by leading as well as following, organisational entities can forge meaningful relationships with their stakeholders (Henneberg, 2006). What would a relationship-oriented party look like? The answer to this question lies partly in posing another: how can loyalty be created? Is it a question of authentically empowering members and giving them a say in policy or a vote in online policy forums, or will we see the rise of loyalty card schemes with party credit cards, hotel discounts or special offers on other products? These are very different ways in which the concept of PRM can be reinforced, but they cannot form the essence of a relationship. The key to the relationship is to cater to modern tastes and conditions, seeing the political relationship as more than just an electoral interaction. Alongside the offer of privileged access to political decision-making elites in parties and policy-implementation structures in government, the bonds of solidarity could be reinforced by actually sustaining and replenishing social networks, that is, using a holistic citizenship concept. This is not a new idea; British Minister Without Portfolio and Labour Party Chairman Hazel Blears wrote in *The Times* on 14 June 2006:

> first, we need to analyse the success of membership organisations such as the RAC or RSPB and learn how to recruit and retain members. Secondly we need to focus on local activities – political or social – which engage people in their communities. If local book groups can involve thousands in local discussion and debate, so can political parties. Thirdly, we need to harness technology such as podcasting, texting and blogging, learning from campaigns such as Make Poverty History.

The keys to PRM are appeals to a sense of involvement, participation and solidarity with others in the political and social sphere, essential to the creation of legitimacy. Mass publics are arguably nothing more than apolitical and inadvertent consumers of political information, who look for heuristics or recognition devices as a way of reducing cognitive effort in the decision-making process (Sniderman et al., 1993; O'Shaughnessy, 2004). Solidarity, on the other hand, is created through interactions with like-minded individuals; there is a commonality of (political) values that serves as a basis of affiliation and attraction (O'Shaughnessy, 2004). This suggests that the social dimension can play a significant role.

A further purpose of PRM is fund-raising, as PRM is arguably as much a revenue-generating strategy as it is an attempt to include voters in the policy development process. Whilst this may seem at first glance a cynical view of relationship-building, it reduces the reliance of parties and candidates on donations from wealthy individuals and lobby groups who expect something in return for their financial support. So PRM can also facilitate a mass donor-base driven by involvement.

Political relationship marketing: panacea of politics (?)

PRM represents an opportunity for all kinds of political actors in that it has the potential to reverse the lack of interest in politics that is evident in most people: the alienated and disinterested citizens. Whilst more traditional political marketing activities such as negative advertising and centralised policy-making contribute to voter apathy (Dermody and Scullion, 2003; Lilleker and Negrine, 2003), PRM could combat that apathy, as the essence of what it offers is a social connection and involvement.

Questions need to be asked about if, and in what way, the use of political marketing concepts in politics changes or affects party systems and the functioning of democracy itself. We have claimed before that '...political marketing can be viewed as a means of neutralising the deeply alienated in society' (O'Shaughnessy, 1990: 15). Such a regaining of trust, the reversal of the erosion of confidence in the political system, hints at the necessity of creating meaningful bonds between political actors and their constituents (Newman, 1999). PRM may be a means to achieve this re-enfranchisement. A further point is that PRM should not lead to the abdication of leadership. The tendency of political marketing towards more 'plebiscitory democracy' (Abramson et al., 1988) is not a new phenomenon (Scammell, 1995). Whilst this abdication of leadership could be induced by an overemphasis on a follower mentality in political marketing (Henneberg, 2006), such tendencies have been observed in the increasing use of focus groups, opinion polls and plebiscitary elements (like grass-roots votes on people, positions and political issues) by many political institutions. However, a market orientation in the sense of a relational approach does not necessarily predispose companies to follow but balances elements of a customer-led with a customer-leading approach (Ormrod, 2005; Henneberg, 2006). Therefore, a relationship-building approach of political marketing management would provide a framework for elements of leadership which are supposedly destroyed by a more traditional, that is, customer- (voter-) led approach (Scammell, 1995).

The merit of PRM, therefore, is that it increases the likelihood that politicians would seek genuine relationships with stakeholders. Sales (votes and support) would follow as a by-product. This contrasts with cruder forms of political manipulation which parties resort to in the absence of relationships with large sectors of the electorate. However, a relationship is something that has to be maintained, not just fabricated at election time. So far parties have been about hired loyalty, material appeals – we as voters and citizens want to internalise loyalty and parties are failing to do this. Much of what occurs in elections is so blatantly manipulative that it probably does more harm than good: solving things at the plastic level. The individual's sense of powerless irrelevance is one of the defining features of the postmodern condition (Bauman, 2000) and manifests itself in the political sphere in such phenomena as low voter turnout and widespread cynicism. In Britain, this voter apathy reached alarming levels (for democracy, anyway): in 2005, first-time voters were more likely to vote in reality television shows than at the UK general election (*Sunday Times*, 13 March 2005).

Currently, the problem is that political actors merely rent the allegiance of their voters by appealing to the electorate on purely economic criteria. PRM would instead appeal to values so that when the inevitable economic downturn occurs, the goodwill that the party or candidate has built up can help it to weather the storm. PRM is a critical orientation for political parties and candidates to adopt if they are to refresh their membership lists and retain voters' allegiance and trust as well as providing legitimacy to their party and to the overall party system. It is probably the most important thing marketing has to offer political actors. Currently, politicians focus on appealing to voters at election time, and impose policy demands on their ideologically driven followers and party members.

We argue that PRM has an untapped potential in the political context, although it is no absolute panacea for the problems facing modern political parties and candidates. As O'Malley and Tynan (2000) point out, there is a real difficulty in creating emotional bonds via technology-mediated interaction. The idea of building and maintaining relationships has such intuitive plausibility that we are apt to forget some of the problems, not least those of sound implementation; for example 'the employment of direct and database marketing in operationalising R[elationship] M[arketing] may actually undermine the process of relationship development, because what marketers call "intimacy" … many consumers view as "intrusive"' (O'Malley and Tynan, 2000: 808). The complaint is that (political) relationship marketing can develop into mere technique with a focus on building databases rather than relationships. As O'Malley and Tynan (2000: 807) remark: 'It may be that the metaphor of interpersonal relationships has been so successful that the academy has forgotten that it is a metaphor which is being used.' Critics suggest that (P)RM too easily becomes a type of business rhetoric, and that attitudes towards consumers continue to represent them as passive targets and deny them autonomy. In politics we have to be particularly sensitive to these considerations. In the end, 'relationship marketing' is a slogan as well as a concept, and like all slogans it directs us to some truths but blinds us to others. For example, the claim is made that social exchange theory, on which the theories of relational marketing are based, overemphasises the role of trust, commitment, communication and mutuality in exchange within consumer markets: 'Social exchange theory ties us into the language and rhetoric of interpersonal relationships, particularly those of marriage' (O'Malley and Tynan, 2000: 807). This represents only a partial view of exchange. Further understanding of, for example, 'interimistic' relationships (Lambe et al., 2000) will broaden our perspective of PRM. We therefore need to base PRM on a clearer and deeper understanding of the essence of political exchanges, be they in the electoral, parliamentary or governmental markets (Peattie and Peattie, 2003; Henneberg and Ormrod, 2013).

Conclusion, implications and further research

More prescriptive theory-building is needed in political marketing research in order to escape purely descriptive studies anchored in existing approaches. While 'explaining events is logically prior to explaining facts' (Elster, 1989: 3), political marketing needs more of the latter. For this purpose, new theory development needs to be encouraged, based on the empirical evidence that political actors use elements of relational marketing. As relational and service-related theories gain considerable influence in contemporary commercial marketing theory (Vargo and Lusch, 2004), it is necessary for political marketing to utilise these prescriptive theories. PRM has been more or less completely neglected by theoreticians despite a twenty-year publication history in this field in commercial marketing theory; this said, very few commercial organisations actually practise relationship marketing successfully. Why, therefore, should parties, candidates or any political organisation do any better?

The practical case for PRM is simply stated. With the professionalisation of politics (Panebianco, 1988) has come voter detachment and disengagement (Richardson, 1995). Parties have become like self-perpetuating clubs, and we reach for the language of the old communist empires to describe them, with words like 'cadre' or 'apparatchik' (Lilleker and Negrine, 2003). The scale of the task is significant; high levels of non-voting combined with mass party membership ostensibly in terminal decline. Public cynicism has apparently become universal in democracies.

The task requires the focus of parties and candidates to be on a range of stakeholders; voters are the main electoral interaction partners, but party members, non-member donors, the media and competitors are also relevant. There is an urgent need to re-engage in meaningful, longer-term and involving interactions. Any tool that might be useful can be explored, and PRM has intuitive plausibility. Of course, PRM is not a panacea; the cynicism and apathy of voters are established and apparently immutable facts and it is difficult to see how they could be countered other than by some measure of relational marketing approach, although how the concept is operationalised and implemented remains open territory for debate.

With the PRM concept we are in fact reviving the practices of an earlier political generation via modern technology and for modern conditions. At one time the party was a social identity definer, but the decline of class-based politics has entailed the demise of the mass-membership party. The British Labour Party maintained close links with trade unions whilst the British Conservative Party itself was a middle-class social network, a social club in the provincial regions. Party functions were social functions. Relationships were mediated through this. Thus there was once a kind of relationship between different political actor groups, as the party was the public political expression of private trade union involvement or performed a social role at the local level. All this has gone; in a postmodern and 'liquid' social order (Bauman, 2000) we seem to focus on rented allegiance rather than relationships. To change this requires membership, the act of joining and of performing some service for the cause, as this stimulates retrospective self-justification and therefore strengthens adherence. Historically, those causes which lack a membership but merely float on media curiosity and the goodwill of a few rich backers do not last long.

There are other reasons why PRM must be treated very seriously, both in the practical sphere and by research in political marketing. If, for example, we move to a more value-based politics, as seems to be the case in the US, relational concepts represent a useful way of exploiting this, since values may embody a more effective basis for sustained relationships than appeals to economic self-interest. There is also the renewed recognition of the significance of maximising the electoral participation of a party or candidate's own voters – 'getting out the vote' – particularly in the closer contests which now arise from political consumerism and the demise of inherited loyalties. People expect to be contacted, and putting a 'face' to the party in every home can only be achieved with volunteers, the local party members and their friends; campaigns that are fought principally in the mass media cannot really leave people with a sense that they own their government in the old way, or are responsible for what it does in their name (as the 80 per cent of the British population who did not vote for the Labour Government in 2005 would doubtless testify).

While the case for the importance of PRM in theory and practice can be made, we suggest that more conceptual as well as descriptive research is needed in order to get to grips with this phenomenon. We have attempted to provide a wide overview of the facets of PRM by putting forward some macro- and micro-views. We are aware that we have maybe raised more questions than we have answered. However, these initial considerations need now to be formalised into a more rigorous theoretical framework, underpinned by discussions of the operationalisation and implementation of the PRM concept and its implication for the whole fabric of electioneering, daily politics and theories of democracy. This should also include the question whether or not PRM may end up being as tenuous as much of the application of customer relationship marketing has proven to be (Bolton et al., 2004). We therefore see efforts that continue our initial discussion of PRM through more specialised studies as a necessary next step of research.

Discussion questions

- Do you think that political relationship marketing can contribute to our understanding of the macro-level of the political sphere?
- Do you think that the adoption of a relationship marketing approach by political parties will be a good thing for politics in particular and society in general?
- Do you think that the introduction of loyalty card schemes like those in commercial retailers are an option for political parties?

Key terms

Relationships   Micro-perspective
Stakeholders   Macro-perspective
Political relationship marketing

Further reading

Bannon (2005): This article develops the commercial understanding of relationship marketing to the political context, and argues that a relationship-based approach by parties can increase voter activity and electoral stability. Relationships can be managed over time and as such can be initiated and ended by both parties and voters (stakeholders), and thus can adapt in line with the dynamic nature of society.

Henneberg and O'Shaughnessy (2009): This article forms the basis of this chapter.

Vargo and Lusch (2004): This article argues that the traditional focus of marketing on transactions has been superseded by a focus on relationships and the co-creation of value. Vargo and Lusch argue that this implies a shift from the importance of the actual products that are produced to the services that these products provide.

References

Abramson, J. B., Arterton, F. C. and Orren, G. R. (1988) *The Electric Commonwealth: The Impact of New Media Technologies on Democratic Policies*. New York: Basic Books.

Arndt, J. (1985) 'On making marketing science more scientific: role of orientations, paradigms, metaphors and puzzle solving', *Journal of Marketing*, 49 (3): 11–23.

Bagozzi, R.P. (1995) 'Reflections on relationship marketing in consumer markets', *Journal of the Academy of Marketing Science*, 23 (4): 272–7.

Baines, P.R., Brennan, R. and Egan, J. (2003) '"Market" classifications and political campaigning: some strategic implications', *Journal of Political Marketing*, 2 (2): 47–66.

Bannon, D.P. (2005) 'Relationship marketing and the political process', *Journal of Political Marketing* 4 (2): 85–102.

Bauman, Z. (2000) *Liquid Life*. Cambridge: Polity.

Blears, H. (2006) 'Party time for democracy', Letter, *The Times*, 14 June.

Bolton, R.N., Day, G.S., Deighton, J., Narayanda, D., Gummesson, E., Hunt, S.D., Prahlad, C.K., Rust, R.T. and Shugan, S.M. (2004) 'Invited commentaries on "evolving to a new dominant logic for marketing"', *Journal of Marketing*, 68 (1): 18–27.

Britt, B. (2005) 'Precision election', *Marketing*, 13 April.

Butler, P. and Collins, N. (1996) 'Strategic analysis in political markets', *European Journal of Marketing*, 30 (10/11): 25–36.

Chernatony, L. de (1993) 'The seven building blocks of brands', *Management Today*, March: 71.

Christopher, M.G., Payne, A. and Ballantyne, D. (1991) *Relationship Marketing*. Oxford: Butterworth-Heinemann.

Dean, D. and Croft, R. (2001) 'Friends and relations: long-term approaches to political campaigning', *European Journal of Marketing*, 35 (11/12): 1197–216.

Dermody, J. and Scullion, R. (2001) 'Delusion of grandeur? Marketing's contribution to "meaningful" Western political consumption', *European Journal of Marketing*, 35 (9/10): 1085–98.

Dermody, J. and Scullion, R. (2003) 'Exploring the consequences of negative advertising for liberal democracy', *Journal of Political Marketing*, 2 (1): 77–100.

Elliott, F. (2005) 'Tories use consumer habits to target voters', *Independent on Sunday*, 6 February.

Ellul, J. (1973) *Propaganda: the Formation of Men's Attitudes*. New York: Vintage Books.

Elster, J. (1989) *Nuts and Bolts for the Social Sciences*. Cambridge: Cambridge University Press.

Ford, D., Gadde, L.E., Hakansson, H. and Snehota, I. (2003) *Managing Business Relationships*. Chichester: Wiley.

Grönroos, C. (1994) 'From marketing mix to relationship marketing: towards a paradigm shift in marketing', *Management Decision*, 32 (2): 4–20.

Hastings, G. (2003) 'Relational paradigms in social marketing', *Journal of Macromarketing*, 23 (1): 6–16.

Heidar, K. and Saglie, J. (2003) 'Predestined parties? Organizational change in Norwegian political parties', *Party Politics*, 9 (2): 219–39.

Henneberg, S.C. (2004) 'The views of an *advocatus dei*: political marketing and its critics', *Journal of Public Affairs*, 4 (3): 225–43.

Henneberg, S.C. (2006) 'Leading or following? A theoretical analysis of political marketing postures', *Journal of Political Marketing*, 5 (3): 29–46.

Henneberg, S.C. and Egbalian, S. (2002) 'Kirchheimer's catch-all party: a reinterpretation in marketing terms', in N.J. O'Shaughnessy and S.C. Henneberg (eds), *The Idea of Political Marketing*. Westport, CT: Praeger, 67–92.

Henneberg, S.C. and Ormrod, R.P. (2013) 'The triadic interaction model of political marketing exchange', *Marketing Theory*.

Henneberg, S.C. and O'Shaughnessy, N.J. (2007) 'The selling of the President 2004: a marketing perspective', *Journal of Public Affairs*, 7 (3): 249–68.

Henneberg, S.C. and O'Shaughnessy, N.J. (2009) 'Political relationship marketing: some macro/micro thoughts', *Journal of Marketing Management*, 25 (1): 5–29.

Hudson, R. (2005) 'E-politics wins a vote of confidence', *Sunday Times*, 13 March.

Hunt, S.D. and Lambe, C.J. (2000) 'Marketing's contribution to business strategy: market orientation, relationship marketing and resource-advantage theory', *International Journal of Management Reviews*, 2 (1): 17–43.

Jackson, N. (2005) 'Party e-newsletters in the UK: a return to direct political communication', *Journal of E-Government*, 1 (4): 39–62.

Johnson, D.W. (1997) *Political Communication in the Information Age*. Berlin: Wissenschaftszentrum Berlin, Bertelsmann Stiftung.

Lambe, C.J., Spekman, R.E. and Hunt, S.D. (2000) 'Interimistic relational exchange: conceptualisation and propositional development', *Journal of the Academy of Marketing Science*, 28 (2): 212–25.

Lilleker, D.G. and Negrine. R. (2003) 'Not big brand names but corner shops: marketing politics to an disengaged electorate', *Journal of Political Marketing*, 2 (1): 55–75.

Lloyd, J. (2003) 'Square peg, round hole? Can marketing-based concepts such as "product" and the "marketing mix" have a useful role in the political arena?', paper presented at the PSA Conference, Leicester, April.

McCarthy, E.J. (1960) *Basic Marketing: A Managerial Approach*. Homewood, IL: Irwin.

Moore, R.L. (1994) *Selling God: American Religion in the Marketplace of Culture*. New York: Oxford University Press.

Newman, B.I. (1994) *The Marketing of the President*. Thousand Oaks, CA: Sage.

Newman, B.I. (1999) *The Mass Marketing of Politics*. Thousand Oaks, CA: Sage.

O'Malley, L. and Tynan, C. (2000) 'Relationship marketing in consumer markets: rhetoric or reality?', *European Journal of Marketing*, 34 (7): 797–815.

Ormrod, R.P. (2005) 'A conceptual model of political market orientation', *Journal of Nonprofit and Public Sector Marketing*, 14 (1/2): 47–64.

Ormrod, R.P. (2007) 'Political market orientation and its commercial cousin: close family or distant relatives?', *Journal of Political Marketing*, 6 (2/3): 69–90.

Ormrod, R.P. and Henneberg, S.C. (2006) 'Are you thinking what we're thinking or are we thinking what you're thinking? An exploratory analysis of the market orientation of the UK parties', in D.G. Lilleker, N.A. Jackson and R. Scullion (eds), *The Marketing of Political Parties*. Manchester: Manchester University Press, 31–58.

O'Shaughnessy, N.J. (1990) *The Phenomenon of Political Marketing*. Basingstoke: Macmillan.

O'Shaughnessy, N.J. (2001) 'The marketing of political marketing', *European Journal of Marketing*, 35 (9/10): 1047–57.

O'Shaughnessy, N.J. (2002) 'Toward an ethical framework for political marketing', *Psychology & Marketing*, 19 (12): 1079–95.

O'Shaughnessy, N.J. (2004) *Politics and Propaganda: Weapons of Mass Seduction*. Manchester: Manchester University Press.

O'Shaughnessy, N.J. (2006) 'The British General Election of 2005: a summary perspective', *Journal of Marketing Management*, 21 (9/10): 907–23.

Panebianco, A. (1988) *Political Parties' Organisation and Power*. Cambridge: Cambridge University Press.

Peattie, S. and Peattie, K. (2003) 'Ready to fly solo? Reducing social marketing's dependence on commercial marketing theory', *Marketing Theory*, 3 (3): 365–85.

Richardson, J. (1995) 'The market for political activism: interest groups as a challenge to political parties', *West European Politics*, 18 (1): 116–39.

Rosenthal, E. (2003) 'The 2004 campaign: the Dean campaign; political challenge 2.0: make a virtual army a reality', *New York Times*, 21 December.

Scammell, M. (1995) *Designer Politics*. New York: St. Martin's Press.

Scammell, M. (1999) 'Political marketing: lessons for political science', *Political Studies*, 47 (4): 718–39.

Smith, G. (2001) 'The 2001 General Election: factors influencing the brand image of political parties and their leaders', *Journal of Marketing Management*, 17 (9/10): 989–1006.

Smith, G. and Hirst, A. (2001) 'Strategic political segmentation', *European Journal of Marketing*, 35 (9/10): 1058–73.

Smith, G. and Saunders, J. (1990) 'The application of marketing to British politics', *Journal of Marketing Management*, 5 (3): 307–23.

Sniderman, P.M., Brody, R.A. and Tetlock, P.E. (1993) *Reasoning and Choice: Explorations in Political Psychology*. Cambridge: Cambridge University Press.

Thomas, E., Clift, E., Peraino, K., Darman, J., Goldman, P., Bailey, H. and Smalley, S. (2004) *Election 2004*. New York: Public Affairs Press.

Vargo, S.L. and Lusch, R.F. (2004) 'Evolving to a new dominant logic for marketing', *Journal of Marketing*, 68 (1): 1–17.

Warren, C. (1996) *Radio Priest: Charles Coughlin: The Father of Hate Radio*. New York: Free Press.

Chapter 8 is developed from Henneberg, S.C. and O'Shaughnessy, N.J. (2009) 'Political relationship marketing: some micro/macro thoughts', *Journal of Marketing Management*, 25: 5–29. Reprinted by permission of Taylor & Francis (www.tandfonline.com).

Strategic Political Postures

After reading this chapter, you should be able to:

- define the concepts of leading and following and apply them to a political party
- state which strategic political posture a party has adopted
- compare the strategic postures of the parties in your system and discuss the results.

Introduction

Political actors such as political parties or candidates are said to develop and follow strategies. These strategies might, for example, consist of a plan of how to win an election campaign (Newman, 1994). To this end, parties may apply political marketing tools to fulfil certain marketing functions that allow them to reach their strategic aims (Henneberg, 2002). It has been stated that it '…has become impossible not to incorporate a marketing orientation when running for political office' (Newman, 2002: 2). However, besides these situation-specific strategies, political parties need to address some more fundamental strategic issues in political marketing. Although these issues are not normally part of campaign-centred political marketing (Newman, 1999), they touch upon the essence of political marketing and thus concern the basic orientation of the party towards political marketing management, that is, which tools the party uses to achieve its aims (Henneberg, 2002).

The aim of this chapter is to develop existing concepts in the commercial literature to the political context in order to provide a framework for understanding the fundamental strategic choice that parties and candidates face. After introducing the concepts of **leading** and **following** we demonstrate how they can help to understand the behaviour of political actors. We then overlay the concepts to form a two-by-two grid and discuss the resulting four generic strategic types that political actors can follow in order to achieve their aims.

Political parties and marketing strategy

While the area of political marketing instruments and their use by political actors is now a commonly researched issue, questions of political market orientation, competitive positioning and the contingencies of strategic frameworks have been largely neglected, with previous studies having mainly used the concept of market positions as analogies for incumbents and challengers or 'nichers' (Butler and Collins, 1996). The basic orientation of a party with regard to political marketing can be called its **strategic posture**. This posture exemplifies in marketing terms how the organisation '... aspires to be perceived (by its customers, employees, and partners) relative to its competitiors and market' (Aaker, 2001: 192). It encompasses one element of what is called a competitive position: how the actor intends to compete (Hooley et al., 2001). These principles of the competitive position are derived from the party's overall goals, its own resources and competences, the market and competitive situation, and the needs of its customers. This posture '... to a large extent dictates the implementation of marketing through elements of the marketing mix ...' (Hooley et al., 2001: 503).

Fundamentally, political parties have two different dimensions to choose from. The party can try to lead; the party knows that its political offering is essentially right. This means that political marketing management is a tactical means to fulfil a certain mission. Leading essentially consists of trying to actively convince others (party members, voters, other stakeholders) of the beneficial nature of a party's political offering. Conversely, a party can choose to follow; the party can guess, anticipate or analyse the wishes of its target constituency and then create a political offering that best integrates and articulates the wishes of the largest possible number of constituency members.

By having to decide their strategic orientation, parties face the same decisions and trade-offs as commercial and non-commercial organisations with regard to their approach towards marketing and customer orientation. Whilst most of the commercial marketing literature identifies these concepts mainly as anticipating and analysing customer demands and, consequently, fulfilling them (Davis and Manrodt, 1996), this description reveals only half the story. It represents the market-driven approach that is based on extensive market research in profitable sub-segments, with new products or product positions based on what customers actually want. In effect, this approach of following customers leads to a policy of frequent incremental improvements. In marketing theory this is often called a customer-led philosophy (Slater and Narver, 1998). However, another expression of marketing and customer orientation is also discussed in the theoretical literature, namely of a creative approach towards offering development, the market-driving approach (Hellensen, 2003). For example, marketing research, product testing and the plethora of modern new product development (NPD) methodology was not able to come up with such an innovative value proposition as Sony's Walkman, nor was it able to show and substantiate the Walkman's immense sustainability in economic terms. Slater and Narver (1998) call this the market-oriented philosophy. The approach of leading is based on conviction even in the face of contradictory evidence, a long-term commitment to understanding customers and empathy with key constituents. However, it must be based on pragmatic knowledge of what is possible and achievable; leading without gaining a followership is not really leading. Leading in a commercial marketing sense means understanding the key components of customer preferences to gain empathy and the ability to judge if one's conviction is a reasonable one in the eyes of the customer. Leading has always been an important positive attribute of politicians.

One caveat needs to be applied to the explanations above. Although leading and following, that is, driving the market or being driven by it, are seemingly antagonistic concepts on a continuum, this is not the case. As will be discussed below, the degree to which both dimensions are applied simultaneously constitutes the specific strategic posture a political party or candidate holds. Leading and following can happen simultaneously as part of a political marketing strategy; this is in line with the approach found in the strategic marketing literature (Connor, 1999). In the following discussion, four postures and their characteristics will be presented as generic options for political parties involved in a competitive situation characterised by democratic elections. It will be shown that the quality and the degree of freedom of policy-making as well as the characteristics of political marketing management instruments change fundamentally with the choice of different political marketing postures.

Strategic political postures

Figure 9.1 shows a representation of four generic postures of strategic political marketing. These can be understood as different competitive positions that political actors can adopt (Hooley et al., 1998). The two dimensions of leading and following are overlaid to produce a two-by-two matrix of strategic options. Complementing the two more extreme postures of either being dominated by a leading approach (**The Convinced Ideologist**) or a following mentality (**The Tactical Populist**), a posture is proposed that scores high on both dimensions, integrating both elements of leading and following (**The Relationship Builder**). The final strategic posture, **The Political Lightweight**, scores low on both the leading and following dimensions and as such this party strategy can be considered to be a non-strategy, as the political lightweight party neither stands by its own convictions nor listens to the *vox populi*. Therefore, this strategic posture will be omitted from the following discussion.

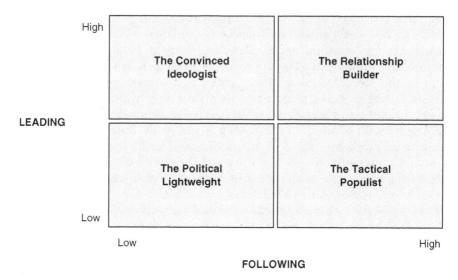

Figure 9.1   Generic postures of strategic political marketing (from Henneberg, 2006a)

Before the main characteristics of the postures are examined in more detail, it is necessary to briefly address questions relating to the relationship of the strategic postures and the development of party systems over time. Traditionally, parties have oriented themselves around cleavage lines (Lipset and Rokkan, 1967), such as bourgeois parties and mass-integration parties that have followed a clear convinced ideologist posture. However, with the crisis of both the classical bourgeois and the mass-integration parties, the emergence of catch-all parties (a classical example of which is the German Christian Democratic Party CDU in the 1950s and 1960s) have meant a move towards following-dominated postures in order to integrate the rather diverse political opinions/preferences across cleavage lines (Kirchheimer, 1966) and the targeting approaches have changed to what is identified in marketing management as an undifferentiated approach (Henneberg and Eghbalian, 2002). Nowadays, it can be argued that this development has been driven to new extremes with a greater emphasis on follower strategies, and consequently more parties are adopting the tactical populist posture. However, this does not mean that the convinced ideologists have become extinct; besides individual candidates, single-issue parties and extremist parties can still be classified as adopting this posture. Green parties and certain neo-communist parties are examples of this use of ideology. The quadrant of the relationship builder seems still somewhat unoccupied (see Figure 9.2).

However, with the backlash against spin and what is perceived as an unashamed emphasis on merely following public opinion, a more balanced approach seems to be one way of recapturing political trust. However, these

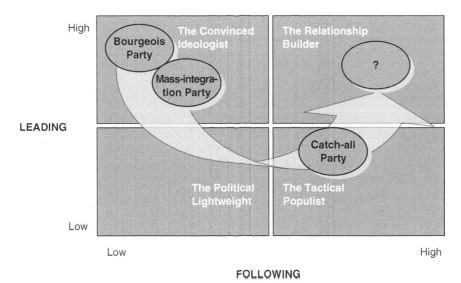

Figure 9.2   Generic postures and political parties (from Henneberg, 2006a)

developments of party postures cannot be exclusively explained by media and technological innovations. These developments have to be seen, at least partly, as long-term strategic decisions (Wring, 2002). The strategic marketing literature suggests that leading (market-oriented) and following (customer-led) can be explained as managerial reactions to environmental characteristics, that is, a following approach is more attractive in a relatively predictable surrounding (Slater and Narver, 1998) where the emphasis is on developing expected offerings, not augmented ones (Slater and Narver, 1999).

Characteristics of the different postures

In this section we will describe the characteristics of the three viable generic postures, the convinced ideologist, the tactical populist and the relationship builder (Table 9.1). It has to be borne in mind that the three postures are generic constructs and therefore a description of their characteristics is always prone to overgeneralisation. The postures are derived from strategic marketing theory and describe what parties would look like that adopt a certain posture. Therefore, the main value of these descriptions is to provide a conceptual framework for further (empirical) investigations. In the conclusion to the chapter several propositions are derived from this framework that will take this approach to the next level of development and abstraction. However, it is important to note that the three viable party postures proposed here overlap to some extent with Wring's (2002) evolutionary model, separating a propaganda phase, a media phase and a political marketing phase of political party development with reference to the UK Labour Party.

The convinced ideologist

The convinced ideologist (CI) party scores high on the leading-scale while its following capabilities are not fully developed. This posture is characterised by a clear focal point for policy-making; a good example of this is ideology or religion where policy content determines the proposition for the convinced ideologist. Voter preferences or shifts in current opinion are secondary as the constituents need to be convinced of the beneficial value of the party's political offering. Public opinion needs to be shaped rather than listened to (Glynn et al., 1999). In operational terms this means that the CI party tries to influence the level of voter support within a framework of socio-economic limitations by stressing the relative importance of ideologically- driven issues; for example, a green party might use political marketing instruments to bring ecological issues to the fore. This gives the CI party a monolithic image and inhibits changes on a strategic level. Therefore, strategic marketing concepts that enable a political party to develop a customer-centred offering like segmentation and targeting, as well as value proposition development concepts (McDonald and Wilson, 2002), are not used as they would interfere with the purity of the political offering.

However, political marketing has a home within a CI party by providing the tools to influence and convince voters in election campaigns using political communication and news management (Henneberg, 2002) whilst also managing donors. The party organisation will typically consist of hierarchies of professional politicians that have limited interfaces with external knowledge networks. Examples of such parties are plentiful; they are typically parties that did not shed their ideological baggage but adopted a much more polished media appearance and used sophisticated election campaign management techniques. However, the essence of their political offering remained largely unchanged. The PDS in Germany, successor to the communist party of the German Democratic Republic (SED), falls into this category. Although still staunchly left-wing, anti-capitalist and anti-establishment, it has adopted a young, fresh and forward-looking image, and was the first party in Germany that employed humour and satire in their election broadcasts.

The tactical populist

The tactical populist (TP) party is diametrically opposed to the convinced ideologist. Being characterised by following more than leading, this party is clearly outward looking, and feeling the political pulse of the electorate is its most important strategic aim. Therefore, strategic marketing techniques are applied to ensure that the political offering is always in sync with public opinion

(Glynn et al., 1999). The main target is to maximise voter support at election time, which means that the TP must be flexible with regard to core character-istics of their political offering. Micro-segmentation and concentration on marginal seats and swing voters might mean that differentiated offerings need to be managed by this party (Smith and Hirst, 2001). On top of being embed-ded in the policy-making process, political marketing concepts also dominate the tactical application and execution of political tools. Besides communica-tion and product functions, political marketing instruments also help with news management and fund-raising. Furthermore, political marketing is used to optimise the tactical requirements of managing the TP party's own grass roots and other core stakeholders. Political marketing becomes a necessary tool for managing what is sometimes called the permanent campaign (Nimmo, 1999), using electoral professionals – think tanks, quasi-independent advisers and communication consultants – who build a shadow apparatus alongside the official party structure (Panebianco, 1988). This development of a separate, parallel organisation of professionals alongside the elected politicians is not a pre-condition for tactical populism but an expected side effect.

Public opinion research also shows that the personalisation of politics and campaigns, especially the prominence of the prime minister, has a direct impact on party popularity and satisfaction levels with government (Lanoue and Head-rick, 1994). An example of this is the British Labour Party of the late 1990s that not only enthusiastically embraced the TP concept but elevated it to the strategic level (Wring, 2002). Their following of the slightest swings in opinion poll results was (in-)famous, whilst campaign and media specialists became members of the political leadership team. To cite another example, Harris (2001) shows that George Bush's 2000 presidential campaign followed a pattern similar to that described as tactical populism (for an overview of this campaign from a political marketing point of view see Newman, 2001). His predecessor, Bill Clinton, showed a similar orientation. However, Clinton went further; he seemed to have used campaign management tactics as a means of governing (Newman, 1994), a true application of Blumenthal's 'permanent campaign' (1982). Clinton's use of the media and understanding of public opinion helped him prevail in adverse situations, like the Lewinsky scandal, by exploiting the public's hesitancy to follow the interpretations of the conservative establishment (Shah et al., 2002).

The relationship builder

The relationship builder (RB) party scores relatively high on both the leading and following dimensions of political marketing. The political offering is developed using political marketing concepts, whilst a clear and trustworthy proposition is created through incorporating ideological roots and long-held overarching political beliefs. In effect this means managing voter support throughout the electoral cycle (Holbrook, 1996). Such an amalgamation of a stable orientation that has the ability to react flexibly to public opinion shifts is in line with contemporary strategic marketing theory. A focus on longer-term relationships, away from a purely transactional focus (winning the next election) by using a relational management concept, is often seen as a paradigmatic shift away from mechanistic marketing mix considerations and the 4P concept (Bannon, 2005). Such an approach would allow an RB party to achieve its long-term aims by locking-in voters and other constituents into a commitment–trust relationship (Morgan and Hunt, 1994). It would mean a time horizon longer than just the next election date, a philosophy of making and delivering on promises, active listening, the use of information in the offering development process and an integrated use of marketing instruments to fulfil the political marketing functions in an interconnected way. The RB party also uses many outside groups and individuals, as would the TP party. The difference between the two, however, is that the TP has two party organisations, an official one and an overlapping shadow one, whilst it is unclear where the borders of the RB party are, as they become blurred through the incorporation of other constituencies, such as voters or donors, into the value-creation process of politics.

Table 9.1 Characteristics of strategic postures (from Henneberg, 2006a)

		Strategic posture		
		Convinced Ideologist	*Tactical Populist*	*Relationship Builder*
Characteristics	Offering development	Content driven	Driven by external forces	Content mediated by external forces
	Use of political marketing concepts	Tactical	Strategic and tactical	Integrated strategic and tactical use
	Focus of political marketing management	Election campaign	Permanent campaign	Permanent relationship management
	Focus of party organisational structure	Party members	Key external stakeholders	Society

Conclusion

Whilst research on how parties use political marketing instruments exists, the lack of emphasis on strategic political marketing, especially with regard to theoretical frameworks of political marketing orientation and strategic positioning, can be seen as a major shortfall in the development of political marketing research as a sub-discipline of marketing and political science. In this chapter we have addressed this lack by developing the commercial marketing strategy literature to the political context, resulting in the two, linked concepts of leading and following. By overlaying the leading and following that a party adopts, three generic types of political parties have been characterised with reference to their stance towards these two elements, which has been described as a strategic posture. Furthermore, the implications of the different strategic postures in fulfilling certain political marketing functions, using political marketing instruments, and the effects on organisational issues have been discussed. While traditional parties with a rigid content-based approach towards policy-making can be characterised as convinced ideologists, modern catch-all parties have moved towards being tactical populists. Both postures are prone to being perceived as either dogmatic or untrustworthy and fickle. A third posture has been proposed that integrates leading and following by using a relational approach towards marketing (Bannon, 2005). The relationship builder party constitutes a theoretical posture that needs to be clarified by empirical research in the political arena.

It becomes clear that political actors can choose from a much wider variety of stances than previously conceptualised, all of which can embrace marketing with differing implications for the use of marketing instruments. These strategic postures, seen as a strategic answer to external as well as internal demands and resources, provide the political organisation or actor with an opportunity to derive a clear strategic position that translates directly into a clear offering. To the other relevant actors, they provide a principled and rigid but predictable political offer, a more volatile but listening and reactive offer, or an integrative approach. Furthermore, a differentiation strategy can be derived from these stances (Hooley et al., 1998). The implications of these postures need to be thought through clearly by the relevant political parties as the posture determines situation-specific strategies and the use of political marketing instruments. A clear understanding of the intended competitive positioning also allows the deployment of so-called isolating mechanisms that protect a chosen posture and ensure its sustainability (Hooley et al., 2001). However, the strategic marketing literature shows that this seemingly analytical process of deriving a strategic posture is a complicated sense-making exercise of limited rationality based on perceptual bias (de Chernatony et al., 1993). These findings should be borne in mind when researching political marketing postures and political market orientation in general.

Discussion questions

- Choose one or more parties from your political system and discuss their levels of leading and following. Where would you place them on Figure 9.1?
- Do you think that the political lightweight is a viable short-term strategic posture? Are there any parties in your party system that show a tendency towards being a political lightweight?
- Do you think that there is an optimal strategic posture for your political system?

> **Key terms**
>
> Leading   The Relationship Builder
> Following   The Political Lightweight
> The Convinced Ideologist   Strategic posture
> The Tactical Populist

Further reading

Henneberg (2006a): This article forms the basis of this chapter, and also includes a number of future research propositions.

Henneberg (2006b): This article demonstrates how the two-by-two grid in Figure 9.1 can be applied to a concrete example, namely British Labour Party leader Tony Blair's strategic posture before and after the second Iraq war in the early 2000s. The article also demonstrates how the strategic postures can be used to understand the dynamic effects of changes in the political environment.

Slater and Narver (1998): This article was the first to explicitly discuss the differences between being customer-led (the commercial equivalent of a following posture) and being market-oriented (the commercial equivalent of a leading posture). Narver and Slater's article argues that, whilst both approaches are useful, it is important not to confuse the two.

References

Aaker, D.A. (2001) *Strategic Marketing Management*. New York: John Wiley.
Bannon, D.P. (2005) 'Relationship marketing and the political process', *Journal of Political Marketing*, 4 (2): 85–102.
Blumenthal, S. (1982) *The Permanent Campaign*. New York: Simon & Schuster.
Butler, P. and Collins, N. (1996) 'Strategic analysis in political markets', *European Journal of Marketing*, 30 (10/11): 25–36.
Chernatony, L. de, Daniels, K. and Johnson, G. (1993) 'Competitive positioning strategies mirroring sellers' and buyers' perceptions?', *Journal of Strategic Marketing*, 1: 229–48.
Connor, T. (1999) 'Customer-led and market-oriented: a matter of balance', *Strategic Management Journal*, 20: 1157–63.
Davis, F.W. and Manrodt, K.B. (1996) *Customer-Responsive Management*, Oxford: Blackwell.
Glynn, D.J., Herbst, S., O'Keefe, G.J. and Shapiro, R.Y. (1999) *Public Opinion*. Boulder, CO: Westview Press.

Harris, P. (2001) 'To spin or not to spin, that is the question: the emergence of modern political marketing', *The Marketing Review*, 2: 35–53.

Hellensen, S. (2003) *Marketing Management*. Harlow: Prentice Hall.

Henneberg, S.C. (2002) 'Understanding political marketing', in N.J. O'Shaughnessy and S. Henneberg (eds), *The Idea of Political Marketing*. Westport, CT: Praeger.

Henneberg, S.C. (2006a) 'Leading or following? A theoretical analysis of political marketing postures', *Journal of Political Marketing*, 5 (3): 29–46.

Henneberg, S.C. (2006b) 'Strategic postures of political marketing: an exploratory operationalization', *Journal of Public Affairs*, 6 (1): 15–30.

Henneberg, S.C. and Egbalian, S. (2002) 'Kirchheimer's catch-all party: a reinterpretation in marketing terms', in N.J. O'Shaughnessy and S.C. Henneberg (eds), *The Idea of Political Marketing*. Westport, CT: Praeger, 67–92.

Holbrook, T.M. (1996) *Do Campaigns Matter?* London: Sage.

Hooley, G., Broderick, A. and Moeller, K. (1998) 'Competitive positioning and the resource-based view of the firm', *Journal of Strategic Marketing*, 6: 97–115.

Hooley, G., Greenley, G., Fahy, J. and Cadogan, J. (2001) 'Market-focused resources, competitive positioning and firm performance', *Journal of Marketing Management*, 17: 503–20.

Kirchheimer, O. (1966) 'The trantormation ot the Western European party systems', in J. LaPalombara and M. Weiner (eds), *Political Parties and Political Development*. Princeton: Princeton University Press, 177–200.

Lanoue, D.J. (1994) 'Prime ministers, parties, and the public', *Public Opinion Quarterly*, 58: 191–209.

Lipset, S.M. and Rokkan, S. (1967) 'Cleavage structure, party systems, and voter alignment', in S.M. Lipset and S. Rokkan (eds), *Party Systems and Voter Alignment*. London: The Free Press.

McDonald, M. and Wilson, H. (2002) *The New Marketing*. Oxford: Butterworth/Heinemann.

Morgan, R.M. and Hunt, S.D. (1994) 'The commitment–trust theory of relationship marketing', *Journal of Marketing*, 58 (July): 20–38.

Newman, B.I. (1994) *The Marketing of the President*. Thousand Oaks, CA: Sage.

Newman, B.I. (1999) 'A predictive model of voter behavior: the repositioning of Bill Clinton', in B.I. Newman (ed.), *Handbook of Political Marketing*. Thousand Oaks, CA: Sage.

Newman, B.I. (2001) 'An assessment of the 2000 US presidential election: a set of political marketing guidelines', *Journal of Public Affairs*, 1 (3): 210–16.

Newman, B.I. (2002) 'The role of marketing in politics', *Journal of Political Marketing*, 1 (1): 1–5.

Nimmo, D. (1999) 'The permanent campaign: marketing as a governing tool', in B. Newman (ed.), *Handbook of Political Marketing*, Thousand Oaks, CA: Sage, 73–88.

O'Cass, A. (2001) 'Political marketing: an investigation of the political marketing concept and political marketing orientation in Australian politics', *European Journal of Marketing*, 35 (9/10): 1003–25.

Panebianco, A. (1988) *Political Parties and Power*. Cambridge: Cambridge University Press.

Shah, D.V., Watts, M.D., Domke, D. and Fan, D.P. (2002) 'News framing and cueing of issue regimes', *Public Opinion Quarterly*, 66: 339–70.

Slater, S.F. and Narver, J.C. (1998) 'Customer-led and market-oriented: let's not confuse the two', *Strategic Management Journal*, 19: 1001–6.

Slater, S.F. and Narver, J.C. (1999) 'Market-oriented is more than being customer-led', *Strategic Management Journal*, 20: 1165–8.

Smith, G. and Hirst, A. (2001) 'Strategic political segmentation', *European Journal of Marketing*, 35 (9/10): 1058–73.

Wring, D. (2002) 'Images of Labour: the progression and politics of party campaigning in Britain', *Journal of Political Marketing*, 1 (1): 23–37.

Chapter 9 is developed from Henneberg, S.C. (2006) 'Leading or following? A theoretical analysis of political marketing postures', *Journal of Political Marketing*, 5 (3): 29–46. Reprinted by permission of Taylor & Francis (www.tandfonline.com).

10 Political Market Orientation

After reading this chapter, you should be able to:

- discuss the relationship between market orientation in the commercial and political contexts
- discuss the implications of member behaviours for a political market orientation
- discuss the implications of stakeholders for political market orientation.

Introduction

Just as market orientation is a central concept in commercial marketing research and practice, **political market orientation** (PMO) is fast becoming a central concept in the field of political marketing. The aim of this chapter is to introduce the reader to the conceptual model of PMO. In order to do this it is necessary to understand the commercial approach to market orientation, which makes up the first section. After this we briefly discuss alternative approaches to political market orientation (O'Cass, 1996, 2001a; Lees-Marshment, 2001a) before finally turning to the core of the chapter, a comprehensive discussion of the conceptual model of PMO.

Political market orientation: commercial origins

The first reference to 'market orientation' occurred in 1960, when Levitt (1960) argued for a change in organisational focus away from the products the business produced to the markets that the business served. One of the examples used by Levitt (1960) was that of the rail companies in the USA. The traditional focus of these companies had been simply 'being a railroad company'. Levitt (1960) argued that had the railroad companies focused on being a means of transport for humans and goods, then it would have been more difficult for the automobile and aeroplane to become the preferred means of long-distance transport.

By the late 1960s, marketing academics began to discuss whether the primary focus on how to sell fast-moving consumer goods like soap and soft-drinks could be expanded to include other markets and product types. More formally, these discussions were concerned with the nature and scope of marketing as a field of research. Led by academics such as Kotler and Levy (1969), discussions centred around whether services and ideas could justifiably be included in marketing research, and whether the behaviour of actors such as hospitals, non-profit organisations and political candidates could be understood using marketing theory (Kotler, 1975). At the end of the 1980s attention again turned to developing a more precise definition of the concept of market orientation. Shapiro's (1988) question 'What the hell is market orientation?' marked the beginning of a formalisation of the concept of market orientation, which initially centred around two alternative approaches, as a set of managerial behaviours (Kohli and Jaworski, 1990) and as an organisational culture (Narver and Slater, 1990). This extended the discussions to include an explicit reference to the consequences of a market orientation, that is, the effects on business performance.

The managerial behaviours approach to market orientation was first proposed by Kohli and Jaworski (1990). This approach consists of three elements: *Intelligence Generation*, *Intelligence Dissemination* and *Responsiveness*. Intelligence is generated about customers and can be from formal and informal sources, for example through market research, analysis of secondary data or as a result of social interactions. Intelligence is disseminated throughout the company by employees, using organisational structures that enable the intelligence to be passed on from the source of the intelligence to the actor who needs the intelligence in their work for the company. Finally, a company that is responsive to the intelligence that has been generated and disseminated develops products and services that meet the needs of customers in a more appropriate way than the company's competitors.

The organisational culture approach was first proposed by Narver and Slater (1990) and focused on the way in which the company was oriented towards its customers and its competitors, and the extent to which the organisation coordinated marketing activities across functional boundaries. Narver and Slater (1990) saw a *Customer Orientation* as an organisational focus on the needs and wants of customers; these could be both explicit, that is, known and demanded by the customer, or latent, where the customer did not realise that they had a need. An example of a latent need is Sony's Walkman, the first portable music player; market research indicated that the market for portable music players would not be viable, but Sony produced their Walkman anyway – and the rest is history. A *Competitor Orientation* refers to being aware of what other companies in the industry are doing, for example, which new products have been released, how much advertising is being used and whether competitors are expanding into new markets. Finally, *Interfunctional Coordination* refers to ability of the organisation to work across different functional areas, for example the extent to which marketing professionals and the scientists working in the R&D department can cooperate to develop the products that customers require.

The perception of the relationship between managerial behaviours and organisational culture approaches to understanding a market orientation has gradually developed from being alternatives to being complementary (Gainer and Padanyi, 2005). The argument is that market-oriented managerial behaviours are unlikely to affect performance unless there is an organisational culture that supports these behaviours, and vice versa. Another important point is that simply possessing high levels of market orientation will not necessarily lead to higher performance; for example, in the computer processor market in the late 1990s resources were focused on the R&D departments as companies such as Intel realised that financial performance was dependent on being the first to develop ever faster computer processors. Finally, a market orientation is dynamic; competitors do not stand still and customer needs and wants change, and so companies have to continuously scan the marketplace to identify trends.

Market orientation of political parties

Market orientation was first mentioned in the political context in the early 1990s (Newman, 1994), but rather than concentrating on the concept, the term was used as an element in a wider understanding of political marketing as part of commercial marketing. The first explicit attempt at developing the commercial market orientation conceptualisation was published by O'Cass (1996). O'Cass followed this in 2001 (O'Cass, 2001a, 2001b) with two articles that investigated different aspects of the market orientation and marketing orientation of political parties. Further approaches were published by Lees-Marshment (2001a) and Ormrod (2005); it is these latter two approaches that comprise the current alternative conceptualisations that dominate the literature.

As pointed out in the commercial market orientation literature as far back as Kohli and Jaworski (1990), a market orientation is not the same as a market*ing* orientation despite their superficial resemblance to one another. A more precise delineation is, respectively, 'an orientation towards the stakeholder markets in which the organisation is present' (market orientation as an organisational orientation), and 'an orientation towards the use of marketing tools and concepts to achieve organisational goals' (market orientation as a function). O'Cass (2001b) was the first to distinguish between a PMO and a political marketing orientation. From a political science perspective, Coleman (2007) sees the difference between a political marketing orientation and a PMO to be 'an important distinction between democratic populism, in which parties pander to ephemeral whims and prejudices, and responsible democratic governance, which regards public demand at any one moment as being but one factor within a historical environment of evolving experiences, reputations and expectations' (Coleman, 2007: 182).

Alternative approaches to a political market orientation

The first explicit attempt to understand the concept of market orientation in the political context was published by O'Cass (1996). In his article, O'Cass follows Kohli and Jaworski's (1990) conceptualisation of a market orientation as an organisational process involving the generation and dissemination of, and responsiveness to, intelligence, and defines a PMO as 'the analysis, planning, implementation and control of political and electoral programs' (O'Cass, 1996: 40). O'Cass (2001b) expands upon this conceptualisation by integrating the three behavioural constructs within a framework developed by Kotler and Andreasen (1991) that distinguishes between an external and internal orientation, with the explicit focus on voters and competitors that characterises Narver and Slater's (1990) conceptualisation. As such, the conceptualisation of a PMO used by O'Cass (1996, 2001a, 2001b) can be considered to be an example of the interdependence approach to PMO. However, O'Cass's (1996, 2001a, 2001b) approach does not aim to develop the commercial market orientation concept to the political sphere, instead providing useful insights into the understanding of the concept by political actors.

Lees-Marshment's (2001a, 2003) contribution to the literature considers a market orientation to be one of three general types of orientation that political parties can adopt, the two alternatives being a product orientation and a sales orientation. Lees-Marshment proposes that the product-oriented party (POP) 'argues for what it stands for and believes in ... this type of party refuses to change its ideas or product even if it fails to gain electoral or membership support' (2001a: 28). The sales-oriented party (SOP) on the other hand 'retains its pre-determined product design, but recognises that the supporters it desires may not automatically want it ... A Sales-Oriented Party does not change its behaviour to suit what people want, but tries to make people want what it offers' (Lees-Marshment, 2001a: 29). Finally, the market-oriented party (MOP) 'designs its behaviour to provide voter satisfaction ... it does not attempt to change what people think, but to deliver what they need and want' (Lees-Marshment, 2001a: 30). This said, the MOP 'will not simply offer voters what they want, or simply follow opinion polls, because it needs to ensure that it can deliver the product on offer' (Lees-Marshment, 2001b: 696), as 'Political marketing identifies the demands of voters but it is still up to parties and politicians to design the policies to meet those needs' (Lees-Marshment, 2003: 28). The MOP is the key to success at election time as 'the basic assumption of CPM

[Comprehensive Political Marketing] theory is that the party which is the most market-oriented wins' (Lees-Marshment, 2001a: 74).

Each of the three party types can be expressed as a multi-stage process (Lees-Marshment, 2001a). The POP process consists of five stages: *Product Design, Communication, Campaign, Election* and *Delivery*. The SOP process consists of six stages. In addition to the five stages that characterise the POP, *Market Intelligence* is moved to after the *Product Design* stage. Finally, the MOP process consists of a total of eight stages, adding *Product Adjustment* and *Implementation* to the six stages that characterise the SOP process. In addition to the extra two stages, the *Market Intelligence* stage occurs before the *Product Design* stage. As such, the structural distinction between the MOP, on the one hand, and the POP and SOP, on the other, is that explicit voter needs and wants are uncovered first and subsequently responded to by designing an appropriate product, the product is adjusted to suit internal opinions, and that there is an explicit implementation phase.

The conceptual model of PMO

Ormrod (2005) argued that the nature of the political marketplace meant that Narver and Slater's (1990) focus on competitors and customers (and, to a lesser extent, employees) was too restrictive; due to their importance to political parties, other stakeholder groups such as interest and lobby groups, citizens and the media play a key role and thus should be explicitly included in the PMO approach. This focus on a wider group of stakeholders is also in keeping with political science models of party organisation which emphasise the importance of the link between parties and society in general (Ormrod and Savigny, 2012).

Ormrod's (2005) conceptualisation of a PMO has undergone several refinements since it was first proposed. From the original conceptualisation in 2005, the PMO model has been investigated and developed in various academic works, for example Ormrod (2007, 2009), Ormrod and Henneberg (2009, 2010a, 2010b) and Ormrod et al. (2007). In addition to this, more recently, Ormrod's (2005) contemporary conceptualisation of a PMO (presented in this chapter) has also been integrated into a wider political marketing strategy construct (Ormrod and Henneberg, 2010a, 2010c; Ormrod et al., 2010) and to party organisational types from the political science literature (Ormrod and Savigny, 2012).

Ormrod (2005) introduced the conceptual model of PMO that, as with O'Cass (1996, 2001a, 2001b), was based on the commercial marketing perception of a market orientation as an integration of the managerial behaviours and organisational culture approaches (e.g. Kohli and Jaworski, 1990; Narver and Slater, 1990). Ormrod's (2005) model consisted of eight constructs, four representing the behaviour of members and four representing the attitudes of party members towards core stakeholder groups in society. The conceptualisation centres around the process whereby information is generated from the four stakeholder groups, integrated into a consistent party offering and communicated out to stakeholders in society with the goal of achieving long-term party aims within a framework imposed by society, thus following the interdependence approach to commercial market orientation (Ormrod, 2007). This represents a pragmatic relationship between the political party and society in that there is an acceptance that the framework imposed by society means that not all of the aims of the party can be realised (Ormrod, 2005). Ormrod (2005: 51) defines a party as market-oriented when:

> its members are sensitive to the attitudes, needs and wants of both external and internal stakeholders, and to use this information within limits imposed by all stakeholder groups in order to develop policies and programmes that enable the party to reach its aims.

Ormrod (2005) presents four constructs that originate in the work of Kohli and Jaworski (1990) and Harrison-Walker (2001), namely **Information Generation, Information Dissemination, Member Participation** and **Consistent Strategy Implementation** (see Figure 10.1). These four constructs represent the behaviours of party members with regard to the flow of information within the political organisation about relevant stakeholder groups in society. The fact that the constructs are arranged in a chain does not imply a dependence relationship, merely the logical flow of information. For example, it is possible for a political party to be extremely proficient at generating information from stakeholders yet not have the organisational structure in place to disseminate this information to those in the party who need the information in their political work.

Ormrod's first 'behavioural' construct, Information Generation, is defined as 'the party-wide generation of formal and informal information regarding all internal and external stakeholders' (2005: 54) and was developed from the work of Kohli and Jaworski (1990). As with Kohli and Jaworski's (1990) construct, information can be generated from formal and informal sources by each party member. Formal information is carried out primarily by the party top, as it consists of conducting market research and analysing the results of publicly available opinion polls. Informal information is far wider in reach as each member possesses their own discrete set of personal relationships and so has the opportunity to contribute in their own unique way (Ormrod and Henneberg, 2010a).

The generated information is then disseminated throughout the organisation to those members who need it in their work for the party (Ormrod, 2005). The Information Dissemination construct, again developed from the work of Kohli and Jaworski (1990), maps this process, conceptualising it as consisting of two dimensions: a willingness to disperse the information and a willingness to receive the information. For example, a party professional responsible for

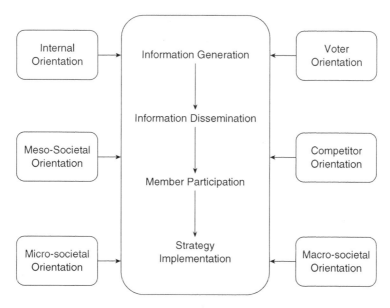

Figure 10.1   The PMO model (developed from Ormrod and Savigny, 2012)

market research may learn about a policy initiative by a competing party. This information is dispersed to the party members who make up the appropriate internal discussion group, who are open towards receiving information that the party professional has generated and has dispersed to them.

After the information has been disseminated to the relevant party members, this information can be used in the development of the party's offering. As parties are legitimised by their members in democratic political systems (Bille, 2003), a specific construct, Member Participation, was included in Ormrod's (2005) PMO model. Ormrod's construct has two dimensions: the breadth and depth of debate in the party. The breadth and depth of member participation correspond to how comprehensively the offering is discussed within appropriate fora, and how thoroughly each element of the offering is debated (Ormrod, 2005). Continuing with the example above, if the party demonstrates a high level of market orientation then the information that was dispersed to the internal discussion group will be discussed in depth by party members. In addition to this, members will also discuss the relationship between the policy and other areas of policy, emphasising that the party offering 'hangs together'.

Finally, the Strategy Implementation construct maps the way in which members at all levels of the party can contribute to implementing the party offering. The Strategy Implementation construct has been developed from Ormrod's (2005) Consistent External Communication construct. Ormrod (2007) provided the first critique of the PMO model by arguing that the Consistent External

Communication construct did not adequately capture the implementation of party strategy by party members. Ormrod (2007) argued that focusing on the relatively straightforward task of communicating the party offering out to stakeholder groups through formal and informal channels ignored the wider implementation of the strategic plan that had been developed in the course of the Member Participation process. For example, simply communicating policy would not take changes in the internal party organisational structure into account, an event that could possibly have a significant impact on the relationships that a party had with various stakeholder groups.

In response to this, in all subsequent work (e.g. Ormrod, 2009; Ormrod and Henneberg, 2010a, 2010b; Ormrod and Savigny, 2012) the construct was re-conceptualised as Consistent Strategy Implementation to take Ormrod's (2007) critique into account. However, Krogh and Christensen (2010) have pointed out that the consistent strategy implementation label is prescriptive and so has been changed to Strategy Implementation to reflect this point of criticism. The fundamental nature of the Strategy Implementation construct remains the same as different members have access to different stakeholder groups; whilst politicians are able to implement a national media strategy and elected members have regular contacts with their counterparts in opposing parties, 'rank-and-file' party activists are more able to implement local strategy and have a much wider contact with citizens through their social interactions. As such it is imperative that party members are aware of potential differences between the decision of what the party offering *is* and their own opinion of what the party offering *ought to be*.

The contemporary conceptualisation of Ormrod's (2005) PMO model is presented in Ormrod and Savigny (2012). This conceptualisation broadens Ormrod's (2005) original work to include six stakeholder groups rather than the initial four; whilst explicit constructs representing the organisational orientation towards competitors (**Competitor Orientation**), voters (**Voter Orientation**) and party members (**Internal Orientation**) are retained, the External Orientation construct (Ormrod, 2005) has been refined into three separate constructs, representing citizens (**Citizen Orientation**), the media (**Media Orientation**), and lobby and interest groups (**Societal Orientation**) (Ormrod and Savigny, 2012). However, despite the change in focus, the underlying nature of the constructs has not changed; each of the six orientations represents a complex set of relationships that can be initiated, developed, maintained and ended if the relationship with the stakeholder is not in tune with the strategic aims of the party.

Narver and Slater's (1990) original Competitor Orientation construct was developed by Ormrod et al. (2010) to allow for the fact that cooperation amongst parties is possible and in some cases necessary for a party to have influence (Lock and Harris, 1996). A good example of this is when parties have to work together in coalition governments. In Denmark, the vast majority of governments are minority coalitions, both left-wing and right-wing. As a result of this, political parties are very aware of whom they cooperate with all the way through the electoral cycle, and this cooperative tradition even affects pre-election rhetoric (Bowler and Farrell, 1992). As a consequence, voters know in advance that a vote for the Danish Liberal Party will lead to a Liberal–Conservative coalition government. Whilst it is not so obvious, in political systems with one-party, majority governments, long-term investment in defence systems or infrastructure may stretch over twenty years or more and so it is important to get cross-party support. British governments up until the 2010 general election are a good example of this; the fact that the Conservative–Liberal Democrat coalition government could exist indicates that the elected representatives of each party, despite a long tradition of opposition, realise the necessity of cooperating with each other.

The Voter Orientation construct was also developed from the work of Narver and Slater (1990) and is the equivalent of a Customer Orientation (Henneberg, 2002). The Voter Orientation construct is focused on the relationship of the party to those stakeholder groups with whom it has a direct, electoral exchange (Henneberg, 2002). There are various ways of grouping voters; a simple way is by classifying voters as loyal voters who always vote for the party, 'swing' voters who make up their mind at each election and those voters who will only vote for other parties. There are also non-voters, for example, the young or otherwise disenfranchised who might not be able to vote at the next election but will be able to vote in the longer term. So if a party displays a high level of Voter Orientation it will be aware of the needs and wants of all groups of voters; however, this does not mean that the party has to deliberately design its offering solely on the basis of a good 'fit' with the needs and wants of all voters (which is in practice impossible) or even a subset of voters.

Ormrod (2005) adapted Narver and Slater's (1990) Interfunctional Coordination construct to be appropriate to the political marketplace; whilst the commercial market orientation literature adopts an approach to internal stakeholders based on bridging functional boundaries (Lafferty and Hult, 2001), political parties tend to be characterised by being more hierarchical in structure (Dean and Croft, 2001). As such, Ormrod's (2005) Internal Orientation construct is conceptualised so as to integrate all members into the various decision-making processes that lead to a consistent implementation of the agreed-upon party strategy. An Internal Orientation consists of two dimensions: the inclusiveness of the party and an acknowledgement of the importance of other party members.

The original conceptualisation of a PMO (Ormrod, 2005) included two dimensions in the External Orientation construct, the media (macro-level stakeholders) and lobby and interest groups together with public sector employees (meso-level stakeholders). The construct was defined as 'the party-wide acknowledgement of the existence and importance of stakeholders in society that are not voters or competitors' (Ormrod, 2005: 60). Kotzaivazoglou (2011) notes that the phrasing 'in society' implies that only stakeholders within the national system are part of the model, although 'supra-national stakeholders' such as the EU and NATO are explicitly investigated in Ormrod and Henneberg (2009).

Ormrod and Henneberg (2011) refined the conceptualisation of an External Orientation to reflect the focus on society rather than simply on 'stakeholders in society that are not voters or competitors' (Ormrod, 2005: 60). In a paper presented at the 2010 International Conference on Political Marketing, Ormrod et al. (2010) argue for a separate Media Orientation construct distinct from an aggregate Societal Orientation construct. This reflects the high importance attached to the media in the political marketing literature. This division of the External Orientation construct into micro- (citizens), meso- (lobby and interest groups) and macro- (the media) elements is reflected in Ormrod and Savigny (2012; Figure 10.1).

Ormrod and Savigny's (2012) Micro-societal Orientation construct is broader in that it represents all citizens in society and not just voters. Ormrod and Savigny (2012) argue that it is necessary to have a separate construct representing citizens due to the sharp difference from voters in the nature of the exchange. The focus on citizens is also maintained throughout the electoral period as opposed to being primarily at election time. Ormrod and Savigny (2012) also introduce the Macro-societal Orientation construct, representing the relationships that exist between the party and the media; this construct is labelled *Media Orientation* in Ormrod et al. (2010) in order to reflect the central position that the media has in the political sphere. The third construct to be developed from the original External Orientation construct of Ormrod (2005) is a Meso-societal Orientation, representing interest and lobby groups in society. These stakeholders are important in that they have the ability to provide parties with support in terms of knowledge and/ or finances (Ormrod and Savigny, 2012).

Summary

The current PMO model consists of two sets of constructs, four representing the behaviour of party members and six representing the orientation of the party organisation towards stakeholder groups in society. The four constructs representing the behaviour of party members are *Information Generation, Information Dissemination, Member Participation* and *Strategy Implementation*, and were developed from the managerial behaviours approach to understand a commercial market orientation (Kohli and Jaworski, 1990; Harrison-Walker, 2001). The six stakeholder orientations focus on citizens, voters, competing parties, the media, party members, and interest and lobby groups. These six orientations have gradually been developed from three constructs first proposed by Narver and Slater (1990) as part of the organisational culture approach to understanding a commercial market orientation to include, most notably, an explicit orientation towards the media, reflecting this stakeholder group's central place in the political sphere.

> **Discussion questions**
>
> - How party members actually behave is difficult to judge from outside of the party, but we can think about how they *ought* to behave. Is it reasonable to think that all party members actively generate information and then pass it on to those who need it in their work for the party? Is it realistic to assume that all party members can and want to contribute to the development of the party offering?
> - Choose a political party that you know well and think about which of the six stakeholder groups that party targets. Is it obvious which stakeholders are targeted? Now have a look at the party website. Which stakeholder groups are targeted here?
> - Do you think that the PMO model has too many stakeholder orientations? Should there be fewer? What about simply having an external orientation and an internal orientation (every actor outside of the party versus every actor inside the party)?

Key terms

Political market orientation	Internal Orientation
Information Generation	Voter Orientation
Information Dissemination	Media Orientation
Member Participation	Citizen Orientation
Strategy Implementation	Societal Orientation
Competitor Orientation	

Further reading

Baines, O'Shaughnessy, O'Cass and Ormrod (2012): This article looks at the alternative construct of political marketing orientation, and discusses the problems that political organisations face when they only focus on political marketing management rather than a wider consideration of the theoretical and conceptual underpinnings of their approach.

Ormrod (2007): This article provides an accessible overview and commentary of the three main approaches to political market orientation and examines the conceptual foundations and research traditions of all three approaches.

Gainer and Padanyi (2005): This article investigates the relationship between market-oriented behaviours, organisational culture and performance in non-profit, service-based organisations. The results indicate that the positive relationship between market-oriented behaviours and organisational performance is mediated by organisational culture.

Ormrod (2011): This book chapter forms the backbone of this chapter. It is written in Danish.

References

Baines, P., O'Shaughnessy, N.J., O'Cass, A. and Ormrod, R.P. (2012) 'Political marketing orientation: confusions, complications and criticisms', *Journal of Political Marketing*, 11 (4): 353–66

Bille, L. (2003) 'Den danske partimodels forfald?', in L. Bille and J. Elklit (eds), *Partiernes Medlemmer*. Aarhus: Aarhus Universitetsforlag.

Bowler, S. and Farrell, D.M. (1992) *Electoral Strategies and Political Marketing*. London: Macmillan.

Coleman, S. (2007) 'Review of Lilleker and Lees-Marshment (2005)', *Parliamentary Affairs*, 60 (1): 180–6.

Dean, D. and Croft, R. (2001) 'Friends and relations: long-term approaches to political campaigning', *European Journal of Marketing*, 35 (11): 1197–217.

Gainer, B. and Padanyi, P. (2005) 'The relationship between market-oriented activities and market-oriented culture: implications for the development of market orientation in nonprofit service organizations', *Journal of Business Research*, 58 (6): 854–62.

Harrison-Walker L.J. (2001) 'The measurement of a market orientation and its impact on business performance', *Journal of Quality Management*, 6: 139–72.

Henneberg, S.C. (2002) 'Understanding political marketing', in N.J. O'Shaughnessy and S.C. Henneberg (eds), *The Idea of Political Marketing*, Wesport, CT: Praeger, 93–170.

Kohli, A.K. and Jaworski, B.J. (1990) 'Market orientation: the construct, research propositions, and managerial implications', *Journal of Marketing*, 54: 1–18.

Kotler, P. (1975) 'Overview of political candidate marketing', *Advances in Consumer Research*, 2: 761–70.

Kotler, P. and Andreasen, A. (1991) *Strategic Marketing for Nonprofit Organizations*. Englewood Cliffs, NJ: Prentice-Hall.

Kotler, P. and Levy, S. (1969) 'Broadening the concept of marketing', *Journal of Marketing*, 33: 10–15.

Krogh, M.R. and Christensen, S.T. (2010) 'Markedsorienteret policyformulering', MSc dissertation, Department of Political Science, University of Copenhagen, Denmark.

Kotzaivazoglou, D. (2011) 'Political marketing in the Greek context: does market orientation exist?', *International Review on Public and Nonprofit Marketing*, 8 (1): 41–56.

Lafferty, B.A. and Hult, G.T. (2001) 'A synthesis of contemporary market orientation perspectives', *European Journal of Marketing*, 35 (1): 92–109.

Lees-Marshment, J. (2001a) *Political Marketing and British Political Parties: the Party's Just Begun*. Manchester: Manchester University Press.

Lees-Marshment, J. (2001b) 'The marriage of politics and marketing', *Political Studies*, 49: 692–713.

Lees-Marshment, J. (2003) 'Political marketing: how to reach that pot of gold', *Journal of Political Marketing*, 2 (1): 1–32.

Levitt, T. (1960) 'Marketing myopia', *Harvard Business Review*, 38 (4): 45–57.

Lock, A. and Harris, P. (1996) 'Political marketing – *vive la différence!*', *European Journal of Marketing*, 30 (10/11): 14–24

Narver, J.C. and Slater, S.F. (1990) 'The effect of market orientation on business profitability', *Journal of Marketing*, 54: 20–35.

Newman, B.I. (1994) *The Marketing of the President*. Thousand Oaks, CA: Sage.

O'Cass, A. (1996) 'Political marketing and the marketing concept', *European Journal of Marketing*, 30 (10/11): 45–61.

O'Cass, A. (2001a) 'Political marketing: an investigation of the political marketing concept and political market orientation in Australian politics', *European Journal of Marketing*, 35 (9/10): 1003–25.

O'Cass, A. (2001b) 'The internal–external marketing orientation of a political party: social implications of political party marketing orientation', *Journal of Public Affairs*, 1 (2): 136–52.

Ormrod, R.P. (2005) 'A conceptual model of political market orientation', *Journal of Nonprofit and Public Sector Marketing*, 14 (1/2): 47–64.

Ormrod, R.P. (2007) 'Political market orientation and its commercial cousin: close family or distant relatives?', *Journal of Political Marketing*, 6 (2/3): 69–90.

Ormrod, R.P. (2009) 'Understanding political market orientation', PhD thesis, Aarhus University.

Ormrod, R.P. and Henneberg, S.C. (2009) 'Different facets of market orientation – a comparative analysis of party manifestos', *Journal of Political Marketing*, 8 (3): 190–208.

Ormrod, R.P. and Henneberg, S.C. (2010a) 'An investigation into the relationship between political activity levels and political market orientation', *European Journal of Marketing*, 44 (3/4): 382–400.

Ormrod, R.P. and Henneberg, S.C. (2010b) 'Understanding voter orientation in the context of political market orientation: is the political customer king?', *Journal of Marketing Management*, 26 (1): 108–30.

Ormrod, R.P. and Henneberg, S.C. (2010c) 'Strategic political postures and political market orientation: towards an integrated concept of political marketing strategy', *Journal of Political Marketing*, 9 (4): 294–313.

Ormrod, R. P. and Henneberg, S. C. (2011) 'Political market orientation and strategic party postures in Danish political parties', *European Journal of Marketing*, 45(6), 852–881.

Ormrod, R.P. and Savigny, H. (2012) 'Political market orientation: a framework for understanding relationship structures in political parties', *Party Politics*, 18 (4): 487–502.

Ormrod, R.P., Henneberg, S.C., Forward, N., Miller, J. and Tymms, L. (2007) 'Political marketing in untraditional campaigns: the case of David Cameron's Conservative Party leadership victory', *Journal of Public Affairs*, 7 (3): 235–48.

Ormrod, R.P., Henneberg, S.C., Zaefarian, G. and de Vries, P. (2010) 'Relationship structures and performance of Belgian political parties', competitive paper presented at the International Conference on Political Marketing, Thessaloniki, September.

Shapiro, B.P. (1988) 'What the hell is market oriented?', *Harvard Business Review*, 66: 119–25.

Chapter 10 is developed from Ormrod, R.P. (2011) 'Politisk markedsorientering', in S. Winther-Nielsen (ed.), *Politisk Marketing*. Copenhagen: Thomson-Reuters/Karnov. Reprinted by permission of Karnov Group.

11 Political Marketing Strategy and Party Organisational Structure

After reading this chapter, you should be able to:

- describe how the concepts of political market orientation and strategic political postures complement each other
- describe how the two concepts can be integrated and the nature of the four strategic profiles
- apply the four strategic profiles to parties in your own political system.

Introduction

Strategic political postures (SPP) and **Political market orientation** (PMO) are central concepts in the political marketing literature (Ormrod and Henneberg, 2010). The two concepts deal with complementary aspects of political marketing, and as such it is useful to integrate the two concepts with the aim of understanding the way in which political actors link their place in the competitive environment with organisational structure and relationship management. This chapter first provides a recap of the concepts of SPP and PMO. Following this, the elements of the two concepts will be integrated to provide four static and dynamic models, forming four strategic profiles. The final section of this chapter will demonstrate the link between the four strategic profiles and political science models of party organisational structure, with a special focus on the network party type (Heidar and Saglie, 2003).

Static and dynamic PMO profiles

In commercial marketing, strategic postures are understood as those organisational positions which companies adopt in order to enable desired perceptions amongst stakeholders in the various markets in which they operate (Aaker, 2001). The fundamental strategic marketing choice is whether to *lead the market* by identifying and fulfilling latent demands (Hellensen, 2003), to *follow the market* by conducting large amounts of research on customer preferences and then developing an offering to fulfil these (Davis and Manrodt, 1996) or to *integrate both strategic postures*, including elements of leading and following in the development of the organisation's strategy (Slater and Narver, 1999). In the political marketing context, a political actor that leads the market focuses on their own offering in the assumption that it is the most appropriate for the relevant legislative context. On the other hand, a political actor that follows the market concentrates on uncovering the needs and wants of the key stakeholder group – usually voters and to a lesser extent the media – and then developing policy to fulfil these needs and wants. As with the commercial conceptualisation of strategic postures, the actual decision is a matter of degree rather than a simple choice between postures (Henneberg, 2006).

The political actor can decide on the level of leading and the level of following that the organisation will adopt. This decision is based upon an evaluation of the effect on organisational performance of the position in the electoral cycle, the political system and the organisational structure. Whilst the political system and the structure of the political organisation are stable over a long time-period, the electoral cycle is dynamic and can result in changes in influence over legislation. As such, the level of leading and the level of following are also dynamic; they can be adapted to reflect changing environmental conditions (Henneberg, 2006).

The strategic choice that political organisations are faced with can be expressed in a two-by-two matrix, thus identifying four SPPs (Henneberg, 2006). The four SPPs are **The Political Lightweight**, **The Convinced Ideologist**, **The Tactical Populist** and **The Relationship Builder** (Henneberg, 2006). There is no theoretical reason why any of the ideal postures is by definition 'better' than any of the others, there is no natural evolution from one posture to another and all four postures can co-exist in any specific political system. Research by Ormrod et al. (2010) has shown that higher party performance is positively related to a higher 'fit' between the ideal and actual strategic profile, rather than with any specific profile, a result which reflects findings of similar investigations in the commercial marketing strategy literature.

The PMO model is developed from the interdependence approach to commercial market orientation (Gainer and Padanyi, 2005) and consists of ten core constructs, four that represent the formal and informal processes of information usage through the political organisation and six that represent the orientation of the political organisation towards key stakeholder groups in society (Ormrod, 2011). These form the basis of a static model that can be used to map the organisational structure. In addition to this, a dynamic model can be identified which maps the relationships between each of the six orientation constructs to the four information-based constructs. These relationships are dynamic, that is, the nature of the relationship can change over time, ranging from initiation to maintenance to termination.

Both SPPs and the PMO model can contribute to our understanding of political organisations. However, in order to gain the maximum benefit of the two conceptual frameworks we can integrate them into strategic political profiles – **PMO profiles** – to gain insights into the interplay between the competitive positioning of the political organisation and the organisation's internal structure. For each of the four SPPs there is a corresponding 'ideal profile' of PMO relationships. Without understanding the ideal PMO profile, the SPP type is meaningless, while *vice versa* focusing only on a specific PMO profile does not say anything about its appropriateness as derived from the profile's relationship with a strategically chosen political posture.

Therefore, each of the four alternative SPPs can be represented as a profile of an unique static organisational model with dynamic relationship patterns. The characteristics of each strategic profile can inform on whether we can expect a strong or weak organisational focus on each of the ten constructs and the expected level of importance of the relationships between each of the ten constructs. In the following we present descriptions of *ideal* PMO profiles for each of the four SPPs; in reality, parties will arrange themselves along the continua such that they are, for example, 'more or less' a tactical populist.

The political lightweight

Henneberg (2006) proposes a strategic type that neither leads nor follows the political market, labelled the political lightweight. The political lightweight is characterised by a lack of focus on both leading and following. There is

Table 11.1   Static and dynamic characteristics of the *political lightweight* SPP (Ormrod and Henneberg, 2010a)

	The political lightweight
Organisational orientation (static model)	The opinions of the members of the political actor's organisation are not considered important when developing the *political lightweight's* offering. Neither are the opinions of stakeholders outside of the organisation. The organisational orientation towards the various stakeholder groups will therefore be without a real focus.
Organisational behaviour (static model)	Little emphasis is placed on including members of the *political lightweight's* organisation in the development of the offering. There are no organisational structures in place to generate information from the stakeholder groups and disseminate this information throughout the organisation. Members do not participate and thus the implementation of strategy is piecemeal and inconsistent.
Relationship profile (dynamic model)	All relationships between stakeholder orientation constructs and the four behavioural constructs will be weak and/or negative. This will also be a characteristic of the relationships between the four behavioural constructs.

only a weak focus on the organisation's own current offering, which is not generally considered to be the best solution. In addition to this, the organisation is unwilling or unable to uncover the needs and wants of stakeholders, both inside and outside of the organisation (see Table 11.1).

It is difficult to argue for a *successful* implementation of the political lightweight strategic posture, as it is precisely the lack of an orientation towards all stakeholder groups that is this posture's defining characteristic. In addition to this, members do not contribute to generating and disseminating information, nor do they take part in developing the party offering or its implementation, which is likely to be confused and without direction.

Ormrod and Henneberg (2010) argue that a party which does not stand for anything cannot be described as a party and so the political lightweight as a strategic posture is nonsensical as it implies that the party strategy is not to have a strategy. However, Kotzaivazoglou (2011) argues that it may be necessary to include the political lightweight posture in future work as the political lightweight strategic posture may be most appropriate in socio-economic situations that are characterised by instability, incomplete information and the need for immediate action that causes short-term austerity but that is in the society's long-term interest; an example of this is the effects on the economies of certain southern European states in the wake of the global financial crisis. A party may not be able to lead according to its own convictions due to environmental pressures; neither can it follow because these very environmental pressures make it impossible to give the population what they want.

The convinced ideologist SPP

The convinced ideologist SPP is characterised by an emphasis on leading the market. This is achieved through an organisational focus on the content of the organisation's own offering, which is then marketed to target stakeholders (see Table 11.2). As such, the primary stakeholders are the party members themselves, together with other stakeholders that have a special affinity with the party due to political sympathies, historical links or coinciding aims (Ormrod and Henneberg, 2009). There is a generally weak focus on other stakeholders such as voters, competing parties, the media and most non-party stakeholders. The internal focus of the party on its members leads to a culture of inclusion, where the organisational structure is such that members have the ability to be heard.

The relationships in the dynamic profile model of the convinced ideologist SPP demonstrate strong, positive relationships between the internal orientation construct and each of the behavioural constructs, as an acknowledgement of the importance of members and their opinions is related to an increased emphasis on listening to other members, passing this information on, participating in the development of the political offering and ensuring its consistent implementation.

Table 11.2 Static and dynamic characteristics of the *convinced ideologist* SPP (Ormrod and Henneberg, 2010a)

	The convinced ideologist
Organisational orientation (static model)	The opinion of party members is central to the development of the *convinced ideologist's* political offering. Some stakeholders outside of the organisation and with an affinity to the political actor through, for example, a common history or similar aims will also be consulted. The organisational orientation will therefore be primarily towards an *internal orientation*, and to a lesser extent outside stakeholders and citizens.
Organisational behaviour (static model)	An emphasis is placed on including as many members of the *convinced ideologist's* organisation in the development of the offering, thus ensuring that the strategy is implemented in a consistent way and all party members feel some form of 'ownership' of the offering. Therefore, *all four behavioural constructs* will be important to a *convinced ideologist*.
Relationship profile (dynamic model)	All relationships between the *internal orientation* construct and the four behavioural constructs are considered to be important. This will also be a characteristic of the relationships with stakeholders that have some form of affinity with the party in question and citizens. These relationships will be strong and positive. On the other hand, the relationships between the *voter orientation, media orientation* and *competitor orientation* and the behavioural constructs will either be weak and/or negative.

To a certain extent this is also a characteristic of the paths from the construct representing the stakeholders in the wider society, although this is a result of the individual sympathies of citizens and the 'double membership' of the party and core interest and lobby groups rather than a focus on *all* of society (Ormrod and Henneberg, 2009). Finally, the relationships between the constructs representing the remaining stakeholders and the behavioural constructs will be weak. It is even possible for the relationships to be negatively related; for example, when the emphasis on voters is increased, the level of member participation in the development of the offering could decrease.

The tactical populist SPP

In contrast to the convinced ideologist, the tactical populist SPP is characterised by a focus on following the market, reflected in the relative importance of stakeholders in the static model. The political offering is developed by listening and responding to the stakeholders that will make a difference at the next election, primarily voters and the media. As such, this type of SPP has a short-term, goal-oriented approach to initiating,

Table 11.3 Static and dynamic characteristics of the *tactical populist* SPP (Ormrod and Henneberg, 2010a)

	The tactical populist
Organisational orientation (static model)	The opinion of voters and the media are central to the development of the *tactical populist's* political offering. Cooperation with competitors is out of necessity rather than preference and the contribution of the party rank-and-file is minimised as there is a risk that this will shift the focus from fulfilling the explicit needs and wants of key external stakeholder groups. Therefore, the key organisational orientations for the *tactical populist* are a *voter orientation* and a *media orientation*.
Organisational behaviour (static model)	Whilst *information generation* from voters and the media is a central characteristic of *tactical populists*, the vast majority of members are passive receivers of the information that is generated, primarily using formal channels. *Member participation* is minimised, whereas a *consistent strategy implementation* is of paramount importance and achieved as a result of the few individuals involved in this activity
Relationship profile (dynamic model)	The relationships between the *voter orientation* and *media orientation* constructs and the *information generation* and *consistent strategy implementation* constructs will be positive, but will be weak or negative with regard to the *information dissemination* and *member participation* constructs. The *internal orientation* construct will have little or no relationship with the behavioural constructs. Only the relationship between the *information generation* and *information dissemination* behavioural constructs will be strong and positive due to the importance of one-way, formal information flows.

maintaining and terminating relationships with stakeholder groups which represent and/or influence public opinion (see Table 11.3). Stakeholders that are not essential to achieving party goals are not afforded resources.

The tactical populist SPP assumes that generating information and disseminating this information throughout the party is essential for developing the party offering, although this is primarily carried out using formal methods such as focus groups, monitoring the mass media and via opinion polls, both publicly available and commissioned, rather than via social interaction at the individual level. The results of this research are presented to the mainly passive party rank-and-file on a need-to-know basis. The passive role of the rank-and-file membership is further underlined in that few individuals are involved in the development and management of the party offering, which enables a large degree of control over how the offering is implemented and perceived by the primary stakeholder groups.

The relationships between PMO constructs for the tactical populist SPP are fundamentally the opposite of those of the convinced ideologist; whilst in the former the party members are the core focus, a party that adopts a tactical populist SPP will down-prioritise members and instead follow key external stakeholder groups. This translates into strong, positive relationships between the Voter Orientation and Media Orientation constructs and the behavioural constructs of Information Generation and Strategy Implementation. This is a result of the necessity of knowing the needs and wants of each of the external stakeholder groups and ensuring that the party line clearly demonstrates an intention to fulfil these.

However, the relationships between the Voter Orientation and Media Orientation constructs, and the Information Dissemination and Member Participation constructs are weak and/or negative; increasing the party-wide focus on any of the stakeholder groups will only affect a handful of members. For example, receiving information that has been gained from voters to the political organisation is central to the success of the tactical populist SPP, but voters themselves do not directly affect the extent to which the information is passed on throughout the political organisation to those who need it.

For a political organisation that adopts a tactical populist strategic political posture it is imperative to know what the important stakeholders want and to pass this on to those in the party who need this information. However, those who 'need to know' are those individuals at the top of the political organisation who formulate the political offering. On the other hand, the relationship between the Information Dissemination and Member Participation constructs will be weak because of the minor importance of rank-and-file member involvement. Furthermore, what little discussion there is between members will not have an impact on the implementation of the party's offering, as this is the responsibility of a small group of members rather than the political organisation as a whole.

The relationship builder SPP

The final SPP is the relationship builder (see Table 11.4). The relationship builder SPP scores highly on both the leading and following dimensions, and therefore parties adopting this strategic posture place an explicit emphasis on acknowledging both the importance and opinions of all stakeholder groups. This said, there will always be some form of trade-off with regard to the extent to which the opinions of each group affect the offering as it is rarely possible to implement 'Texan taxes with Scandinavian welfare benefits' (Henneberg and O'Shaughnessy, 2007: 20). Resources can be prioritised according to, for example, the stage on the electoral cycle, the party ideology or socio-economic forces.

The inclusive focus of the relationship builder is reflected in the activity of party members, who consider it their responsibility to generate and disseminate information. The general emphasis of the party is on wide member participation in the development of the party's offering. Whilst there is a 'party line', there is an acknowledgement that the personal opinions of individual

Table 11.4   Static and dynamic characteristics of the *relationship builder* SPP (Ormrod and Henneberg, 2010a)

	The relationship builder
Organisational orientation (static model)	The *relationship builder* will underline the importance of acknowledging the existence and opinions of all stakeholder groups, although there will be a prioritisation due to the limited resources available to build and maintain relationships.
Organisational behaviour (static model)	Information will be generated from both formal and informal sources, with members feeling a responsibility to both disseminate this information to those who need it and to participate in the development of the party's offering. Whilst the 'party-line' will be known and implemented, members are free to have and express their own opinions.
Relationship profile (dynamic model)	All relationships between constructs will be strong and positive.

members may not exactly reflect the party offering, as parties are an aggregation of all member opinions; however, as long as the party line is known and implemented, members are free to express their own opinion.

Finally, building on the argument that leading and following are not mutually exclusive, the focus of the relationship builder is on managing relationships such that emphasis is placed on uncovering the opinions of central stakeholder groups, bearing in mind the limitations imposed by the scarcity of resources. This will have a positive impact on the generation of information and its dissemination throughout the organisation, which in turn informs the internal debate and enables the implementation of the agreed-upon strategy.

PMO profiles and party organisational structure

Whilst in theory none of the profiles is expected to perform better than any other (the exception being the political lightweight SPP), choosing a specific strategic profile implies choosing a configuration of the static model together with the relevant dynamic relationships (Olson et al., 2005). The implication is that political actors can optimise the use of scarce resources when developing and implementing strategies and offerings to help them achieve their aims. In practice, however, party system characteristics and organisational structures and capabilities limit the feasible strategic postures a party can aim to achieve. For example, in theory, political systems characterised by few parties (such as the UK and the US) favour the tactical populist and relationship builder strategic political postures as parties must uncover and aggregate the diverse needs and wants of large numbers of voters into one political offering. On the other hand, a small party in a proportional electoral system with a political offering based firmly on a particular ideology may aim to influence policy via coalition-building rather than gain an overall majority. In this latter situation, the favoured SPP for a small party is the convinced ideologist.

When seen through the lens of a strategic profile, attention is drawn to the relationships that exist between parties, on the one hand, and stakeholders such as voters, competitors and the wider environment in which parties are situated, on the other, and how each of these stakeholders have differing interests and expectations of how these interests will be met. Moreover, strategic profiles highlight how this tension between interests is translated into party strategy (Ormrod and Henneberg, 2010). For example, there is considerable debate as to what the key objectives of parties are; indeed, elements of the party offering may conflict and members on different 'wings' of large parties may disagree greatly on internal policy proposals. It is generally accepted that there is a tension between the desire to adhere to the traditional ideological position of the party and party cohesion versus legislative responsibility (Strøm and Müller, 1999). A common observation is that parties need to choose different strategies for different arenas and the choice of one strategy may well influence the outcome or the choice of another (Wolinetz, 2002).

Voters are a central component of political science research, as central as the customer is in the commercial marketing literature. It is widely recognised that political parties are no longer able to rely on traditional bases of support from specific voter segments. This can be a result of voters moving away from their party of traditional allegiance without replacing this with a new allegiance ('dealignment'; Sarlvik and Crewe, 1983) or as a result of changes in more general voting patterns, both sudden and over a period of time ('realignment'; Heath et al., 1985). However, it is these traditional bases of voter support that have been assumed in much of the party organisation literature, with the main focus on the voter–party relationship. For example, Kirchheimer (1966) accepted that parties had to reach out to many different segments of the electorate; Panebianco (1988) noted the increasing volatility of an opinion electorate and the rise of careerist politicians; and Katz and Mair (1995) and Heidar and Saglie (2003) highlight structural and institutional factors which shape the party as an organisation for representing voter opinions.

Understanding the activities and offerings of competing parties in the political system may be necessary to achieve the party's own long-term aims (Ormrod, 2005). In political systems with a strong tradition for single-party government, this can consist of an 'arms-length' assessment of the strategic market positions adopted by competitors and then positioning the party accordingly (Butler and Collins, 1996), although limited cooperation may be necessary for long-term investments such as in infrastructure or defence systems. On the other hand, in party systems that are characterised by coalition and/or minority governments it may be necessary for parties to collude (Detterbeck, 2005) and modify their pre-election rhetoric to allow for post-election cooperation (Bowler and Farrell, 1992). Compromises may also have to be made between local, federal and national political interests (Henneberg and O'Shaughnessy, 2009). With Katz and Mair's (1995) 'cartel party' type, the focus on the competitor is slightly different and draws attention to ideas of cooperation between parties and states to maintain the parliamentary *status quo* (Detterbeck, 2005), both in terms of the increase in the state funding of parties (outside of the UK and US) and an increasing campaign emphasis upon state-regulated electronic media.

Narver and Slater (1990) introduced the concept of interfunctional coordination in their conceptualisation of a market orientation. An organisation that is characterised by high levels of interfunctional coordination will ensure that different functional areas communicate when developing the organisation's offering. In the political context this reflects the extent to which party members recognise that their co-members can contribute to the success of the party, irrespective of their position in the party hierarchy or their activity level (Ormrod, 2005). Whilst the role of members in political parties is a common theme in the political science literature, this is not the case in the political marketing literature, with few articles dealing specifically with members (Lilleker, 2005). Here there are parallels with the network party which draws attention to the ways in which new ICTs can play a role in enabling members to participate in developing the party offering (Gibson and Ward, 2009), which in turn supports a consistent interpretation of the offering (Shapiro, 1988).

Whilst a focus on voters, competing parties and the internal membership has direct roots in the commercial market orientation literature, Ormrod (2005) argues that it is necessary to include an explicit focus on the societal context within which the political organisation exists. Whilst not well researched in the commercial market orientation literature (Kang and James, 2007), the inclusion of an explicit orientation towards various important groups in society makes it possible to understand the interplay of member orientations towards the media, citizens, and interest and lobby groups whilst retaining a wider focus. Citizens are conceptualised as distinct from voters because of the nature of the exchange relationships that exist between each of them and parties; for example, the interaction between voters and the party occurs simultaneously (on election day), whilst the interaction between citizens is ongoing throughout the electoral period (Henneberg and Ormrod, 2013).

So rather than an orientation towards society as a whole as originally proposed by Ormrod (2005), the PMO model considers a holistic interpretation of 'society' to be conceptually exogenous to the model, with the specific stakeholder groups forming the elements that are endogenous to the model (Ormrod, 2011). Society as an overarching construct can be described as 'transient and turbulent' (Heidar and Saglie, 2003: 222) which affects the ability of party leaders to implement specific strategies that are necessary to achieve long-term aims. This results in a tension: party leaders have to make tough decisions on behalf of their organisations (Strøm and Müller, 1999: 1), yet the decisions made by party members – especially in the case of the convinced ideologist strategic type – may inhibit leaderships from pursing their strategic aims.

Once the strategic profile has been identified, the party invests resources to develop the appropriate stakeholder relationships whilst reducing the resources that are used to maintain others; a good example of this is the removal of the block vote from the trade union members in the British Labour Party during the party's 'modernisation' process in the mid-1990s, a response to opinion poll data which revealed that Labour was widely perceived as being 'unelectable' (Gould, 1999). In addition to this, strategic profiles can provide information about the way in which information is used in the party; for example, Pedersen and Saglie (2005) found that inactive members did not use the party intranet for participation, indicating that other methods could be more efficient at including the rank and file in the offering development process.

The PMO profile can arguably be used to understand other party organisational typologies. For example, Panebianco's (1988) electoral/professional party type emphasises the role of the party top and the estrangement of the volunteer membership; in this case only the party top would exhibit high values of market orientation focused on the importance of voters and the media at the expense of the membership, with information being disseminated to volunteer party members on a need-to-know basis. In the following section we provide a specific link between the elements of the profiles and the political science literature concerning party organisational structure. We focus on the example of Heidar and Saglie's (2003) network party to demonstrate how PMO profiles can help us understand the orientation of parties towards stakeholders and the associated member behaviours.

The PMO profile of the network party

Heidar and Saglie's (2003) network party emphasises that parties are embedded within an environment characterised by dynamic relationships of different strength, duration and intensity, and where relationships with stakeholder groups outside of the party can directly impact upon internal offering development processes. It also provides a stark contrast to the more common perception of political marketing as being most appropriate for understanding the behaviour of parties that exhibit characteristics of Panebianco's (1988) electoral/professional party model, that is, a focus on those activities of party professionals and elected members that support the sole aim of winning elections. The conclusion of Heidar and Saglie

(2003) is that parties are increasingly embracing network organisational structures, but that the extent to which they do this will vary according to existing organisational structures and party goals (Gibson and Ward, 2009).

Heidar and Saglie (2003) develop Koole's (1994) 'modern cadre party' and to a lesser extent Duverger's (1954) 'mass party' by integrating the internal and external environments within a single 'network party' model, acknowledging that party tradition is as essential to a party's identity as its responsiveness to the technological and social dynamics of the political sphere. This permeability of the boundaries between the organisation and its environment reflects the 'double membership' of party and other organisations that is especially visible in the case of the convinced ideologist SPP. Heidar and Saglie's (2003) network party model has seven core characteristics that centre on the relationship between the party elite and wider membership, the way in which the party is organised and financed, and the party's relationships with internal and external stakeholders. When developing the party's offering, the network party is arranged around 'thematic network structures' that enable a greater inclusion of external stakeholders in internal discussions (Heidar and Saglie, 2003). The network organisational structure also enables members and non-members to be more selective in the issues to which they contribute, thus enabling interest and knowledge to drive participation in the thematic networks (Heidar and Saglie, 2003). In this sense the idea of stakeholders in the PMO is useful as here it is possible to isolate the sources of information which in turn are used to inform party strategies.

For a typical network party, specific stakeholder groups are prioritised together with an explicit emphasis on the importance of information in the offering development process via thematic networks (Heidar and Saglie, 2003). As a PMO is not an 'either–or' proposition, members can be market-oriented to a greater or lesser degree depending on, for example, their level of activity or position in the party hierarchy. Again, here there are parallels in the political science literature. Membership ballots as proposed by Heidar and Saglie (2003) and Katz and Mair (1995) are a mechanism through which party elites are able to bypass existing institutional party structures and have direct access to party members. What becomes clear is that the party literature and the PMO highlight two sides of the same coin and the ways in which party elites can seek both to include and exclude information gathered from the membership. Moreover, what is also highlighted here is the way in which the tensions between these competing interests may lead to privileging of one set of stakeholders over another; stakeholders themselves may have conflicts of interests. What the PMO facilitates is clear exposition of these competing interests and how these serve to shape party strategy.

For the members of a network party, the ICT-based organisation of the party facilitates the dissemination of generated information to those members who want to participate in developing the party offering (Gibson and Ward, 2009), which in turn supports a consistent interpretation of the offering (Shapiro, 1988). Integrating thematic networks into the organisational structure of the party supports the internal orientation of party members. By extension this is also valid for other, sympathetic stakeholders in the political sphere (Heidar and Saglie, 2003); it is acknowledged that selected citizens, and interest and lobby groups, can also contribute with their knowledge and opinions on elements of the offering (Ormrod, 2011). At election time there is a change in the focal stakeholders that reflects the nature of political competition both before and after the election (Bowler and Farrell, 1992).

Conclusion

A PMO perspective does not simply proscribe particular tools from the realm of political marketing management, and neither does it limit its explanandum to the structural boundaries delineating the party offering or to a professional focus towards marketing this offering. Instead, understanding the nature and extent of the party's level of PMO towards each of the stakeholder groups and the effect this has on the behaviour of party members can be used to construct a strategic profile. The strategic profile can in turn be used to inform organisational decisions regarding the development of the party's offering, rather than being the reason for them (Ormrod and Henneberg, 2010). Thus an explicit awareness of strategic profiles draws attention to the way in which key stakeholders are identified as important to the organisation.

Strategic profiles are limited in that they cannot provide answers to normative questions regarding to what extent parties *should* strive towards being facilitators of stakeholder participation in the democratic process, or which party structure is the most appropriate to enable the desired level of participation. However, strategic profiles can provide a framework for understanding the development and management of the relationships that exist between members and important stakeholder groups, together with providing an analytic foundation for integrating the organisational structure with appropriate strategies and tactics with which to achieve party aims. In short, concepts developed from the commercial marketing literature can be integrated and used to help understand rather than replace existing political science models of party organisation.

Discussion questions

- Think about the political parties in your national system. Which of the four alternative postures do these parties adopt? Use the PMO profile to support your arguments.
- Is there an ideal PMO profile in your national party system?
- Is the PMO profile of the political lightweight possible to use in practice?

Key terms	
Strategic political postures	The Tactical Populist
Political market orientation	The Relationship Builder
The Political Lightweight	PMO profile
The Convinced Ideologist	

Further reading

Ormrod and Henneberg (2010): This article forms part of the backbone of this chapter (along with Ormrod and Savigny, 2012). Reading the original article will provide you with a more detailed understanding of the relationship between strategic political postures and political market orientation.

Ormrod and Savigny (2012): This article too forms part of the backbone of the chapter (along with Ormrod and Henneberg, 2010). Reading the original article will help you to understand the relationship between political market orientation and alternative party organisational types as discussed in the political science literature.

Henneberg (2006): This article provides an in-depth treatment of the four strategic postures.

References

Aaker, D.A. (2001) *Strategic Marketing Management*. New York: Wiley.

Bowler, S. and Farrell, D.M. (eds) (1992) *Electoral Strategies and Political Marketing*. London: Macmillan.

Bowler, S. and Farrell, D.M. (eds) (1992), *Electoral Strategies and Political Marketing*. London: Macmillan.

Butler, P. and Collins, N. (1996) 'Strategic analysis in political markets', *European Journal of Marketing*, 30 (10): 25–36.

Davis, F.W. and Manrodt, K.B. (1996) *Customer-Responsive Management*. Oxford: Blackwell.

Detterbeck, K. (2005) 'Cartel parties in Western Europe?', *Party Politics*, 11 (2): 173–91.

Duverger, M. (1954) *Political Parties: Their Organization and Activities in the Modern State*. London: Methuen.

Gainer, B. and Padanyi P. (2005) 'The relationship between market-oriented activities and market-oriented culture: implications for the development of market orientation in nonprofit service organizations', *Journal of Business Research*, 58 (6): 854–62.

Gibson, R. and Ward, S. (2009) 'Parties in the digital age – a review article', *Representation*, 45 (1): 87–100.

Gould, P. (1999) *The Unfinished Revolution: How the Modernisers Saved the Labour Party*. London: Abacus.

Heath, A., Jowell, R. and Curtice, J.K. (1985) *How Britain Votes*. Oxford: Pergamon Press.

Heidar, K. and Saglie, J. (2003) 'Predestined parties? Organizational change in Norwegian political parties', *Party Politics*, 9 (2): 219–39.

Hellensen, S. (2003) *Marketing Management*. Harlow: Prentice Hall.

Henneberg, S.C. (2006) 'Leading or following? A theoretical analysis of political marketing postures', *Journal of Political Marketing*, 5 (3): 29–46.

Henneberg, S.C. and Ormrod, R.P. (forthcoming) 'A triadic interaction model of political marketing exchange', *Marketing Theory*.

Henneberg, S.C. and O'Shaughnessy, N.J. (2007) 'Theory and concept development in political marketing: issues and an agenda', *Journal of Political Marketing*, 6 (2/3): 5–31.

Henneberg, S.C. and O'Shaughnessy, N.J. (2009) 'Political relationship marketing: some macro/micro thoughts', *Journal of Marketing Management*, 25 (1): 5–29.

Kang, G.-D. and James, J. (2007) 'Revisiting the concept of a societal orientation: conceptualization and delineation', *Journal of Business Ethics*, 73: 301–18.

Katz, R.S. and Mair, P. (1995) 'Changing models of party organization and party democracy: the emergence of the cartel party', *Party Politics*, 1 (5): 5–28.

Kirchheimer, O. (1966) 'The transformation of Western European party systems', in J. LaPalombara and M. Weiner (eds), *Political Parties and Political Development*. Princeton, NJ: Princeton University Press, 177–200.

Koole, R. (1994) 'The vulnerability of the modern cadre party in the Netherlands', in R.S. Katz and P. Mair (eds), *How Parties Organize: Change and Adaptation in Party Organizations in Western Democracies*. London: Sage, 278–303.

Kotzaivazoglou, I. (2011) 'Political marketing in the Greek context: does market orientation exist?', *International Review of Public and Nonprofit Marketing*, 8, 41–56.

Lilleker, D.G. (2005) 'The impact of political marketing on internal party democracy', *Parliamentary Affairs*, 58 (3): 570–84.

Narver, J.C. and Slater, S.F. (1990) 'The effect of market orientation on business profitability', *Journal of Marketing*, 54: 20–35.

Olson, E.M., Slater, S.F. and Hult, G.T.M. (2005) 'The performance implications of fit among business strategy, marketing organizational structure, and strategic behavior', *Journal of Marketing*, 69 (July): 49–65.

Ormrod, R.P. (2005) 'A conceptual model of political market orientation', *Journal of Nonprofit and Public Sector Marketing*, 14 (1/2): 47–64.

Ormrod, R.P. (2011) 'Politisk markedsorientering', in S. Winther Nielsen (ed.) *Politisk Marketing*. Copenhagen: Karnov Group, 207–236.

Ormrod, R.P. and Henneberg, S.C. (2009) 'Different facets of market orientation – a comparative analysis of party manifestos', *Journal of Political Marketing*, 8 (3): 190–208.

Ormrod, R.P. and Henneberg, S.C. (2010) 'Strategic political postures and political market orientation: towards an integrated concept of political marketing strategy', *Journal of Political Marketing*, 9 (4): 294–313.

Ormrod, R.P. and Savigny, H. (2012) 'Political market orientation: a framework for understanding relationship structures in political parties', *Party Politics*, 18 (4): 487–502.

Ormrod, R.P., Henneberg, S.C., Zaefarian, G. and de Vries, P. (2010) 'Relationship structures and performance of Belgian political parties', competitive paper presented at the International Conference on Political Marketing, Thessaloniki, September.

Panebianco, A. (1988) *Political Parties: Organisation and Power*. Cambridge: Cambridge University Press.

Pedersen, K. and Saglie, J. (2005) 'New technology in ageing parties: internet use in Danish and Norwegian parties', *Party Politics*, 11 (3): 359–77.

Sarlvik, B. and Crewe, I. (1983) *Decade of Dealignment*. Cambridge: Cambridge University Press.

Savigny, H. (2008) *The Problem of Political Marketing*. New York: Continuum.

Shapiro, B.P. (1988) 'What the hell is market oriented?', *Harvard Business Review*, 66 (November/December): 119–25.

Slater, S.F. and Narver, J.C. (1999) 'Market-oriented is more than being customer-led', *Strategic Management Journal*, 20: 1165–8.

Strøm, K. and Müller, W.C. (1999) 'Political parties and hard choices', in W.C. Müller and K. Strøm (eds), *Policy, Office, or Votes? How Political Parties in Western Europe Make Hard Decisions*. Cambridge: Cambridge University Press, 1–35.

Wolinetz. S.B. (2002) 'Beyond the catch-all party: approaches to the study of parties and party systems in contemporary democracies', in R. Gunther, J.R. Montero and J. Linz (eds), *Political Parties: Old Concepts and New Challenges*. Oxford: Oxford University Press.

Chapter 11 is developed from Ormrod, R.P. and Henneberg, S.C. (2010) 'Strategic political postures and political market orientation: toward an integrated concept of political marketing strategy', *Journal of Political Marketing*, 9 (4): 294–313. Reprinted by permission of Taylor & Francis (www.tandfonline.com).

12 Symbolism in Political Marketing

After reading this chapter, you should be able to:

- describe the concept of the symbolic government
- identify the use of symbolism, rhetoric and imagery in communications by political actors
- identify symbolic acts by political actors and what these acts,attempt to achieve.

Introduction

Communication has always been a central activity in political marketing; without being able to get the message out, voters and other stakeholders will not be aware of what the politician or party is offering and will be less inclined to give their support. Whilst much has been written about the use of tools from commercial marketing and how they can contribute to getting a candidate elected through a modified marketing process, little has been written on the way in which governments use symbols to justify their policy initiatives rather than looking at the processes surrounding concrete message development and communication. Therefore, in line with the focus of this book on theory and concepts, we go one level of abstraction upwards from communication tools and focus on the **symbolic government**. To illustrate this complex subject – symbolic government – we will draw on the work of O'Shaughnessy (2003, 2004) and use the rather extreme example of the British Labour Party in government between 1997 and 2002, a period during which journalists become increasingly aware of the communication style that characterised the symbolic government. In addition to this, we use the case of the Labour Party's justification for entering the war against Iraq to demonstrate how symbolism can be linked to a specific event.

The symbolic government: a new idea in politics?

The importance of managing a government's communication is increasingly rivalling the management of the state itself; modern leaders are continually aware of the **symbolism** of the **rhetoric** and **imagery** that they are communicating to stakeholders, and how this symbolism may enhance or distort the leader's status. Thus presidential adviser Dick Morris warned Clinton about his appearance, with a rock star, on a yacht, in Martha's Vineyard: the accumulated associations of all of these elements were offensive to Middle America. The symbolic government of Ronald Reagan was managed via a series of symbolic visual episodes (e.g. Reagan on the Dunkirk beaches) that telegraphed the core values of his presidency. Symbolic people were also incorporated into these episodes, such as the teenage volunteer among the homeless introduced by Reagan. During the wars in Afghanistan and Iraq, all of George W. Bush's actions were permeated with symbolism – the flying jackets, the backdrops of military personnel, the jet landing on the aircraft carrier, and so on (O'Shaughnessy, 2004). However, symbolism can backfire when it is exposed as being a manipulation, as when boxes of ostensibly American export goods, used as a backdrop by Bush, were exposed by the *New York Times* as having their 'Made in China' labels taped over.

The use of symbols to persuade is what Mayhew (1997) calls 'the rhetoric of presentation', since the display of symbols is generally more persuasive than political arguments put forward in a discussion. **Symbolic acts** have been at the heart of politics almost since recorded history began. What is often regarded as great political leadership is in fact the supreme sensitivity to symbols and a mastery of their manipulation. Mahatma Gandhi, for example, was the magician of symbols; the symbolism of his clothing and the spinning wheel, with their message of simplicity and self-reliance, spoke both to his followers and to the British imperial rulers he wished to influence. Gandhi's Great Salt March was a masterpiece of symbolism, with its message that India's natural bounty, sea salt, was being absurdly taxed by her colonial rulers (O'Shaughnessy, 2003).

Symbolic government is a style of government where the creation of symbolic images and actions and celebratory rhetoric have become a principal concern (O'Shaughnessy, 2003). This is equally valid for opposition political actors, but is more extreme in incumbents, hence our primary focus on symbolic *government*. Appearances do not just matter to the symbolic government; they are central to the way in which voters are communicated with. Symbolic government is a relatively new kind of government; this is not to say that previous regimes did not engage in it frequently, but what was once just one of several tools of government has now graduated into becoming its central organising principle, absorbing therefore much of the energy of government.

Outside of the home of spin in the USA, an increase in the importance of image management could already be seen in Europe in 1990s Britain. In the mid-1990s, the media did not quite know what to make of the new political communications advisers, many of whom had been imported from the USA. The comprehensiveness of the way in which all aspects of communication were managed by the 1997–2002 Labour government was partly a response to many years of sustained media persecution of especially Labour politicians, as exemplified by the *Sun*'s (8 April 1992) eight-page feature entitled 'Nightmare on Kinnock Street' as its preamble to the 1992 general election. Due to its frequency, many people simply took it for granted that the Labour government (and increasingly the parliamentary opposition) professionally manipulated – put a **spin** on – the images, press releases and communications that the public received. It was not only because of its use in the political sphere that 'spin' became a household word: 'spin' also became a popular term in the field of entertainment, for example in soaps (*The West Wing, Spin City*) and dramas (Kosminsky and Jackson's *The Practice*).

So how does this chapter differ from other accounts of the rise of rhetoric and imagery in politics? Our central argument is that, although the processes and mindsets that focus on presenting a favourable account of political events to the media are well understood, the larger picture is often ignored – the extent to which the entire apparatus of government has become preoccupied with the pursuit of managing symbolism through the use of rhetoric and imagery. The word 'spin' is descriptively inadequate, as a 'spin government' would primarily concentrate on the processes involved in developing effective sound bites. It is obvious, however, that much more is going on. Symbolic government is arguably a more nuanced and more substantial concept, with 'spin' being but one of many tools with which to communicate with voters through the mass media (O'Shaughnessy, 2003).

The idea of symbolic government

The modern symbolic government is therefore not the same as a government which uses rhetoric and symbolic actions from time to time as one of a number of governing instruments. The persuasion concept forms the essence of the political culture of a symbolic government, and as it lacks a guiding ideology or core beliefs, at least in the eyes of its critics, it may even seem that the purpose of power has become power itself. Symbolic governments campaign permanently, and what is critical to them is the appearance of momentum. The symbolic government is also government by narratives, small stories by which governments account for their daily work, and by meta-narratives, the big themes that provide a coherent structure for the understanding of the smaller narratives. The symbolic government tells stories about itself, and a good story beats logic or reason (Simmons, 2000).

Symbolic government is unthinkable without leaders who are actors as well as enactors; they perform. In America this is arguably a consequence of the tripartite role of the US president as figurehead, chief executive and commander-in-chief of the armed forces. Ronald Reagan defined the essence of the symbolic presidency, and his successors are his imitators. President Clinton's use of symbols and rhetoric was in some ways a development of the Reagan politics of imagery. Reagan's intimate rhetorical style was reflected in Clinton's 'I feel your pain' pose, and Labour Party leader Tony Blair's style owed much to Clinton's example of how a left-leaning leader can successfully appeal to the middle class.

The structure of symbolic government may be seen as comprising a number of components. Key amongst these are the constant assertion of progress in all areas of government; using statistics as 'proof' and to confuse the issue in question; symbolic actions and subjects of attack; exaggerated language; the generation of 'tableaux' (symbol-rich theatrical scenes such as photo opportunities with politically significant groups); an acute sensitivity to imagery and its management; and, on occasion, the manufacture of enemies or targets of derision (O'Shaughnessy, 2003). As can be seen, the two central components of symbolic government are rhetoric and symbolism, that is, the verbal and the visual. These components are in essence based on image: one creates images from language, the other from vivid pictures. In contrast to other styles of governing, the verbal and visual are interdependent in the context of symbolic government.

The foundation for symbolic government: Labour in opposition

Political parties and governments have always used persuasion in some way or another to achieve their aims. Until recently this was mainly in the form of rhetoric, but with the rise of the mass media and voting rights to all citizens over the age of 18, a more accessible method of communication had to be developed. The Labour Party discovered this to their cost in the general election of 1983; the party leader, Michael Foot, was seen as a competent orator but lacked media presence. Whilst not the only reason for the Labour Party's defeat at the election, it did not help. A similar demonstration of the power of the mass media came in the 1992 general election, when the mainly Conservative-supporting newspapers made a concerted effort to discredit the Labour Party. Despite leading in the opinion polls at the beginning of the campaign, the power of the mass media to influence voters was demonstrated and, once more, the Labour Party was defeated.

Lessons were also learned by the Labour Party from the various scandals that befell the Conservative government between 1992 and 1997. A good example of this in the context of rhetoric and symbolic actions is the government's handling of the BSE crisis in the mid-1990s. BSE (Bovine Spongiform encepha-lopathy) is a degenerative brain disease that can be passed to humans through contaminated meat from certain areas of the animal (principally the brain and spinal column). The Conservative government saw the BSE crisis as a technical problem that could be solved with a technical solution, the culling of poten-tially infected cattle. The Conservative government did not fully recognise the role of rhetoric and symbolic actions in an event that was characterised by public safety fears that could not be changed by logical argument. Government press releases concentrated on explaining the technical features of the disease and the government's response in equally technical terms; symbolic actions were not well thought through, such as Agriculture Minister John Gummer eating a hamburger at a photo opportunity and offering it to his daughter. The mass media were forced to create their own, more graphic explanation that could be understood by the general public (which they did with much enthu-siasm), and Gummer's symbolic action was framed by the media as being in bad taste rather than emphasising that British beef was safe to eat.

Obviously, something had to change in the Labour Party if it was to regain power. Apart from the obligatory election of a new party leader, the Labour Party realised that it would have to change the way in which it communi-cated with voters. These changes towards the comprehensive use of symbol-ism began in earnest in 1994 following the untimely death of Labour leader John Smith. With the election of Tony Blair as party leader, several initiatives were put in place to ensure victory in the subsequent general election which would take place in 1997 at the latest. Public concerns over the historically close links between the Labour Party and the trade unions were acted on in 1995 with the repealing of Clause IV of the Labour Party constitution (which emphasised the working class as the key group that the party would repre-sent), and efforts were made to reach out to employer organisations and business leaders to demonstrate that the Labour Party was willing to sup-port the interests of the private sector. The Labour Party also realised that the majority of voters used the mass media as the main source of their political information, a result of a decreasing involvement in politics and the rise of the 'floating voter', individuals who base their voting choice on immediate needs rather than partisan, class-based loyalties (Zuckerman, 1982). Political news was becoming 'consumed' rather than actively sought out by voters, and so the Labour Party began to tightly manage how it was presented in the media through its rhetoric and symbolism.

Rhetoric

Rhetoric is at the core of political persuasion. Rhetoric emphasises the precise meaning of the words that are used in the description both of the problem and the alternative solutions that exist, and these descriptions can vary in persuasive content. Descriptions connect a theme with our key emotional concerns, thus raising the possibility of a change in perspectives. The power of rhetoric has been suspect from antiquity: it was pseudo-reason, seen as using symbols of rationality to bypass the scrutiny of reason. Plato attacked orators for possessing beliefs rather than knowledge. Mason (1989) argues that rhetoric can only ever flourish in the realms of opinion, for the activity of persuasion never permanently ceases, and that rhetoric only fails if it is possible to be completely certain.

Rhetoric is often considered to be synonymous with the word 'empty'. As a judgement of value, the use of the word 'empty' is arguably legitimate, but as a judgement of significance this is not true. Rhetoric provides something around which thoughts can be structured: an image, words or a feeling (Mason, 1989). Language does not simply declare a stance on an issue; it provides a biased perception of that issue. Foulkes (1983) and the wartime diarist Victor Klemperer (1998) argue that one of the rhetorical achievements of the National Socialist (Nazi) Party of the Third Reich was to ensure that specific words and phrases entered everyday language, so much so that they became embedded in the culture. Words and phrases are not neutral tools but embody perspectives, and control over the language of the discussion enables control over the perception of the issue; the 'Newspeak' developed in George Orwell's novel *Nineteen Eighty-Four* is a classic example (Orwell, 1949). Language is not merely the vehicle for articulating our thoughts; it creates meaning, making us think in certain ways: 'language does more than merely express reality; it actively structures experience ... language and linguistic devices structure how we think about things' (Umberson and Henderson, 1992). Language and rhetoric are active agents for the creation of perception.

The British Labour Party used several rhetorical elements in the 1997 general election campaign and continued this after winning a majority in the British parliament (Jones, 1999: 22). Campaign slogans such as 'education, education, education', 'tough on crime, tough on the causes of crime' and 'it's time for a change' were all more about reflecting the public mood than about concrete policy pledges. Austin (1976) terms these sound bites as 'performatives', where the aim is to focus on the dramatic element of the phrase. Austin (1976) contrasts this with 'constative' statements that can be true or false – truth and falsehood are not relevant to sound bites phrased in a performative style. This performative rhetoric was continued in government, the prime example being the 1999 budget that contained headlines such as 'building a better society'.

The rhetorical vision

In addition to performative rhetoric, the Labour Party developed certain policies based on the rhetorical value of the policy rather than on research into the needs of society. Thus the political vision of the party was based to a certain extent on the political rhetoric of the party, hence the term **rhetorical vision**. Symbolic governments emphasise the way in which rhetoric is linked with an image – a rhetorical vision – of an 'ideal state', rather than as a measured response to a felt need or an analysis of the results of the needs of society. An example of this was the Labour Party's vision of sending 50 per cent of the British population to university (O'Shaughnessy, 2003). The question is, why precisely 50 per cent? There had been no investigation into the educational profile needs of British society that had recommended this figure and, when announced, the proposal had not been costed to see whether it was financially feasible or not.

As a rhetorical vision, 50 per cent was, however, a number that suggested democratic empowerment and participation of half the population in an institution that had until recently been the preserve of a small elite. Opponents could be declared elitist by definition since they were against the plan to encourage a larger percentage of the British population to become university educated. Thus the rhetorical vision arguably led the development of the specifics of policy, rather than the other way round. This method of policy development was also a characteristic of the 1997 election campaign: uncosted promises on class sizes, tax, jobs, health service and crime, communicated as 'big ideas' for a stakeholder society (O'Shaughnessy, 2003).

Spin and the presentation of policy

The rhetorical aspects of symbolic government are often called 'spin' by the general public. The ancestry of spin lies with Cicero and Aristotle and rests upon the recognition that all events are open to interpretation; this is why history books continue to be written, as historical 'facts' are interpreted differently by different people at different points in time. Indeed, for Nietzsche, all thought arose out of alternative perspectives; there are no 'true' facts, only interpretations. Putting a spin on a particular policy means framing the policy – spin-doctoring – in a way that connects the policy to the concerns of the target audience, to their values and sense, and their lack of control over the issue of concern. Spin involves providing the intended audience with an interpretation, especially an interpretation that is memorable and coherent, and successful spin quickly gains acceptance as the perspective from which the policy is viewed.

Putting a spin on an issue involves carefully developing the style and tone of the language – the specific words – that are used to present that issue. An example given by Boardman (1978) is of a denial by President Nixon that uses words in such a way that what he did not say is more important than what he actually did say: 'none of these [illegal activities] took place with my specific approval or knowledge'. A superficial interpretation leads to the conclusion that Nixon did not know about the illegal activities. However, note the use of the word specific – how could Nixon know about every single one of the illegal activities? Replace the word 'specific' with 'general' and the quote takes on a whole new meaning. Nixon could quite possibly have given his 'general' approval to carry out illegal activities without interfering with how his commanders decided to achieve the 'specific' goals of the administration.

Equally, though, spin is about concealing the negative aspects of the policy for the target audience, often by confusing people or boring them so that they look no further. Spin is about selectivity, being 'economical with the truth', as the originators of the policy recognise that the media and general public usually have a limited attention span. Budget proposals under the British Labour government were presented in such a way as to make it difficult to follow the way in which the tax system was structured. For example, it was necessary to read different chapters to calculate the taxes that citizens paid, and capital spending was excluded. Some commentators accused the Labour government of disguising tax increases behind technical language, and towards the end of the party's first term in government in 2001, newspapers that supported the opposition Conservative Party were claiming that British people were paying one billion more in tax than when Labour came to power in 1997 (*Daily Telegraph*, 23 May 2001). However, due to the spin put on the presentation of these changes to the tax structure, individuals and even the media were not able to decipher these new taxes; for example, whilst not immediately obvious, the abolition of pension funds' ability to reclaim dividend tax credits amounted to a £6 billion a year annual tax on retirement savings (Draper, 1997).

Spin can also be used to describe a policy initiative in particularly glowing terms. In one period, Labour Party leader Tony Blair made fifty-three speeches and used the word 'modernisation' eighty-seven times. The following press release – where the word modernisation is used (only) three times – illustrates the way in which a simple initiative can be described in such a way as to paint a more positive picture than is arguably necessary:

> 'Mr Milburn will be creating a top-level NHS modernisation board to drive through the changes in the NHS. In a move designed to overturn traditional Whitehall bureaucracy and hierarchy, board membership would include the brightest and best modernisers in the health service. The changes signal a vote of confidence in front line clinicians and managers who are consistently trail-blazing new ideas. These are the people at the rock face with the experience and enthusiasm to drive home the modernisation programme.'
>
> (Quoted in *The Times*, February 2001)

So the question is, what exactly is being announced in this press release? Despite the positive, dynamic language – a vote of confidence for the trail-blazing, front line, top-level, brightest and best NHS modernisers at the rock-face – the simplest interpretation is that Mr Milburn is setting up a committee. Along with the words praising NHS staff, an enemy is created: the traditional Whitehall hierarchy and their bureaucracy. It almost seems to be taken from the plot of a Hollywood movie, where the heroes (the NHS) and villains (the civil service) fight against each other, and in true Hollywood style the heroes always win. One thing that must be remembered is that the press release did not lie; however, its presentation – the spin that was put on the initiative – arguably exceeded that which was necessary to get the message about the initiative across to the relevant audience.

Symbolism

Symbols are flexible in that each individual has their own interpretation of the meaning of the symbol, although specific symbols may mean a very similar thing to a wide variety of people. A symbol is understood by most people to be a visual image or a tangible object, but a symbol can also be a sequence of expressive actions. Statistics can also provide support to symbols if they are used to illustrate a particular perspective on a policy initiative; they provide quantifiable, empirical 'proof' of the importance or success of a particular initiative.

Symbolic actions

The Labour Party used symbolic actions, in the form of policy initiatives, to demonstrate to the general public that the government was dealing with the problems of society. For example, the Labour Party announced that crime committed by children would be cut by introducing curfews for under-tens and formal punishment for juvenile offenders, and that schools would be improved by enabling teachers who did not live up to certain performance criteria to be fired in four weeks. Other social problems were to be tackled by adopting the European Social Charter and the introduction of a minimum wage (Draper, 1997). However, critics pointed out that these initiatives tended to be in the form of solutions that were designed to solve the immediate problem rather than tackle the underlying cause.

A symbolic government uses symbolic actions to a large extent as policy initiatives give an impression of dynamism which can be used to silence those critics who complain about official inactivity. Symbolic actions in the form of policy initiatives were used to such a degree by the Labour government that some argued that policy initiatives were the only way in which the party could deal with social problems. Probably the most visible example of this were the policy initiatives announced by Home Secretary David Blunkett at a rate of more than one a week between June 2001 and April 2002 (*Daily*

Telegraph, 16 April 2002). Many of these initiatives involved creating commit-tees or slight changes to existing legislation, such as a task force to protect children on the internet, new guidelines for tackling drug dealers on housing estates, a crime summit to be held at the prime minister's London residence at 10 Downing Street and a new advisory panel for victims of crime.

Symbolic statistics

Modern society is characterised by the use of statistics in order to 'prove' that a particular perspective on an issue or policy initiative is the most appropriate. Traditional rhetoric, with its focus on persuasion by the use of words, is considered to be less powerful unless the arguments are supported by scientific evidence. Symbolic governments use statistics both as support for policy initiatives but also as symbols of the success of previous policy initiatives. At one point, the Labour government realised that it was becom-ing vulnerable on issues related to healthcare. On 11 April 2002, statistics were announced that demonstrated that the number of patients who had been waiting for an operation for more than fifteen months had been reduced to only two; however, the average amount of time that people had waited for an operation had gone up. It is probably important to remember the quote often attributed to British prime minister Benjamin Disraeli: 'There are three kinds of lies: lies, damned lies and statistics.'

The Labour Party made wide use of statistics by setting quantifiable per-formance criteria to assess the success of institutions such as schools, the police and hospitals. As symbolic governments need succinct, easy-to-interpret numbers that can support their claims, having several statistics for each per-formance measure makes persuasive communication more difficult. Therefore, the Labour government popularised the use of single figures such as hospital waiting lists or school league tables based on exam results as the criteria against which state institutions could be judged. However, in some cases this led to somewhat dubious practices: 'in one case, patients were asked by telephone when they were going on holiday, then given dates for their operations in that period' (National Audit Office, 19 December 2001). In addition to this, qual-itative data was simply not used – what could not be measured did not figure in the success criteria.

Implementation of symbolic government

Control

Symbolic government is not just about accepting that rhetoric and spin are essential tools in modern political communication, but that symbolism is ingrained in the very philosophy of the party. Control over the party message is the alpha and omega; party professionals – whether they are elected representatives or hired political managers – have to make sure that there is consistency in everything that is communicated by the party. Party professionals in a symbolic government also have to make sure that discipline is maintained amongst members to accept party policies, as successful persuasion is consistent persuasion. This can sometimes lead to a backlash by certain members of the party; the Labour Party went to great lengths to ensure that members who protested against the party leadership were sidelined and that internal political debate, when it occurred, was kept behind closed doors and a united front was provided for the cameras.

This importance of control via centralised command was one of the central lessons that the Labour Party learned from the election campaigns run by US President Bill Clinton, and this lesson was applied both in the immediate campaign period leading up to the 1997 general election and in the much longer 'pre-campaign campaign' period from 1995 on. Before the election campaign proper began, a comprehensive plan was drawn up that coordinated photo opportunities, news conferences, campaign posters and party political broadcasts (Jones, 1997). During the campaign itself there was an emphasis on control – nothing was left to chance and the number of potentially uncontrollable events was kept to a minimum; Labour Party leader Tony Blair only spoke directly with the press three times (*Independent*, 1997) and even the cheering crowds who met Blair on his arrival at 10 Downing Street were choreographed (*Sunday Times*, 1997).

Rebuttal and media manipulation

Rebuttal can be understood as a process that a political party can use to demonstrate that claims made by an opponent are false (Baines, 2001). Rebuttal is a key activity of a symbolic government in that it enables the party to integrate rhetoric, spin and statistics in one message that demonstrates that the accusation made by competing parties or the media is false as the problem has already been addressed using a policy proposal or initiative that is linked to the overall rhetorical vision of the party. The Millbank headquarters of the Labour Party functioned during the 1997 election campaign as the hub of a complex information analysis, storage and retrieval system called 'Excalibur' which enabled instant access to documents, speeches, statistics, backgrounds and press cuttings (Jones, 1997). Campaigners and representatives in the field were linked via the internet, telephone and fax to the Excalibur system, which enabled them to quickly answer any challenges using up-to-date knowledge; that the system was centrally located enabled the top of the Labour Party to remain in control of the overall message.

The symbolic government recognises the importance of the media as the main channel through which the symbolic vision is presented to voters.

There is to a certain extent a joint reliance of political parties and the media; parties need the media to communicate their message whilst the media needs content in order to sell its product (Róka, 1999). In contrast to countries where the media is a state monopoly (the former Soviet Union and North Korea) or where political leaders own or have the openly partisan support of certain media (Berlusconi in Italy), parties in some democracies, including Britain, do not own or control newspapers or television stations. Thus media manipulation is distinguishable from media propaganda, where influence over the message is a result of private wealth or state control. So in Britain, political parties in general, and symbolic governments in particular, must rely on the integration of symbols, spin, images and the party's rhetorical vision to shape the message that is received by voters.

The Labour Party recognised that the both the media and the party message had to be controlled if the party was to successfully transmit its symbolic vision to voters. This was the core strategy for electioneering and subsequently for governing; the campaign culture permeated government. The central strategic and communications unit coordinated messages across government departments and organised spin-doctoring activities. The media was manipulated by giving private briefings to journalists who adopted a pro-governmental view on issues. The government also enjoyed the services of seventy special advisers, as the Labour government recognised that, in order to successfully pursue advocacy, it was necessary to employ advocates (O'Shaughnessy, 2003). Traditionally independent government press officers insisted that government departments ought to provide information, not advocate government policy, but after the first year in power, the Labour Party had replaced twenty-four of the forty-four department heads and deputy heads.

The consequences of symbolic government

Symbolic government has consequences, both immediate and long term. The immediate effect of the presentation of a party's rhetorical vision through spin and symbolic actions is to provide the public with a 'feel-good factor', creating positive images and symbols of the new society that the incumbent party will take them to. However, in the long term there is inevitably a difference between the rhetorical vision provided by the government and the reality in which voters find themselves. Symbols of the new society do not materialise as policy initiatives are designed to provide solutions to immediate problems, rather than tackling the wider problems in society at their roots. The fact that the reality that voters find themselves in is very different from the rhetorical vision of the government leads to cynicism amongst voters – the promises of a bright new future have been broken. As the mass media becomes more and more aware of the difference between the party's rhetorical vision and the reality in which voters find themselves, the symbolic government is forced to exert even more control over the way in which its messages are presented to voters. This inevitably results in an attempt to further manipulate the media; at its worst, the symbolic government can assume authoritarian characteristics in its handling of the media.

Media manipulation

An example of how the symbolic government manipulates the media is through the incumbent's use of information. If the symbolic government does not want information to be found, it can make it difficult for the media to do its job of keeping the government in check. At the same time, the symbolic government feeds the media with large amounts of information on trivial policy initiatives in order to keep the media busy. Spin, rhetoric and symbolic actions are made artificially dramatic in order to provide the print media with interesting stories that can help sell newspapers, despite the openly adversarial relationship between the symbolic government and the media.

The Labour Party when in government was good at feeding the press with large amounts of information; in addition to this, the party began to announce existing policy initiatives as fresh news, to reallocate general funding to specific initiatives and to hide the source of spending promises behind symbolic statistics. For example, 'When Alan Milburn announced ... that ward sisters would be given £5000 to improve their patients' environment it was welcomed ... But six weeks later the Department of Health informed hospital trusts that the policy was to be funded via a cut in their capital allocation' (*The Times*, 2000; see also Jones, 1999). Another example was when the respected *Times Higher Education Supplement* demonstrated that the Labour government had chosen to include compulsory tuition fees from the parents of students (an amount which over three years would reach £1.2 billion) as part of public investment in higher education (*THES*, 24 November 2000).

Authoritarianism

Sometimes, symbolic governments go one step further from manipulation and become authoritarian. Rather than simply feeding the media with large amounts of irrelevant information and letting the media work out the good stories, the authoritarian symbolic government will actively try to prevent the media from independently reporting on a particular event. This is where the symbolic government's need for control over the images that voters are exposed to begins to influence democratic rights.

For example, the Labour Party leadership did its utmost to silence internal party debate, and during the foot-and-mouth epidemic (a disease that affects cattle), newspaper reports made accusations about bullying and even illegal exercise of state authority. In this latter case, it was reported that officials tried to stop newsmen filming from public roads, blocked cameramen and threatened camera crews when they tried to enter government 'territory' (*Daily Telegraph*, 3 August 2001). Reporters were made to strip in public and their equipment was ruined by being sprayed with disinfectant. Journalists on public roads spoke of being put in the back of police vans and, for much of the crisis, farmers seeking reimbursement for disinfecting their farms had to sign the Official Secrets Act.

Selling war: the case of Britain in Iraq

The event that illustrates the way in which the Labour Party used all the aspects of a symbolic government was in conjunction with the wars in Afghanistan and Iraq. During the run-up to the declaration of war there were frequent press complaints about the level of disinformation that was provided by the Labour government. On 22 March 2002, the government briefed the media that a biological warfare laboratory had been found in Afghanistan and that the Iraqi government in Baghdad was supplying al-Qa'ida with weapons of mass destruction. The Pentagon questioned the accuracy of these claims, but only after the print deadline for newspaper headlines, and, in another case, the Special Boat Service had intercepted a freighter off the Sussex coast under suspicion that it was carrying anthrax or bomb materials; in spite of newspaper headlines such as 'Armada of Terror' and continued claims that a plot had been foiled, only sugar was ever found (*Independent*, 31 March 2002).

This exercise in disinformation became visible when it was revealed that the government had borrowed large parts of an old PhD thesis without acknowledgement (and without even correcting the grammatical errors) to help create a public dossier on Saddam Hussein. This work 'related to events around the time of the Gulf War in 1991' (*Daily Telegraph*, 8 February 2003), 'but was presented by the British government as up-to-date. The dossier also plagiarised from Jane's Intelligence Review.' However, the document was not simply plagiarised, it was also altered (*Sunday Times*, 9 February 2003). For example, the phrase 'helping opposition groups' was changed to 'supporting terrorist organisations', and 'monitoring foreign embassies' became 'spying on foreign embassies'. In spite of this, Colin Powell still praised this dossier in his presentation to the United Nations Security Council on Wednesday 5 February 2003.

If public opinion was to support a war with Iraq, it was essential for the Labour government (and their American allies) to demonise Saddam Hussein and his regime. Saddam Hussein, it was argued, ought to be removed from power in Iraq as he was a direct threat to the safety of the West through both his alleged weapons of mass destruction and his alleged close link with Osama Bin Laden. However, if this threat was to be believed, Saddam Hussein needed to be seen by public opinion to be a truly evil man, capable of just about anything. So in the lead-up to the war, the British Foreign Office drew up a twenty-three page report which described in detail the various torture methods employed by Saddam Hussein's security services (*Daily Telegraph*, 3 December 2002). The press briefing where this report was presented by the Foreign Office also included a video show depicting the beating and execution of prisoners, and of course the famous scenes after the gas attack on Kurdish villages.

The existence in Iraq of weapons of mass destruction received formal endorsement in a dossier presented to the Cabinet Office's Joint Intelligence Committee, published on 24 September 2002. Tony Blair argued that the government had 'as clear evidence as you can get that he [Saddam Hussein] is continuing with his weapons programme and the threat is real, serious and continues' (*Guardian*, 24 September, 2002). Blair added that Saddam Hussein would 'launch an external attack on his neighbours'. The report also said that Iraq could deploy chemical and biological weapons within forty-five minutes; Blair 'mesmerised' the House of Commons with its details (*Guardian*, 30 May 2003). By late April 2003 Secretary of State for Defence Geoff Hoon was claiming that such weapons might have escaped detection because they had been taken apart and buried (*Independent on Sunday*, 27 April 2003). In February 2003, a Sky TV poll revealed that many Britons had become convinced of the truth of these claims – 79 per cent believed that Saddam Hussein possessed weapons of mass destruction whilst only 21 per cent doubted the claims (*Sun*, 6 February 2003). The existence of weapons of mass destruction became the principle justification for war.

However, the press rapidly became sceptical about the existence of weapons of mass destruction. On 27 April 2003 the *Independent on Sunday* carried a headline: 'Revealed: how the road to war was paved with lies.' The newspaper claimed that there was no evidence for either chemical, biological, nuclear or banned missile activity by the Iraqi government. From the beginning of June 2003 onward, the claim that public opinion had been deceived into participating in the war in Iraq became the single biggest issue in British politics (e.g. *Guardian*, 2 June 2003) and the biggest crisis in the history of the Labour government, with Communications Adviser Alastair Campbell failing to answer charges that the now notorious dossier was essentially a fabrication. British public opinion came quickly to believe that they had been manipulated into fighting the Iraq War (ICM poll results 24 August 2003). Labour Party leader Tony Blair's claim that Iraq could launch weapons of mass destruction in forty-five minutes looked increasingly questionable; was the dossier based on fact or was it simply a case of spin to justify participating in the war?

Conclusion: the future of symbolic government?

Four days after Osama Bin Laden was killed by US Special Forces, US President Barack Obama laid a wreath of flowers at Ground Zero in New York in memory of those who lost their lives in the terrorist attack on the World Trade Center on 9/11. President Obama did not make a speech on this occasion and television cameras were not allowed close to the ceremony. This was a symbolic action in that people in the US and all over the world recognised the significance of the events behind the wreath-laying ceremony. However, the idea behind the symbolic government is that it is a governing *philosophy*; one might ask whether President Obama actually had a choice whether to visit Ground Zero or not. If President Obama believed that he did not have a choice, then the way in which he carried this out, without making a speech or turning the ceremony into a photo shoot, is an indication of the recognition by politicians that symbolism in the style used by the British Labour Party in their first term in office is no longer a viable strategy. The wreath-laying ceremony was, however, accompanied by a visit by the President to the Firehouse in Manhattan that lost fifteen firefighters in the 9/11 terrorist attack. Here, Obama did make a speech and cameras were allowed close to the President. The media was quick to ask whether the Firehouse event was nothing more than a symbolic action in the run-up to the presidential election campaign to be held in the autumn of 2012.

Before the general election of May 2010 the Labour Party admitted that it had used spin excessively in the early years of its period in office; it promised that it would now stop using spin and deal frankly with the public. So the Labour Party admitted its guilt and promised not to do it again; or is the Labour Party's announcement just a symbolic action designed to provide voters with a rhetorical vision of a future society without spin? This underlines one of the difficulties of separating the use of symbols as a government communication tool and symbolism as a government philosophy, but what is certain is that the media and citizens have learned over the past fifteen years to recognise symbolic government when they see it. It seems that symbolic actions have become so ingrained in our politics that sometimes politicians have to perform symbolic actions to show that they care, and to provide a rhetorical vision to prove that they are addressing the needs of society. The Labour Party's apology for using spin demonstrates that politicians must tread a thin line: they have to get their message out to voters through the media without turning that message into an empty symbolic action; President Obama's visit to New York on 4 May 2011 may have given us a clue as to where that line is.

Discussion questions

- Go to the home page of one of the parties in the parliament in your country. Look for a press release and try to write down the central message of the press release. Can you do this in fewer words than the party has done?
- Now try it from the other perspective: choose a story about a government policy initiative that is reported in a newspaper or on the television and try to write a press release in the style of the one in this chapter.
- Look on the web site of a newspaper or television station in your country for a report that includes an image of a politician. Is this a case of symbolic government or the use of symbols as a communication tool by a government?

Key terms

Image management   Symbolism
Rhetoric   Symbolic actions
Rhetorical vision   Symbolic government
Spin

Further reading

Axford, B. and Huggins, R. (2002): This chapter in Henneberg and O'Shaughnessy's (2002) edited book discusses the link between political marketing and postmodern trends in society. Postmodernism in politics emphasises symbols and signs, and thus links the current chapter to broader themes in society.

O'Shaughnessy, N. J. (2003): This article forms the basis of this chapter.

O'Shaughnessy, N. J. (2004): This book discusses the relationship between politics and propaganda in modern political marketing. The book argues that the three elements of propaganda – myth, rhetoric and symbolism – are consciously used to appeal to our emotions rather than to our reason.

References

Austin, J.L. (1976) *How to Do Things With Words*. Oxford: Oxford University Press.
Axford, B. and Huggins, R. (2002) 'Political marketing and the aestheticization of politics: modern politics and postmodern trends', in N.J. O'Shaughnessy and S.C. Henneberg (eds), *The Idea of Political Marketing*. Westport, CT: Praeger.

Baines, P. (2001) 'Marketing and political campaigning in the US and the UK: what can the UK political parties learn for the development of a campaign management process model?', doctoral dissertation, University of Manchester.

Boardman, P. (1978) 'Beware the semantic trap: language and propaganda', *Etcetera*, 35 (1): 78–85.

Daily Telegraph (2001) 'How Brown can quietly raise taxes to 50% of income', Ian Cowie, 23 May. www.telegraph.co.uk/comment/4262364/How-Brown-can-quietly-raise-taxes-to-50-per-cent-of-income.html.

Draper, D. (1997) *Blair's 100 Days*. London: Faber and Faber.

Foulkes, A.P. (1983) *Literature and Propaganda*. London: Methuen.

Independent on Sunday (2003) 'Revealed: how the road to war was paved with lies', Raymond Whitaker, 27 April. http://archive.truthout.org/article/revealed-how-road-war-was-paved-with-lies.

Jones, N. (1997) *Campaign 1997*. London: Indigo Books.

Jones, N. (1999) *Sultans of Spin*. London: Orion Books.

Klemperer, V. (1998) *I Shall Bear Witness: the Diaries of Victor Klemperer 1933–41*. London: Weidenfeld & Nicolson.

Mason, G. (1989) *Philosophical Rhetoric*. London: Routledge.

Mayhew, L.H. (1997) *The New Public*. Cambridge: Cambridge University Press.

Orwell, G. (1949) *Nineteen Eighty-Four*. London: Secker & Warburg.

O'Shaughnessy, N.J. (2003) 'The symbolic state: a British experience', *Journal of Public Affairs*, 3 (4): 297–312.

O'Shaughnessy, N.J. (2004) *Politics and Propaganda: Weapons of Mass Seduction*. Manchester: Manchester University Press.

Róka, J. (1999) 'Do the media reflect or shape public opinion?', in B.I. Newman (ed.) *The Handbook of Political Marketing*. Thousand Oaks, CA: Sage.

Simmons, A. (2000) *The Story Factor: Secrets of Influence from the Art of Storytelling*. New York: Perseus Publishing.

Umberson, D. and Henderson, K. (1992) 'The social construction of death in the Gulf War', *Omega: The Journal of Death and Dying*, 25 (1): 1–15.

Zuckerman, A.S. (1982) 'New approaches to political cleavage: a theoretical introduction', *Comparative Political Studies*, 15 (2): 131–44.

Chapter 12 is developed from O'Shaughnessy, N.J. (2003) 'The symbolic state: a British experience', *Journal of Public Affairs*, 3 (4): 297–312. Reprinted by permission of John Wiley & Sons.

13 Conclusion: Research Agendas for Political Marketing and Political Marketing Management

After reading this chapter, you should be able to:

- identify specific areas of political marketing that can be addressed by future research
- identify specific areas of political marketing management that can be addressed by future research.

Introduction

This final chapter proposes two research agendas, one for **political marketing** and the second for **political marketing management**. Whilst not comprehensive nor authoritative, the aim is to pinpoint areas of **theoretical** and **conceptual** research that can help us to understand both political marketing and political marketing management. As such, we advocate the adoption of the *wide* interpretation of political marketing. As this is a continuation of existing lines of research, we also advocate a more rigorous and engaging redefinition of research foci. We believe that political marketing theory should be developed to the extent that it provides an alternative research lens on politics itself. Whilst contentious, this has the potential to widen the domain of political marketing research and to engage in more meaningful ways with political scientists and other 'established' academic traditions in the area of political studies.

The first point that needs to be clarified is whether there is actually any generic content of political marketing. We need to acknowledge the fact that there are researchers – especially amongst political scientists – who are of the opinion that political marketing is theoretically and conceptually irrelevant to the political context. We argue that it should be central to our understanding, not only of modern elections but also of the conduct of government and democracy itself, the *wide* interpretation of political marketing. At the most basic level, political actors have borrowed commercial marketing techniques, such as targeted ones (direct-mail) and general ones (television advertisements). However, political actors have also adopted many operational and strategic concepts from commercial marketing such as segmentation and competitive positioning, together with market research techniques such as focus groups and opinion polling. This said, the adoption (or more usually, unquestioning transference) of methods and techniques from commercial marketing does not collectively add up to strategic political marketing. Strategic political marketing requires there to be some level of recognition, even if not fully articulated, that elections and democracy itself are a competitive marketplace, voters participate in a political exchange and citizens are consumers of a political offering, and that this development is underpinned by the rise of an advanced consumerist material culture. This fosters a homogeneous society and fickle party allegiances – a post-loyalty society perhaps. The political consequences of this recognition are profound, and need to find their equivalent focus in research content.

Parties and other political actors cease to be exclusively internally or ideologically driven, and as a result of this the political process refocuses on the citizen as a consumer of a political offering and on the competitive interpretation of voter needs and wants. In the most basic explanation of political marketing, parties, governments, single-interest groups and other stakeholders begin to ask what voters want and how they want it, rather than what parties think that voters ought to have. The content of theories and concepts of political marketing have to be nuanced because the phenomena in question are in essence based on a political science approach; the volatility, pressure, intensity and instantaneous characteristics of political marketing are all contextual characteristics that differentiate political marketing from commercial marketing. Whilst political marketing represents a specific research phenomenon, its explanatory conceptual frameworks draw on the slower and less publicly scrutinised realm of business. As a result of this there is the danger of naïvety in some research where issues specific to political marketing are not examined, simply adopted at face value into a marketing agenda. Many of the agenda points discussed below represent clear deviations from commercial marketing. Thus, whilst political marketing conceptualises some of the relationships in political and electoral communication effectively, serious conceptual issues arise in the search for a comprehensive and literal application of marketing to politics. The specific characteristics of political marketing need to be adapted with regard to the focus on specific content aspects. The purpose of the following research agendas is to stress the particularism of political marketing by highlighting issues that we believe merit further conceptual and theoretical emphasis in order for political marketing to become a rigorous branch of mainstream non-profit marketing theory and as a complementary and relevant field to political studies.

A research agenda for political marketing

Theories and concepts in political marketing need to be empirically investigated; whilst the development of concepts is crucial for the initial phase of a new discipline, this development must be complemented by empirical studies that allow for an assessment as well as fine-tuning of initial concepts and provide pointers towards further research issues. Analytical and empirical studies, especially international or comparative studies using rigorous, higher-level qualitative or quantitative methods, are still rare. Much existing empirical research is used to underline a descriptive argument. It is necessary to go beyond description towards more prescriptive concepts about how to run election campaigns, how to develop optimal policy offerings and how to position a party vis-à-vis stakeholders such as voters, the media and donors. Empirical research can provide the input for the necessary analyses regarding the contingencies of these concepts, enabling political managers to optimise the use of their scarce resources.

To re-engage with the breadth and depth of existing marketing theory, research on political marketing needs to 'let go' of the easily adaptable but unhelpful fixation on the instrumental/managerial interpretation of marketing. In order to achieve relevance and influence, theories and concepts of political marketing need to be influenced by developments in the commercial and non-profit marketing discipline at large. Furthermore, theories and concepts of political marketing also need to be influenced by developments in the field of political science. Mere lip service to theories and concepts from political science hampers a better understanding of the political sphere (Scammell, 1999).

Emphasis on relationship-building and collaboration within a political market (instead of a purely transactional concept) can potentially increase the success and performance of political parties in their dealing with a variety of stakeholders (Bannon, 2005). Such an approach must also be seen in conjunction with more plebiscitary aspects of democratic life at the macro-level as well as the possibility of re-engaging with voters, citizens and other stakeholders at the micro-level (Henneberg and O'Shaughnessy, 2009). The existing foundations in customer relationship management (CRM) and the literature on international marketing and purchasing (IMP) provide many interesting concepts. Furthermore, research undertaken in contemporary marketing practice (CMP) on how organisations balance transactional and relationship elements as well as the Nordic School of services marketing can be of interest as the political offering is an amalgamation of candidate characteristics, issues stances and overarching ideology, which together with deferred implementation has a substantial overlap with service-based offerings. A relational approach to political marketing would address the ontological areas of exchange and qualified market characteristics as well as taking into account the social embeddedness of the political sphere within a wider systemic framework.

Several studies have recently highlighted the potential of public relations and public affairs concepts for marketing, especially in 'communication organisations' like political parties (Newman, 2005). Whilst communication aspects are a well-researched area in political marketing management, this research often consists of constructs that are not fully linked into a marketing framework. Arguably, a more integrative approach towards communications and political marketing management is needed. Related conceptual domains such as identity and reputation management (corporate identity management) are also in a position to broaden our understanding, just as public relations (PR) and integrated marketing communications (IMC) are at the heart of political marketing management. It can even be argued that commercial marketing theory can learn from communication practices in the political sphere. Therefore, one research focus for political marketing lies in integrating the existing theories of IMC and PR so, together with existing communication studies on politics, a theory of political communication that is integral to an understanding of political marketing management can be developed. This will allow for interaction and interrelation characteristics of political actors to be researched, in line with a 'qualified market' ontology.

Issues of the effectiveness and efficiency of political marketing management have not been sufficiently addressed. It is still debated to what degree political marketing management actually affects the performance of political actors. On the micro-level, how does political marketing influence individual voters in their decision-making? On the macro-level, how is the fabric of political life itself being changed by the ubiquitous use of political marketing management in political discourse? Disturbingly, the question of the performance of political parties and candidates in terms of strategic management requirements has not been addressed. Questions such as what kind of resources and capabilities do parties and candidates need, what functional requirements do they have to fulfil, how can they best allocate their scarce resources and what processes are used in doing this are also largely unresolved. A link to a resource-based or a competence-based view of the organisation could help illuminate these strategic issues, linking them with mainstream organisational strategy as well as performance (Hunt and Lambe, 2000). This would help political marketing research work towards a more general 'theory of political management' that is oriented towards a wide variety of internal and external stakeholders and which acknowledges the embeddedness of management decisions within a wider social sphere (Baines and Lynch, 2005). Whilst research needs to focus on existing research strands in political marketing management, conceptual developments on the level of political marketing theory are also necessary. Using a *wide* interpretation of political marketing theory presupposes a clarification of the ontology and epistemology of political marketing.

In terms of research foci and research methodologies, the idea that political marketing is structurally part of the socio-cultural make-up of society means that we must also consider the functioning of democratic systems. The relationship of political marketing with different concepts of democracy, especially a more 'plebiscitary' democracy, have to be made explicit and the notion of identity in a postmodern world needs consideration. This ought to go beyond existing ethical considerations and should be anchored in ethical theories that are connected to a market-oriented understanding of political actors, and beyond utopian views on how voters ought to behave and make decisions. In general, the way in which voters and other stakeholders are represented and how these actors make sense of the political sphere can be brought back into the focus of ethical research. This would allow for a redressing of the balance; thus the dominance of the current party and candidate-focused research practice would be challenged. A shift in applied methodologies would also need to go with this change in focus, balancing the more quantitative orientation of studies of voting with a more qualitative understanding of a market-oriented theory of voter behaviour. The exchange paradigm of commercial marketing theory provides a unique and differential perspective on what constitutes a 'good' interaction and adapted interpretations of 'exchanged value' can help assess the appropriateness of frameworks for political interactions and exchanges as well as those marketing instruments that are employed. A 'political macro-marketing theory' would be a main aim of this research area.

A further issue concerns developing a voter behaviour theory that is more aligned with current political exchange phenomena. Traditional voter behaviour concepts such as those of the 'Columbia' or 'Michigan' schools, the economic rational-choice school or the socio-psychological school do not provide adequate insight into what effect political marketing management has on voter perceptions, attitudes or behaviour. Often this is due to the fact that either their main focus is not on the individual voter but on groups of voters or the electorate in general, or they use long-term, structural explanatory constructs that are not affected by political marketing management activities. This precludes a cognitive understanding of voters. On the other hand, tendencies towards more cognitive psychology-influenced voting behaviour research allow for the use of consumer behaviour theory to be integrated. Knowledge of how people purchase market offerings can foster knowledge about how voters react to certain political marketing management activities and political offerings, or how citizens perceive policy promises and their implementation. Therefore, a theory of market-oriented voter behaviour would answer questions regarding impact and appropriateness of strategies and tactics based on theories and concepts from political marketing in a way that mainstream voter behaviour research (and normative theories of democracy) may not be able to achieve. This would address issues regarding exchange as well as structural connectedness. It is noteworthy that this research area was in fact one of the first to develop in political marketing theory but has produced only limited interest in the meantime (Newman, 2002).

Representation and sense-making in commercial economic exchange situations are embedded in a net of primary and secondary interactions and interrelations that are extremely complicated (Ford et al., 2003). However, the political sphere shows even more complex structures and processes, with several interaction 'markets' of competition (the electoral, parliamentary and governmental markets), a disconnection between value exchange (policy promises at elections and the implementation of these promises), and organisational resource generation via state funding, membership fees and donations. Intermediaries such as the media play a much more important role as facilitators or influencers of political interactions and exchanges. All stakeholders are strongly linked via feedback mechanisms. Entity-focused or dyadic exchange theories cannot get to grips with the inherent complexity of politics. Therefore, a triadic interaction-based approach to politics is pivotal in providing a macro-picture of politics that enriches the ways political scientists and political marketers perceive their field of interest.

A research agenda based on an epistemological understanding of political marketing theory opens up another issue, one that is thrown at commercial management theories on a regular basis, that of 'conceptual imperialism' and overreach (O'Shaughnessy, 2002). However, in a pluralistic environment many new insights are gained at the flexing points of theories, where friction between competing theories, based on different epistemologies, exists. If there is an overreach then the insights gained should be shallow or not appropriate in relation to other explanatory constructs. Marketing theory needs to be willing to accept and engage with other disciplines and their specific starting points for analysis. In any case, management studies and marketing are an eclectic methodological mix of other disciplines. Management studies and marketing should not strive for hegemony in explaining political phenomena but should show relevance through their theories, a relevance in a wider sense that makes it inevitable for researchers of any discipline to consult them in their search for knowledge in politics (Ormrod and Savigny, 2012). Currently, the field of political marketing research is a considerable distance away from reaching this aim.

A research agenda for political marketing management

The purpose of this book has been to address issues concerning the theoretical and conceptual foundations of political marketing research, but what about the implications of an increased focus on theory and concepts for political marketing management research? In this section we discuss those political marketing management activities that we perceive to be most in need of being addressed: the permanent campaign, the nature of political leadership, the image of the party leader or candidate, that political marketing management is a mediated phenomenon, the use of symbolism, the importance of values, political messages that are characterised by deceit and fantasy, and the implications of outsourcing political marketing management activities to quasi-autonomous single-issue groups. Whilst this is by no means a comprehensive list, it aims to provide a tentative research agenda for political marketing management.

The permanent campaign

In consumer marketing, campaigns tend to occur at regular intervals, for example at major sporting events. This was once the case in politics, but politicians have learnt during the course of the twentieth century that they have to campaign ceaselessly to remain in office, especially by creating positive images of themselves and celebratory rhetoric. Winston Churchill was filmed at the head of police and troops during the Siege of Sidney Street in 1910, and the Reagan presidency was based around managed visual imagery from the very beginning, where Reagan's inaugural address in January 1981 mutated into a travelogue of the major Washington monuments. What is new in contemporary political marketing is the integration of managed images into the daily activity of governing; what once occurred at intervals now influences policy-making and policy implementation. Therefore, political marketing management activities become 'permanent', that is, necessary activities for political actors whatever the stage on the electoral cycle. As such, political marketing theories must go beyond the election campaign and embrace more dynamic conceptualisations that take this permanence of campaigning into account. One set of questions revolves around the nature of the political exchange as a triadic interaction; are there political marketing management activities that are more important in a specific interaction, which stakeholders should be prioritised, and what are the consequences of the interplay between electoral interactions during campaigns, parliamentary interactions during the development of legislation and governmental interactions during policy implementation as part of the overall political system?

Leadership and public opinion

One key issue that is worthy of further theoretical treatment concerns the ability to know the public mind versus the ability to know the consumer mind. By referring to the concept of 'voter orientation', we touch upon one of the central concepts in political market orientation. In politics, the ability to know the needs and wants of interaction partners is very difficult, not least because people seek incompatible objectives such as the desire for 'Texan taxes and Scandinavian welfare benefits' (Henneberg and O'Shaughnessy, 2007). Hence, opinion pollsters can get wildly different data on many key political topics via subtly different shades of emphasis in the wording of questions to voters. Public opinion is often tentative, confused or even contradictory. Persuasion and leadership is still very important and it is the task of political leadership to guide these trade-offs and articulate the parameters of what is possible. Political actors cannot blindly follow public opinion; neither can they ignore public opinion. This needs to be integrated within political marketing theory and political marketing management practice in order to qualify the naïve understanding of a voter orientation. Otherwise, it will be difficult to relate political marketing theory and concepts to the reality of political marketing management.

Leader image

The political offering is a mixture of the elements of policy, party impression and its history. However, leader image can perhaps be seen as the central and unifying core to this idea. The leader has to be attractive, credible, strong and caring. However, the characteristics of political leadership and their perception are not fully understood despite the impact of leadership attributes on performance and their halo-effect on other aspects of the political offering. The failure of the British Conservative Party in the decade following their 1997 landslide defeat can be partly blamed on their failure to produce leaders who were both attractive and credible, or at least able to communicate and deliver these leader attributes effectively. Few commercial organisations are so dependent on the idiosyncrasies and credibility of an individual, yet this is often one of the central tasks of political marketing management, one constrained by the publicly received record of that person. Political marketing management can succeed with repackaging, repositioning and makeovers such as the 'New Nixon' of 1968 (McGinnis, 1969), which is testament to its power, but we lack a clear conceptual understanding of how the perceptions of leaders affect, amongst others, relationships with voters, the media and other stakeholders in both presidential and party-based political systems.

Mediated phenomena

This book has identified the issue of exchange and interaction processes as theoretical and conceptual themes. The flipside of this is the phenomenon of mediation that characterises political interactions. Commercial marketing only experiences mediation to a limited extent via consumer watchdog programmes and the occasional media critique of commercial organisations and advertising campaigns. In political marketing, on the other hand, the mass media generally acts as the link between the different public and political spheres and interferes with and influences the political exchange, especially the electoral and governmental interactions. Thus, political marketing management cannot ever be wholly detached from the mass media. Political texts (a collective term for communications, adverts, images and speeches and so on) are an element of the mediated context. So central is media coverage of phenomena in the political sphere that the mass media itself is often the principal target of political marketing management activities. Political texts are political events in their own right with independent political consequences, depending on reception by public and media. They represent potentially volatile, combustible material. The mass media not only relays the text but also interprets the text, and over that interpretation the party in a free society has influence but not control. Political marketing theory and concepts that do not take mediation into account fall short of representing rigorous research in this area.

Symbolism

The generation of images that include the public as participants and the creation of contexts for the communication of symbols – symbolic tableaux – has become an integral part of modern political marketing management. Resonant settings, symbolic imagery and the creation of meaningful contexts are testament to politicians' understanding that a picture is worth ten thousand words. This is a different world to the corporate one, and even in extreme crisis no corporate PR strategy is likely to use these methods. However, for political discourse, the creation of symbolic tableaux is a way of communicating the parties' civic and social identity to the public and other stakeholders by stimulating media attention. Politicians recognise that the consumer of political information is an inadvertent consumer. In today's political environment, images resonate far more than a speech or written text to the extent that we may now legitimately speak of visual rhetoric. The issue of symbolism as part of political marketing management therefore needs further conceptual elaboration, integrating already existing models of communication studies within the framework of political marketing theory.

Values

Political marketing management is intertwined with the construct of value. In commercial marketing theory, values are linked to specific offering characteristics that enable certain desired outcomes for the customer, whilst the offering itself is linked to basic needs. However, in the political exchange, the link between political ideas and values is much more direct. Political marketing offerings are values in and of themselves. Values such as environmentalism or protection of our children are central to the political mobilisation of citizens. When Goebbels said that no one ever died for the eight-hour day, he was suggesting a distinction between materialism and idealism, which is also relevant here. Politicians, single-interest groups and governments do not just appeal to our economic self-interest or collective class interest alone, and the impression that they do so represents a serious misreading of contemporary campaigns and politics. For example, the agenda of George W. Bush may have been unsuited to the needs of working-class America (such as his rejection of anything resembling a national health system), but many working-class citizens nevertheless voted for him. This was despite the US involvement in the war in Iraq and high levels of unemployment. The appeal was based on values: Bush's strategy of opposing gay marriage and successfully associating Democrats with that idea resonated with many Americans' accumulated frustration over the dominance of the liberal social agenda.

Political marketing management and policy development is driven by such a value-based agenda, particularly so when we include the activities of partisan, non-affiliated actors such as the 527 groups in the United States and single-issue groups in the United Kingdom. The special attraction of values in political messages is that they do not entail any precise, and therefore controversial, policy prescriptions. Political vulnerability is reduced when appeals are made to values relative to more rational, and thereby prescriptive, appeals. Better, as Labour Party leader Tony Blair did in the United Kingdom, to lend to the forces of law and order rhetorical support than initiate tough, and therefore politically divisive, policies. For example, the value-based slogan 'tough on crime, tough on causes of crime' was integrated with the visual rhetoric of the image of Blair placing flowers on the memorial to a dead policeman (Brandreth, 1999). Questions here relate to the implications of values for relationship management, symbolic government, and the effects on individuals in particular and society in general.

Deceit

Deceit in political marketing management needs to become a topic that is not just moralised about but rigorously conceptualised with regard to both its practical use and its impact on stakeholders at the micro-level as well as to its overall effects on democratic systems at the macro-level. Open deceit is uncommon in commercial marketing practice, but it is engrained in political marketing management. Johnson (1997) reminds us that a study of 2000 US political commercials between 1952 and 1992 found that 15 per cent contained some unethical passages; a follow-up study for the 1996 US presidential campaign found 20 per cent of the 188 commercials examined made questionable claims, such as news conferences that were never held, debates that never took place and audio or video tricks that were used to stereotype or ridicule opponents.

Much of course has been written on the ethics of consumer marketing, but there are always constraints, such as truth in advertising laws, professional standards and self-regulating bodies. Whilst commercial marketing is prone to exaggeration, cases of verifiable lying are rare. Yet we constantly forgive politicians and other political actors (such as the media) their two-facedness and the consequences of their deceitfulness. This is ultimately a question of 'symbolic government', the core of which is rhetorical pronouncements and the pursuit of public imagery without moral conviction. For example, Dick Cheney's announcement in 2001 of a review of consequence management in a terrorist attack remained simply that – an announcement. All political campaigns exaggerate of course, but many also create events that did not happen and distort those that did. Whilst much description of this particular aspect of political marketing management exists, we do not know much about how this fits with wider relationship management activities, how stakeholders make sense of this deceit and how it impacts on the wider exchange and interaction systems in politics.

Fantasy

A further content issue that political marketing research needs to deal with conceptually is that of fantasy. Consumer marketing, and specifically advertising, often uses fantasy as a persuasive appeal; for example, an offering can be associated with some utopian or dream-like desired state, whilst political fantasies are firmly embedded in negative-type appeals. Negative adverts do not make the mistake of asking for belief, but instead are based on political fears, animosities and phobias. These feelings are not imposed or coerced, but rather voters, citizens and the media are invited to join in as co-producers. An example of an extreme negative advert was run as part of the recall election campaign of Republican Governor Scott Walker of Wisconsin. Using an image of a toddler who had been beaten to death, the advert blamed Walker's Democratic opponent for the 'controversial aftermath' (Moore, 2012). In more general terms, how does this blatant use of fantasy affect the relationship between the candidate and other stakeholders? Is this only a characteristic of a specific strategic posture, or is it a more general phenomenon? What about the implications for the individual on the one hand, and society in general on the other?

Outsourcing the campaign

In the political marketing sphere, parties no longer have the organisational monopoly let alone the ability to shape and control the political agenda, especially during election campaigns. Other actors become important: for example, single-issue groups shape the agenda on everything from feminism to environmentalism, and a parallel political marketplace forms. In the United States one mutation of the single-issue group phenomenon has been the so-called 527 groups and their participation in elections by running private campaigns that vocalise their own agenda. These actors run simultaneous campaigns outside of the candidate's official campaign. These simultaneous campaigns can effectively subcontract the negative aspects of the candidate's campaign to an outside group, leaving the candidate to run a dignified campaign. Thus, in the 2004 US presidential election, a group of Republican supporters, the 'Swift Boat Veterans for Truth', made their mark: the 'Swifties' claimed that Kerry lied about his medals and had called his comrades war criminals. The failure of Kerry to respond to this libel left sufficient doubt in the minds of the public; the irony was that Bush did not fight in the Vietnam War at all. No commercial business would use its marketing activities to challenge and distort facts about its competitors in this way, even though commercial organisations can sometimes be co-opted into behaving in this way in an election campaign, as happened during the Bush campaign. However, these supplementary actors – commercial or otherwise – do not feature in most political marketing conceptualisations and therefore constitute an important aspect of future political marketing research.

Conclusion

Research on political marketing has now established itself as a lively subdiscipline of marketing, producing considerable numbers of academic articles and books each year. However, few of these contain references to the theoretical and conceptual underpinnings of political marketing and political marketing management. Whilst the current research limitations in political marketing can be explained by the dominant focus on the narrow interpretation of political marketing theory, the wider interpretation that we advocate frames a new research agenda for political marketing – and thus political marketing management – that can provide new directions and less restricted conceptual horizons. As such, the research agendas presented in this chapter inherently encompass 'friction points' with other disciplines such as political science that we believe can only help stimulate further cross-disciplinary discussions and counteract any stagnation in the field.

However, commercial marketing thought is fragmented around several different schools of research, and research into political marketing is affected by – and may indeed be part of – this fragmentation process simply by representing a very specialised application of commercial marketing theory. However, a substantial aspect of building theories and concepts in political marketing may be dependent on being able to partition the field under investigation, and this is arguably an important aspect of research in political marketing that has not been conducted satisfactorily. We believe that this is due to the fact that many existing commercial marketing concepts have been imported into politics without theoretically getting to grips with the differences between the two research fields. Whichever way individual researchers choose to go, we argue that more research into the theoretical and conceptual underpinnings of political marketing are necessary in order to build a solid foundation on which to understand political marketing management as a practical activity.

Discussion questions

- We know that it is necessary to understand the theoretical and conceptual foundations of political marketing, but which issues do you think are the most important to start with?
- How will a wide interpretation of political marketing affect the way in which negativity – deceit and fantasy – are included in future election campaigns? What about the effects on political relationship management and the strategic posture that parties and candidates can adopt?
- More generally, it is necessary to link theory and concepts with practice. Which areas of political marketing theory and concepts can help us to understand the nine political marketing management issues?

Key terms

Political marketing	Theory
Political marketing management	Concepts

Further reading

Henneberg and O'Shaughnessy (2007): This chapter is based on some of the work published in Henneberg and O'Shaughnessy's (2007) article in the *Journal of Political Marketing*.

Henneberg (2008): This chapter is based on some of the work published in Henneberg's (2008) article in the *Journal of Political Marketing*.

References

Baines, P. and Lynch, R. (2005) 'The context, content and process of political marketing strategy', *Journal of Political Marketing*, 4 (2): 11–27.

Bannon, D. (2005) 'Relationship marketing and the political process', *Journal of Political Marketing*, 4 (2/3): 73–90.

Brandreth, G. (1999) *Breaking the Code*. London: Weidenfeld & Nicholson.

Ford, D., Gadde, L. E., Hakansson, H. and Snehota, I. (2003) *Managing Business Relationships*. Chichester: Wiley.

Henneberg, S.C. (2008) 'An epistemological perspective on political marketing', *Journal of Political Marketing*, 7 (2): 151–82.

Henneberg, S.C. and O'Shaughnessy, N.J. (2007) 'Theory and concept development in political marketing: issues and agenda', *Journal of Political Marketing*, 6 (2/3): 5–32.

Henneberg, S.C. and O'Shaughnessy, N.J. (2009) 'Political relationship marketing: some micro/macro thoughts', *Journal of Marketing Management*, 25 (1/2): 5–29.

Hunt, S.C. and Lambe, C.J. (2000) 'Marketing's contribution to business strategy: market orientation, relationship marketing and resource-advantage theory', *International Journal of Management Reviews*, 2 (1): 17–43.

Johnson, D. (1997) 'Political communication in the information age', paper presented at the Wissenchaftszentrum Berlin/Bertelsmann Stiftung, February.

McGinnis, J. (1969) *The Selling of the President 1968*. New York: Trident.

Moore, L. (2012) 'Which Wisconsin?', *New York Review of Books*, July.

Newman, B.I. (2002) 'Testing a predictive model of voter behavior on the 2000 U.S. presidential election', *Journal of Political Marketing*, 1 (2/3): 159–73.

Newman, B.I. (2005) 'Political marketing and public affairs', in P. Harris and C.S. Fleisher (eds), *The Handbook of Public Affairs*. London: Sage, 379–93.

Ormrod, R.P. and Savigny, H. (2012) 'Political market orientation: a framework for understanding relationship structures in political parties', *Party Politics*, 18 (4): 487–502.

O'Shaughnessy, N.J. (2002) 'The marketing of political marketing', in N.J. O'Shaughnessy and S.C. Henneberg (eds), *The Idea of Political Marketing*, Westport, CT: Praeger, 209–20.

Scammell, M. (1999) 'Political marketing: lessons for political science', *Political Studies*, 47 (4): 718–39.

The **Conclusion** is developed from Henneberg, S.C. and O'Shaughnessy, N.J. (2007) 'Theory and concept development in political marketing: issues and an agenda', *Journal of Political Marketing*, 6 (2/3): 5–31, and Henneberg, S.C. (2008) 'An epistemological perspective on research in political marketing', *Journal of Political Marketing*, 7 (2): 151–182. Both reprinted by permission of Taylor & Francis (www.tandfonline.com).

Index

Page numbers in *italics* refer to figures and tables.